A Singing Mouse at Buckingham Palace

and other amazing animal stories from the nineteenth century

Richard Sugg

For my Mother,
with love and thanks

Contents

Part One: At Home.

Dogs

Cats

Mice

Birds

In the Saddle

Field and Farmyard

Part Two: On Safari.

Apes

Claws

Slither

A Mixed Menagerie

Elephants

Introduction

Animals bring people together. Day by day in parks, streets, country walks or pubs dogs draw otherwise random strangers into conversation – sometimes into friendship, now and then even marriage. Meanwhile, with the internet offering a seemingly inexhaustible supply of tumbling puppies, talented kittens, and assorted fluffiness of all shapes, colours and sizes, you can make contact with your friends merely by sending them one of these gems via e-mail or social media. (And who has not at some point forwarded to a woman the puppy sent to them by another female friend – wondering nervously at the same time if this is not a subtle form of virtual adultery?)

In this book animals bring people together in some very surprising ways. A humble old lady sends a kitten to Queen Victoria. An equally impoverished couple from a London slum capture a singing mouse, which presently finds itself summoned to Buckingham Palace for a command performance. Over in Downing Street those ferocious political enemies Benjamin Disraeli and William Gladstone are united in their affection for a cat called Tom, chief mouser to the cabinet. In St Louis a starving family is saved by a charitable woman, summoned to their wretched hovel by the pleadings of their pet dog. In Grenoble the entire town is united in its mourning for the dead Charlemagne, a chimp who once saved a child trapped in a well. Loose groups of bystanders are welded into united audiences, gaping breathlessly from riverbanks and seashores as they watch people rescuing animals and dogs rescuing people (to say nothing of the performance of a mouse-teasing kitten in Moorgate railway station). And thanks to the reach of the nineteenth century press, many of these stories more indirectly draw readers together, as they follow improbable animal feats, including the career of Railway Jack, a dog famous for riding trains in the 1880s, and whose death in 1890 seems to have been mourned by much of the nation.

Needless to say, animals can also divide people. How should they be treated or kept? Should they be eaten? How close to humans should they get? (Someone who loves to stroke dogs, for example, might be appalled at the idea of one sleeping in its owner's bed.) The division which came to fascinate me when assembling these stories was rather different. It is, simply, the divide between ordinary pet-owners, farmers, zoo keepers and so forth, and animal experts. In recent years some of the best books on animals have been written by this latter group. But for a long time zoologists or academics speculating about animals seemed frequently to suffer from a strange blindness about their supposed Specialist Subject. They would assert with absolute confidence and a wealth of jargon that animals did not have consciousness or feelings; could not think, and did not have genuinely loving relationships with their owners or fellow creatures. Everything that in a human would pass for intelligence would in an animal be seen as instinct; where a person appeared altruistic, the animal was secretly self-interested, or just following the automatic evolutionary habits of its group or species. Imagine a sheepdog torn from its Scottish Highland home to the misery of Victorian London. Imagine that finally it returns and, in the words of its shepherd master, bounds around the hills so wildly that the man fears it will go mad with joy. For a long time, there were plenty of animal experts who would tell you that this dog was not happy.

In so many cases, if you wanted to know the most interesting, surprising and important things about a dog, cat, parrot, elephant or chimp, you were much better off asking pet owners, animal trainers or zoo-keepers. For one thing, these people spent a lot of time with their animals, and tended to actually look at them, rather than looking vaguely through a set of dubious ideas *about* animals. More subtly, they were likely to see different things just because of the way they treated animals, gained their trust, nurtured their skills and intelligence, and so forth.

It is of course possible to misunderstand animals just because you love them. A zookeeper recently told me about a case in which a child managed to fall into a gorilla enclosure. Immediately the lead male gorilla came up and stood over the fallen child – leading to widespread admiration for the way it protected the boy from its pack. In reality, it was almost certainly protecting the pack from the boy. Decoding the behaviour of wild animals can, then, be a tricky business. But there remains something sadly comic about the historic and still partly lingering divide between the exalted experts and the supposed amateurs. And it is probably no accident that one of the professionals who has learned some of the most interesting things about animals lately is Rupert Sheldrake: a Cambridge-educated biologist who has taken the trouble to repeatedly consult pet-owners, and who has also been increasingly marginalised, by the scientific mainstream, as some kind of dangerous heretic.

Having said all this, I should add that I have been repeatedly surprised, when preparing this book, by all the things I didn't know, or the things I thought I knew. At face value, this book looks very different from my previous work on cannibals, the soul, vampires, ghosts and poltergeists. But in fact there is one interesting similarity. Much of what has interested me in earlier works has been findings which challenged false or overly-rigid divisions: for a long time body and soul blurred into one another in ways which recent thought has tended to forget. The study of medicinal cannibalism startled me and many others by showing that ideological lines between savage and civilised often crumbled to dust in a period when European royalty was eating people for medicine. More recently, my sense of the hard line between mind and body was upset by the numerous accounts of people who were quite literally scared to death: a process in which the mind seemingly takes the body down with it.

In the end, animals are animals and not people – and in some ways it is good to appreciate them for what they are. But writing this book has certainly made me think very hard about how lines are drawn between humans and animals. These lines are often so taken for granted that we might forget how artificial they can be. For example: when we see or hear talking monkeys, dogs driving cars, cats playing pianos, elephants painting, chimps riding bikes and sawing at violins, laughter is inevitable. Is some of that laughter often just slightly nervous, an involuntary release of unease, at the sense that they are getting a little too close for comfort? Even, perhaps, faintly uncanny?

We can of course love and respect what we laugh at. A good general rule for selecting these stories from hundreds of others was: if it doesn't make you laugh, it might make you think. Quite a few, I suspect, can do both. Oscar Wilde once observed that anyone who tries to exhaust a subject always exhausts their listeners. The same probably goes for readers, and it would be especially foolish to try and exhaust a subject as joyously abundant and varied as this one. Indeed, among other things, it would shoot up the length and the price of the book quite alarmingly. My aim with the Century series has been to offer readers books which people (rather than academic libraries) can afford. I have been impressed and touched by all the people who did buy *Mummies, Cannibals and Vampires*, which cost about £28 new in paperback. But I would certainly think twice myself when faced with that price tag, however interesting the work looked.

It is partly for this reason that my first animal collection has no pictures. If readers often feel that a given tale or moment is crying out for one, well… I often thought the same. With luck I may be able to get some into my second volume, and also onto my website. *A Century of Supernatural Stories* and *A Century of Ghost Stories* each presented a hundred stories from the nineteenth century press. In the present case I found such an abundance of stories – many short but memorable - that I have upped the count to two hundred. I like the nineteenth century because there is a lot of data available, and because its writers had a knack of making a story vivid and detailed in relatively few words. But my next volume will be a different kind of century – probably running from 1846 to 1945, and weighted in favour of the twentieth century. I have also started to collect material for an eighteenth century edition.

Can we be sure that all these stories are true? I certainly did discard one or two gems on the grounds that they were probably not. A story about the prodigious intelligence of dogs, for example, related how, with their owners away on holiday, one dog got down the photo album and began showing the other one all the places where the family might have gone. Whilst this was evidently deliberate satire, I was not quite so sure about the mourning dogs of America. When a death occurred in the family, these animals unsuccessfully attempted to get into the cupboard where all the black crepe was stored. Determined, however, to emulate all the black-clad mourners around them they upturned a bottle of ink and dyed themselves a suitably funereal colour instead… Good – but probably a bit too good to be true. Of the present selection, the tale of the ship's parrot and its impromptu choir is perhaps the most doubtful, though nevertheless a bit too good to exclude. Where relevant, I have noted that a particular story lacks family or place names – but in many cases other details are precise and realistic.

The book is structured to follow the animal experience of most typical readers. Hence dogs, cats, and more homely British animals form the first part, and take up a little more space than the wilder things of the second. Part two, meanwhile, reminds us just how many wild or dangerous animals could be seen in Britain in the nineteenth century – often in places where you least expected. A very small handful of these stories have appeared elsewhere; but those were ones which, in a book on animals, it seemed a shame to omit. On the whole I have been struck by how surprising most of these tales were; and how close they have come to be being buried in the great mountains of newsprint from which they were unearthed.

I would love to hear from pet owners, zoo-keepers, farmers or anyone else who has any stories relevant to those given below. I would also love to hear from any readers with views on any of the questions raised here. Just a few possible ones include: which animals should have statues or other monuments? Should animals have their own Dictionary Of Animal Biography? If so, who should be in there, and why? Should animals be allowed to attend funerals and churches? Time now, however, to get our paws and our muzzles dirty, as we romp back through a century of surprising histories – ranging from the extraordinary to the simple ordinary magic of everyday animal life.

richardjsugg@yahoo.co.uk

At Home

Dogs

When I first began lecturing in 2001 a veteran colleague assured me that 'if you've pleased them all - you've failed...' – an adage which comes to mind here as I open up a total of fifty three dog stories, comprising almost a quarter of my entire tally. What can I say to cat-lovers, or indeed those afraid of dogs? Perhaps, for one thing, that dogs, in Britain and elsewhere, do seem undeniably the most popular tame animal there is. Indeed, recalling my plea for a Dictionary of Animal Biography, we might remind ourselves how many dogs already have whole novels or films shaped around them, from Virginia Woolf's *Flush* (inspired by the dog-napped spaniel of Robert and Elizabeth Barrett Browning) through to James Herbert's *Fluke*, Paul Auster's *Timbuktu* and Lasse Hallstrom's movie, *A Dog's Purpose*.

By the time that Charles II's brother James disgraced himself in 1682 (during a storm at sea in which men were drowning on all sides) by shouting 'Save the dogs and Colonel Churchill!' Britain's love affair with dogs was already centuries old. Nowadays, when even the most besotted dog-lover could probably not hope to watch all the internet clips of dogs driving cars (well do I recall the day when one of my female colleagues lost an afternoon's work to this gem), rescuing other dogs, and generally tumbling about in puppyish folly, there seems little chance of their ever being toppled, even by that most adorably fluffy entity, the kitten.

It has been many years now since I owned a dog. I must have been about sixteen when we brought home a bouncing and madly affectionate Alsatian-Collie-cross puppy from the Dog Rescue Centre. I can still recall the way that Sally managed in puppyhood to wag not just her tail but her whole body, when reunited with us after a separation of a few hours, and the impossibly comic look of an animal whose Alsatian ears were almost as big as her head. Sadly, I also recall my first experience of real and shattering grief – when Sally was hit by a car outside our house and killed, at little more than a year old. No one close to me had ever died at this stage, and the following morning I stumbled through my familiar paper-round in a state of numbed and tearful shock.

We hardly need to venture through all the famous bequests of money made to pet dogs or cats (sometimes at the expense of human relatives) to realise how all-consuming love for a pet can be. Although far from an expert in this area, it strikes me that our love affair with dogs depends on their distinctive mixture of sameness and difference. They can attach themselves to people with an intensity and a fidelity that humans often fail to match. At times we seem to know them, and they to know us. My friends have a golden retriever, Isabelle, a lady of a certain age whose red coat (the standard golden retriever colour for the American breed) is now nobly silvered with grey about her ever-hungry chops. At one point I would see this beast frequently when my friends lived in the middle of Durham, but when they moved to the suburbs this stopped; until one evening when Isabelle and I were reunited on the Durham river bank by Hild Bede College. At first her frenzy of greeting seemed much the same as any other. But when she was presently pulled away (possibly because I was trying to eat something) Isabelle gave an unusual whimper of dismay, prompting us all to wonder about the dog's memory of a person she had not seen for over six months.

And yet… just when we think we know this almost human creature, the dog will remind us that it is, after all, an animal – whether by rolling in badger dung, or sinking like some red-coated and doe-eyed Thing From the Swamp into a bog of mud just before its long-suffering mother is due to take it back home by public transport.

Funnily enough, one of the things below which reminds us of this second quality is also something which humans would love to be able to do, and indeed to even understand. Take all the dotcom silicone valley space age billion dollar rocket science technology you can think of, shake it up in a superconducting atom blaster at a thousand miles per minute and… watch it fall *dead* in the water next to the brain of the dumbest dog, when it is set the task of travelling home 200 miles, on a route it has never used before. This, I hope, is something even cat-people or bird-fanciers can marvel at – as are many of the great dog rescues we will encounter in this opening chapter. We begin, happily enough, in the beautiful city of Durham.

1. Seventy Miles: with a Muzzle and no Map…
'A fox terrier dog, nearly seven months old, belonging to Mr Kingsford, of University College, Durham, has had a most remarkable walking tour. It had been reared by P.C. Bowe, the University constable, and on Tuesday 2nd August, it was taken by its master, Mr Kingsford, from Durham by train. On arriving at York station the dog escaped out of the carriage. It was at that time muzzled. Shortly before nine o'clock on Sunday morning last, five days after the dog escaped from York, P.C. Bowe observed it coming down his yard on the Palace Green, Durham. It was still muzzled, and was in a very thin and weak condition, being hardly able to crawl down the yard. About three inches of chain was attached to its collar, and the leather at the top of the muzzle was worn

and frayed, as if the dog had attempted to get loose. Its feet were very much blistered, and its nose was bruised, the latter probably having been caused by the animal's endeavours to get rid of the muzzle. There is little doubt (says the *Durham Advertiser*) that the poor animal travelled on foot from York to Durham,
a distance of nearly seventy miles, without any food.'
The Dundee Courier & Argus, 18 August 1892.

Like myself, some readers may have endured train journeys from York to Durham which make a half-starved and muzzled trip on bare feet seem appealing by comparison. By the time that this nameless animal hobbled back onto Palace Green, the wandering dogs of the nineteenth century must between them have covered thousands of miles, in Britain alone. Many such adventures will by now have been lost to us. But an impressive number have survived, and, whilst admiring our terrier's hardiness, padding seventy miles without food, we will find that his escapade was by no means the most startling of these. Already, though, this York-Durham trip raises one of the most intriguing questions posed by such stories of the canine homing instinct.

     Just how do dogs *do* this? The instinct, although apparently not quite universal, is clearly very common. My mother, indeed, recalls an example of it from her childhood in the 1940s, when their dog Pat was frightened by a sudden trumpet blast from a Scout band in the park, and hurtled off out of sight – only to turn up minutes later back at their house, around half a mile away. Clearly sense of smell alone cannot account for this uncanny skill – as we will see, many of the dogs in question, like the Durham terrier, took the correct route home, even if first brought down it by train or boat. In an age when the dreary robot tones of the satnav draw on enormous reserves of technology to guide drivers to their destinations, there is something romantically touching and mysterious about this inbuilt, homegrown ability, apparently lodged somewhere beyond reason in the brain of a dog. As we will see, whatever underpins this strange knack, cats also possess it.

2. Celebrity Dogs (I): Carlo the Actor.

'A new serio-comic spectacle, under the title of "The Caravan" was brought forward at Drury Lane Theatre on Monday night, with the aid of much splendid scenery and decoration. Muneral, the Spanish regent, is in love with the Marchioness of Culatrava. In order to forward his aims, he sends her husband [prisoner] in a close caravan to Barcelona, on his way to Mexico, and wishes even to starve him on his road; from this fate he is saved by Blabbo, the driver. The Marchioness follows her husband; the tyrant finding her inexorable, tears her child from her arms, and throws it into the sea. There is, on this occasion, a piece of real water on the stage, into which the dog Carlo leaps, and saves the infant ... The house was crowded to the very avenues. Mr Bannister, accompanied by the dog, gave it out for a second representation amid the loudest plaudits.'
The Bath Chronicle, 8 December 1803.

'The Dog Carlo. This day is published, price 1s., embellished with several beautiful engravings and his portrait, by permission of his owner, *The Life of Carlo*, the famous dog of Drury Lane Theatre, and the principal performer in The Caravan.'
The Morning Chronicle, 20 October 1804.

As Jan Bondeson explains in his recent book *Amazing Dogs*, Carlo's career had at this point only just begun: by 1806 he was touring the provinces, and come 1808 he was too busy to appear as Crab in a revised *Two Gentlemen of Verona*. His biography, though fictitious, was also a hit, and had been penned by the children's author Eliza Fenwick after she attended a Carlo performance filled with enchanted boys and girls. As Bondeson further notes, part of Carlo's popularity was down to a genius for improvisation rivalling that of Shakespeare's famous clown, Will Kemp. 'Once, he pushed the Marquis over and reclaimed the food he was supposed to share … Sometimes, the audience distracted him with their shouts of "Carlo! Carlo! Carlo!" and made him jump about and bark excitedly; at other times, when … bored, he lay down on stage and did not move a muscle.' Readers accustomed to the modern rigours of Health and Safety may also be interested to know that the rescue scene featured a real child, rather than a dummy. 'In March 1804, the mother of the child actor demanded that Carlo was replaced, since her son had been "terribly bruised" from the acting dog's powerful jaws'. Judging that the child was much less of a star than Carlo, the manager (adds Bondeson) simply 'got hold of a less squeamish child actor' instead (*Amazing Dogs*, 71-74).

The initial story that Carlo was the dog of a London butcher may well have been fabricated. As late as September 1880 *The Caravan* was still recalled as a piece which, after its debut, 'commenced a career which reached nearly 100 nights … By a contrivance new at Drury Lane, but often used at Sadler's Wells, a large tank of real water was placed on the stage and the dog sprang from a rocky elevation directly the child was thrown in. The water was procured easily enough, but considerable difficulty was experienced in obtaining the dog, which was at last hired from the proprietor of a neighbouring eating house.

During the first and second rehearsals, Carlo infinitely preferred sniffing the footlights to taking the jump; but, by some contrivances in the arrangement of the scenery, and the constant care and guidance of [actor Jack] Bannister, he was eventually drilled into perfect correctness. The effect literally electrified the audience ... "Thanks to my friend Carlo", wrote [playwright Frederick Reynolds], "I cleared £360, simply by a dog jumping into a small tank of water"'.

The dog also enriched 'the owner of the eating house, which was afterwards celebrated as "Johnson's Alamode Beef House" in Clare Court, Drury Lane. As Carlo's master would take no recompense but an occasional ticket to the Theatre for his friends, Sheridan obtained for Johnson a wine and spirit licence, thus considerably enhancing the profits of the establishment, and enabling him eventually to retire with a fortune. The house is alluded to by Charles Dickens in *David Copperfield*, and is the place where he came with a small piece of bread, and purchased a fourpenny plate of alamode beef to eat with it.'
The Era, 5 September 1880.

In the decades after Carlo hung up his collar, canine thespians were bounding without pause across the nation's stages. At the Theatre Royal, Leeds, in October 1883 audiences thrilled to *Mardo; or The Nihilists of St Petersburg*, featuring 'a den of wild hyenas, the wonderful acting dog Jack, and the two performing bears, Frank and Jenny', as well as 'the burning of a bridge and hut, and the realisation of a Siberian snowstorm' (*The Era*, 6 October 1883 – the hyenas, in case anyone is wondering, were played by dogs). *The Wild Violet*, at the Queen's Theatre, Birmingham, was a prairie drama boasting an acting dog, a den of hyenas, and a horse (*The Era*, 8 December 1894), and later in the 1890s Mr Nat Emmett and his acting dog Tiger had the whole week tailored to their skills at the Adelphi Theatre, Liverpool. Here viewers flocked in for *The Forest of Bondy* (first staged in Paris in 1814), *The Dog of the Standard*, *Dark Deeds*, *The Miser's Dog*, and *The Dog Detective* (*The Era*, 22 February 1896).

Be assured that neither Carlo nor his canine successors were the strangest actors to appear on the nineteenth century stage. We will, in our closing pages, be sending on the elephants and the camels…

3. Dog Rescues Dog.
'A few days ago a gentleman residing at a watering place on the Cowal shore resolved to drown a terrier which was in a diseased condition, and he accordingly hied himself with the animal to the pier, and, attaching a stone to its neck with a stout cord, committed it to the deep. The murderous act was observed by a large Russian dog belonging to a resident, and which was sunning itself on the pier. The body of the terrier had scarcely reached the bottom when the other dog plunged from the pier, dived, rose to the surface with the cord which attached the unfortunate terrier to the stone in its teeth, and swam to the shore, where it landed the terrier still alive, but, as the saying is, "in a very exhausted state from its immersion." The conscience-stricken owner immediately hurried home with it in his arms, and has, we are informed, made a solemn vow that whetever its fate may be it will not be

drowning by his hands.'
The Liverpool Mercury, 23 September 1863.

Although this is the most unusual incident of dog rescue I have come across, it is not the only one in which a dog saves another dog. In addition to what we will see below, we have a modern case from Chile which readers can watch for themselves on film: when one dog is struck by a car on a terrifyingly busy highway, another manages to reach it, and drag it to safety using its paws, rather than its teeth.[1] It is possible that these Chilean dogs were particular friends. But if not, the bravery of the rescuer might well seem all the more commendable. Perhaps Carlo's initial difficulties in training might have been more quickly overcome, had he been sent to rescue not a child, but a helpless puppy...

4. Dogs Hold a Funeral.

"'A curious incident of the sagacity and imitative habits of dogs came to our knowledge a day or two ago ... it can be substantiated by affidavits from several persons of the highest standing, members of the family in which it occurred, some of whom are ladies. Previous to the war, Governor Charles A. Wickliffe was an extensive slave-owner, and each one of his negroes owned one or more dogs. In 1860 one of these dogs, a spaniel, manifested symptoms of hydrophobia, and was shot by Judge Wickliffe, the Governor's son. Immediately after the shooting, all the dogs in the place collected around the body of their dead companion, and, after prolonged howling, prepared for a funeral. 'Old Bull', the largest and fiercest dog, took the body in his mouth and started for the woods south of the Governor's residence. The other dogs formed into a regular procession, and in a single file followed the body to the woods. They selected a tree just outside of the fence, and at the foot of it dug a grave, in which Old Bull deposited the body, and all the dogs joined in covering with earth the remains. After the grave had been filled, all united in more howling, which was kept up some ten or fifteen minutes, when they dispersed."'

Freeman's Journal, 11 September 1875, citing *Bardsdown Record,* Kentucky.

Did this really happen? The precise details (Wickliffe's name, the breed of the dog, and the symptoms of hydrophobia) certainly suggest that something did. Let us assume for a moment that the report is entirely accurate. If so, it would seem to imply that the dogs had seen other funerals, and perhaps the burial of one or more dogs in previous times. As the case of Minos the Skye terrier will show presently, dogs can perform some impressive feats if properly trained. What is of course intriguing about our Kentucky funeral is its relatively spontaneous character. It seems to have involved imitation and genuine grief, rather than any human intervention.

Two further questions might well be springing up in readers' minds. One: do dogs feel grief? And: are they capable of forming an orderly funeral procession? The remarkable case of Margarita Suarez suggests that the answer to both questions is indeed Yes. During her life this noted animal lover every day fed up to twenty stray dogs and cats in her home city of Cuernavaca in Mexico. Margarita died in March 2015. While her body was lying in a local chapel prior to her funeral, a number of dogs wandered in and kept a vigil there during the night –a phenomenon which Margarita's daughter Patricia described as 'something wonderful … on the saddest day of my life'. This clearly did happen, and pictures of the respectful dogs can be seen in online newspaper coverage. Moreover, it was also stated that,

"On the day of the funeral on March 15 the dogs formed a procession behind the hearse and returned to the funeral home, only leaving once the body was being prepared for cremation".[2]

A still more impressively faithful vigil was kept by Ciccio, the German shepherd dog of one Maria Margherita Lochi, after she died in November 2012. Having been taken regularly to the church of Santa Maria Assunta in San Donaci, Puglia by Maria during her lifetime, Ciccio now went and sat there day after day. Was he waiting, remembering, or paying tribute? Whatever his motivations, he was certainly decorous. According to Father Donato Panna: "He's there every time I celebrate Mass and is very well behaved - he doesn't make a sound, I've not heard one bark from him in all the time he has been coming in".[3]

It is probably not too whimsical to feel that these cases raise an interesting question about animal rights. Namely: should mourning dogs be allowed into churches? Personally, I suspect that a fair few Protestant churches would be rather less welcoming than those Mexican or Italian chapels (although Protestants themselves varied, as our next story shows). But I should certainly like to know what readers think – especially when they have read about the Welsh singing dog we will meet below. We will also see that Railway Jack, one of the most famous British dogs of this age, had an odd fondness for funerals, and was equally respectful during his attendance.

5. A Shaggy Dog Story.

'The residents of Windsor and the castle, where [Queen Victoria] is at present residing, were greatly startled and shocked last evening by the report of a murderous attempt which had been made upon the life of Lady Florence Dixie, whose travelling experiences and recent strictures upon the Land League Organisation are well known. Sir Beaumont and Lady Florence are living at

"The Fishery", a pretty villa, about three miles from Windsor, and situated upon the Berkshire shore of the Thames ...

Shortly before four o'clock in the afternoon Lady Florence Dixie, accompanied by a large favourite St Bernard dog, named Hubert, left the grounds and went for a stroll on the Windsor road ... Suddenly her Ladyship was confronted by two persons attired as women ... who came along the highway towards her...' The remainder of the story is best told by Lady Florence herself, who shortly afterwards, 'at her husband's request, gave an account of the outrage. Her Ladyship had just returned from a walk, attended by two or three gentlemen as an escort [when she gave her statement] ... She was clad in a red tight-fitting jersey, with red skirt and hat ... there was a ruddy glow upon her cheeks, as she recounted the affair, without apparent tremor ...

"I first saw the men who attacked me standing in the road, near Captain Brocklehurst's ... they were far too tall for women, ... [and] they were big and strong ... At that moment my attention was attracted to a soldier and a young woman who were walking down the road towards Windsor. I was standing just outside the little gate leading to the shrubbery, and I was thinking what a fine-looking man the soldier was. The two men came up behind me and asked me the time. I had no watch and could not tell, but I told them it was about twenty minutes to five, I thought. I then passed from the gate down the footpath ... when I saw them coming up behind me a second time. They did not then speak ... I then became suspicious of their intentions. One of them ran forward and caught me by the neck and threw me down upon the ground. The other man ... stabbed at me with a dagger. The dagger at the first thrust went against the steel of my corset. Then he pulled it out and stabbed again. I caught at it by the handle, and cut my hand and saw the bright steel. Mud was thrust in my mouth, and I then received a blow upon the head, and swooned, and heard no more ... My dog Hubert came up some time during the attack ... When I recovered consciousness I found myself upon the ground, all alone. The dog had gone probably to follow the men ... Whether the dog bit the men or not I cannot say; but he flew at the man who was stabbing me, and pulled him back. It was after I was over the fence the dog came up. I have no doubt he saved my life."

'The dog Hubert' (continues our reporter) 'has no marks or wounds upon him. His master states that he is an inoffensive animal, and though he would pull a man off who attacked him, he would seize by the clothes and not hurt anyone.' This report also added that, at the spot where Lady Florence had been thrown down, 'evidences of the terrible struggle which ensued are clearly discernible, the disturbed turf and soil being impressed by the nailed brogues of the men and the dog's feet.' At the same time this report seemed to sound a note of scepticism when it described how Lady Florence, during her statement, had held up her wounded hand 'covered by a narrow patch of plaster ... Neither her fingers nor any other portion of her hand were marked in any way, and ... no bruise of any kind ... was observable about either her Ladyship's face or neck.' The paper also expressed

surprise that two alleged Fenians would be so inexpert in their attack, and that Hubert should receive no wounds whatsoever.
The Standard, 19 March 1883.

On 31 March *Punch* seemed to amplify this sceptical note. Nominally congratulating Hubert on his heroism, it went on to ask of him various awkward questions, such as how he had managed to contend with two assailants at once; and why, if he had (as might be expected) torn one of the dresses to shreds, no trace of the material was to be found. The writer insisted that Hubert comply with 'the request of all England, for full information' and not 'simply wag your tail and say, "Bow, wow, wow!"'

Dixie's biographer, Dorothy Middleton, adds that 'Sir William Harcourt, the home secretary, declared in the House of Commons that the story was unconfirmed, and nothing further followed'. Given the status of Lady Florence and her husband, this sounds like a polite way of saying that the whole incident was fabricated; and indeed Doug MacGowan argues that it took years 'for Florence to recover her good name'.[4]

If she invented the story, then... why? We can only guess. Possibly to cover up a genuine incident, which was somehow embarrassing or scandalous to herself? At the darker end of the spectrum of conjecture, there is also the chance that she fabricated the affair to help discredit the cause of Irish land reform (cf her 'recent strictures upon the [Irish] Land League Organisation').

Despite the evidently very reasonable doubts about the attack, Hubert became (writes Bondeson) 'the most famous dog in Britain ... A gentleman sent Hubert a silver-studded collar, and many people sent him bones, beefsteaks and other treats'. Lady Florence turned down at least two offers of money for Hubert, including one from 'a showman who wanted to exhibit the dog in a music hall', although 'she consented to Hubert becoming the special invited guest at a dog show in Durham, where he was awarded first prize.' Hubert was also present, though not competing, in the Bristol, Clifton and West of England dog show in January 1885, where he was lauded as the dog 'who so successfully defended her Ladyship from the attack of the footpads'. To cap all this, Hubert was photographed by Mr Snook of Windsor, and a copy of the image sent to Queen Victoria (*Amazing Dogs*, 200-201).

6. Religious Freedom.
'In New Boston ... one of the canine species attended regularly a Methodist Episcopal Church in one of the villages near that city. The animal attended all the services, behaving most decorously for a dog. The doorkeeper, however, having treated him rather rudely when attending a funeral, he became offended and went off and joined the Congregationalists, at whose place of worship he became a regular attendant.'
The Illustrated Police News, 17 June 1876.

7. Uncanny Rescue.
'A Broughty Ferry* lady ... gives an account of a strange occurrence by which her husband was saved from being run down in a ferryboat. The gentleman was just about to step into the ferryboat to cross the river, when a large retriever rushed upon him, caught hold of his trousers with its teeth, and at the same time set up a constant howl. It was only after considerable difficulty that he could get himself released, and by that time the ferryboat had been shoved off into the river. The gentleman naturally felt much annoyed at being prevented from crossing; but his feelings were changed

when, a minute later, he saw the ferryboat run down by a steamer which had approached without noticing the boat.

The passengers were thrown into the water, but fortunately the crew of the steamer were successful in saving them all, some being very much exhausted, however. While thinking of the singular means by which he had been saved from the accident, the gentleman could not help noticing the conduct of the dog, which followed closely at his heels. He tried every means to get rid of it during the day; but in the afternoon the animal was still following him, and he was obliged to take it home with him. The dog has now been installed as watchman of the house, and has already shown great attachment to the gentleman and his family.'
Edinburgh Evening News, 12 September 1878.
*Broughty Ferry lies on the Scottish coast, four miles east of Dundee.
A whole minute seems quite a long time between the dog's intervention and the collision between steamer and ferryboat (and indeed, the steamboat must have been some way off for our gentleman to have missed it). This raises an intriguing question. Did our retriever somehow see into the future, rather than merely guessing what was about to happen? There is evidence to suggest that a small number of people possess the faculty of precognition – some years ago, for example, a friend of mine and her mother both dreamed, on the same night, of a road accident at a certain spot in the nearby countryside. The next day an accident occurred in that exact place, resulting in a death.

In his book *Dogs That Know When Their Owners are Coming Home*, Rupert Sheldrake gives cases where dogs protect their owners just before a blackout or a heart attack. Noting that this may often be due to the animal picking up 'some subtle change in the person's behaviour …movements, or … unusual smells', Sheldrake adds that such anticipations have also occurred when the animal and the person are in different rooms, or yet further apart. Again, some readers will probably have their own stories here.

8. Taxing Times.

'Among the humours of the Southwark election, the palm must be awarded to a large brown and white retriever dog, who, acting the part of a boardman, might have been seen perambulating the Old Kent Road, decorated with a blue tie, and a card dependent from his neck with the legend:

> What have the Tories done for the likes of me?
> Raised my tax by 2s 6d.'

Penny Illustrated Paper, 10 April 1880.

This increase actually seems to have been less harsh than originally designed: in April 1879 dog-owners were heatedly denouncing a proposed raise from 2s 6d to 7s 6d.

9. A Dog Detective: I.

'About two months ago the sum of £46 in bank notes was stolen from a warehouse in George Street, Glasgow, by a man employed on the premises. The thief had concealed himself in the warehouse before the closing hour, and after every person had left he broke open several desks and abstracted the cash, the greater portion of which he concealed under a stone in a field in the northern district.

It so happened that when the thief was in the act of concealing the notes a retriever dog, belonging to a young man residing in New City Road, was amusing itself near the spot, and after the money had been hidden, the dog appears to have uncovered the parcel of notes and carried the cash home. It is alleged that the owner of the dog was present when the animal entered with the cash in his mouth, and that the mother of the young man observed that the parcel was composed of bank notes. The latter denies that his dog ever brought a parcel of notes to the house. It is somewhat remarkable also that when the thief of the cash was apprehended he admitted the charge, and told the detectives that he had concealed a portion of the money in a park. The officers took him to the park, and he pointed out the spot where he had concealed the notes. The retriever dog was there, and it was with some difficulty that the officers could complete their search, in consequence of the dog barking and leaping round them. The money, it was discovered, had been carried off. The young man and his mother have been apprehended pending an investigation into this somewhat strange case.'
Cheltenham Chronicle, 12 July 1870.

10. A Doggie Robber.

'Mrs Knight ... and her sister were returning about 6 o'clock [in] the evening from Pancras Church towards Battle Bridge [when] a shaggy dog, resembling a drover's dog, unaccompanied by any person, jumped suddenly up from the roadside, and laying hold of the reticule* she had in her hand with his teeth, forcibly snatched it from her, and crossing off the road, made his escape: her reticule contained a pound note, a sovereign, 18s in silver, a silver thimble, a pair of silver spectacles, and several other articles. The constable stated, that a dog answering the same description, attacked a poor woman on Saturday evening, near the Veterinary College, and robbed her of a bundle containing two shirts, some handkerchiefs, and other things, with which he ran away, and that the poor woman was so frightened, it had nearly cost her her life. There were several other charges made against the same dog, which is supposed to have been trained up to the business, and that his master must be at some place not far distant. The officers undertook to be on the alert to apprehend this depredator, or else to shoot him.'

Trewman's Exeter Flying Post, 18 September 1817.

*A small handbag. Interestingly, handbags closer to the size of modern ones were still novel objects of suspicion in the late nineteenth century. A policeman who spied a woman with one of these might look on her rather as later officers would view a dubious youth in a hood – given that the more capacious bags quite often contained rocks, hurled by suffragettes through windows in their campaign for the vote.

It would be intriguing to know just how this dog was 'trained up to the business'. Did the training, for example, have to involve a real woman? We can presume that our furry robber aimed only at delicate females, especially as men were not in the habit of carrying conveniently accessible reticules.

11. Lassie Sent Home:
Or, The Shepherd, the Actor and the Sheepdog.

'Mr Henry Irving was in Scotland two or three summers ago,* and on one of his walks he frequently met a shepherd with a fine collie. He took a fancy to the dog, and a few days before leaving he said to the Highlander, "I will give you £50 for your collie." The shepherd seemed surprised at the amount offered, and was struck with sadness, for he was poor and wanted the money, yet he had formed so strong an attachment to the dog that he could not bear the thought of parting with it. After deliberating for a while, he said, "Na, sir, I weel na tak the fifty pund." "Well then," said Mr Irving, "I will give you 60 if you like to bring the dog to my hotel within three days." The man stood looking down at his dog and was silent, and Mr Irving walked away.

At the end of three days one of the hotel servants said that a shepherd had called to see Mr Irving. The Highlander and his dog came in, and the man said that although he did not want to part with the collie, as he was poor and had a family to support, he could not afford to keep a dog worth £60, and he had decided to accept the offer. The poor fellow took the money and thanked Mr Irving. He looked once very hard at the collie, which whined and tried to lick his hand; then he threw his arm over his eyes and ran out of the room.

Mr Irving brought the dog to London, but the rumble of the city and the crowds in the street seemed to confuse him. He grew more and more unhappy, and after a few days the great actor began to regret his bargain, for he had only succeeded in making himself, the shepherd, and the dog thoroughly miserable. A few

days after his return, Mr Irving took his dog into Kensington Gardens, and for a moment the poor creature brightened at the sight of a few sheep that were grazing under the trees, but soon discovering that they were not his own flock, and that his master was not near, he lapsed into his usual dejection. After this, it was very difficult to get him to take any food, and as he soon lost his fine appearance and grew lean, Mr Irving decided to give him his liberty. So he returned him as a present to the Highlander, who afterwards wrote that the dog was so overjoyed to get back home that he leapt upon his old master's shoulders, and then ran about the hills so wildly that he (the shepherd) feared for a time he would go mad.'
The North-Eastern Daily Gazette, 23 November 1893.
*In fact, the date of this visit seems to have been 1878.

To most of us, it seems so obvious that this dog was wild with joy that the point scarcely needs labouring. Yet, as we have seen, many experts on animal behaviour have been at pains to deny or doubt the existence of emotion in dogs, cats, parrots, primates or elephants (to name just a few of the more likely candidates). Jeffrey Masson and Susan McCarthy, on the other hand, have made a powerful case for taking animal emotion seriously, and some of the examples they use to support their argument are similar to this one. Could we get a dog to replicate, in a laboratory, the romping ecstasies of that Scottish collie? I doubt it. So: how can we be sure that it was really happy? Sometimes, common sense really is the best approach…

From the 1870s until his sudden death in 1905, Irving (knighted in 1895) established himself as a national icon in the world of theatre – both as actor and as owner and manager of the Lyceum, where he showcased, among others, the great actress Ellen Terry.

Interestingly, Irvine's biographer Robertson Davies notes that the actor, aged around eleven, was first introduced to popular entertainment when his father took him to see Van Amburgh, the great lion-tamer of the day. Irving is also now remembered as the model for Stoker's Dracula, having strongly influenced the author's idea of the Count's physical and psychological qualities.

Perhaps most interesting to us, however, is Irving's legendary generosity. He came from a relatively humble background in Cornwall, and in his early years as an actor endured a great deal of hardship. As Davies shrewdly notes, by the time of his success and affluence, 'he tipped with the open hand of a man who had known real poverty, and laughed when Ellen Terry told him in desperation (using the most dreadful of Victorian accusations) that such tipping was "common". But the guineas flowed on, and when Irving died every cabman in London tied a crepe ribbon on his whip'. Now, a knighthood is one thing; but that, surely, is the way to be remembered when you go.

12. Brain Beats Brawn.

'A correspondent sends us the following: "In my neighbourhood there live two large and ferocious cats, which consort together for the purpose of feloniously assaulting any unfortunate dog they may happen to meet. Their *modus operandi* was as follows: having selected their victim they would lie in wait for him behind a wall; then they would spring out, and while one jumped on his back and dug its claws into him, the other would lacerate his countenance in a manner frightful to behold.

One day they treated in this manner ... a young collie, who naturally was much astonished and alarmed by their sudden onslaught, and fled precipitately with his tail between his legs. Next time, however, he turned the tables on them by pretending not to notice them till they attacked him, when he got rid of the cat who sprang on his back by running under a fence, and then he returned to the charge; and slew the other cat, while the first, thinking it unsafe to risk further combat, fled for its life, and did not stop until it had put a good distance between itself and the dog, who by his sagacity had put a stop to the ill-treatment of his canine fellow creatures.'

The North-Eastern Daily Gazette, 3 February 1887.

13. Woof and Safety.

'Everybody will agree that Mr Sheil, the magistrate, acted with admirable discretion in recommending the directors of the Aquarium to use a dummy baby instead of a real one for a sensational performance in which a collie dog rescues an infant from a house on fire and descends a fire escape with it in its mouth. It was highly exciting, said the promoters of the "show", but there was no danger to the child, and they therefore asked the magistrate's permission to employ a nine month old infant in the performance. "No", said Mr Sheil, "you won't get permission from me for such a thing." "But", urged a promoter, "the father of the baby is here, and he will tell you that the dog is a most sagacious creature – in fact it rocks the baby's cradle." "I don't care", replied the magistrate; "I can't believe that spectators would experience pleasure in seeing a child in such a position, and there is always the risk of some accident happening. No, no; you needn't attempt to argue. I don't care what you say, I shall not sanction it. A dummy will

do just as well, and you will have to use it instead of the baby if the performance be given." Surely the sagacity of the animal can be as well displayed on a harlequinade infant as on a real and helpless child. The dog itself, if it really be sagacious, will feel much more comfortable with a dummy in its mouth than a living being.'
The Yorkshire Herald, 25 September 1893.

Readers will notice the great strides made by Health and Safety since the days of the heroic Carlo and his infant co-stars.

14. A Near Miss.

'The other day, after the three o'clock train for Dumfriess had left Annan Station, a collie dog was observed near to the bridge complacently trotting along in front between the rails on which the train was travelling. The driver blew the whistle loudly to frighten the dog off the line, but when the train had come within a short distance of him, the collie came to a standstill, turned to the right-about, and barked furiously. The observers expected to see the dog run over, but just as the train came up he suddenly ducked his head, and lay flat on the ground until it had passed over him. He then essayed to stand, but he must have been struck by some portion of the engine, and been somewhat stunned, for he was unable to keep his feet, and rolled down the embankment. After a time he recovered, and quietly went his way home along the line. The dog has been in the habit of running after passing trains, but since this adventure it is observed he has given up the practice.'
The Evening Telegraph, 26 June 1886.

15. Celebrity Dogs (II): Railway Jack.

'Few people who travel on the London, Brighton, and South Coast Railway know what a distinguished character has a free pass on every branch of the line, of which for several years he has taken daily advantage. It is between two and three years ago that a fox terrier, big in bone, and not over well-bred, jumped into a train that was leaving Brighton for Horsham, and settled himself in the guard's carriage. Little notice was taken of him at first, but after a time he began to be a person of great interest. No one knew where he came from or to whom he belonged; but every day he was ready for an early start in an early train. Sometimes he went to Portsmouth, sometimes to Horsham; sometimes only to nearer stations; but the most remarkable part of his arrangements was that he always got to Brighton in time to go by the last train to Lewes, where he always slept, leaving again by the first train in the morning.

When the friend from whom I first heard this story ... last heard of Jack he still continued this practice, and always spent the night at Lewes station. About a year ago the London, Brighton, and South Coast Railway began to look upon him as one of their regular servants, and presented him with a collar bearing this inscription: "Jack -- London, Brighton and South Coast Railway Company." My friend told me that on one occasion, some months ago, he traced Jack's movements on one especial day, and probably it was a good sample of many another. He arrived from Brighton by a train reaching Steyning at 10.50; there he got out for a minute, but went on by the same train to Henfield.

Here he left the train, and went to a public house not far from the station, where a biscuit was given to him; and, after a little walk, took a later train to West Grinstead, where he spent the afternoon, returning to Brighton in time for the last train to Lewes.

He was rather fond of the Portsmouth line but never, I believe, has come so far as London. He generally takes his place on or by the guard's wheel, and sits looking out of the window. It would be very interesting to know in what the fascination of this perpetual railway travelling consists. It certainly shows an immense amount of instinct and observation, and the regularity and punctuality of Jack's daily life are a lesson to many a two-legged traveller. Whether he considers himself sub-guard, or director, or general overseer, no one can tell, but there is, it seems, an idea of duty in his movements; what he has to do (or thinks he has to do) he does faithfully, and so far is a telling example to his fellow travellers on the London, Brighton, and South Coast Railway.'
The Huddersfield Daily Chronicle, 2 June 1881.

'The interment took place on Friday of Mr Bryant, for many years platform inspector at Eastbourne station, and who died under somewhat painfully sudden circumstances a few days ago. Besides a large number of the railway staff at Eastbourne, Polgate, Hailsham and other stations, the members of the Eastbourne Manual Fire Brigade, to which the deceased was for years attached, and a large number of tradespeople, attended. A singular fact in connection with the funeral was the presence of the celebrated railway dog "Jack".

This remarkably sagacious animal has not been seen in town since the dog show in September, but on Thursday it arrived on one of the trains about midday, and taking up a position near the hearse, not only followed the corpse to the cemetery, but entered the chapel, and in common with the other mourners took a look at the coffin after it had been lowered into the grave. This incident would be less significant were it not for the fact that the dog turned up in an equally singular manner, and conducted itself in the same orderly way, at the funeral of Isgar, the late head porter, at Lewes a few weeks since.'
Portsmouth Evening News, 5 November 1881.

After what we have seen of that canine Guard of Honour during the last farewell to Margarita Suarez, we can well understand Jack's sober devotion at these Victorian funerals (although how he knew to get to them is another mystery ranking with that of dogs' homing abilities.) What makes Jack still more remarkable, however, is the way in which he quickly became one of Britain's greatest animal celebrities. This status was already strong early in 1882 when, as Bondeson points out, the wealthy Mrs J.P. Knight of Brockley presented Jack with a silver-mounted collar. On it were inscribed the words: 'I am Jack, the L.B. and S.C. Railway Dog. Please give me a drink, and then I will go home to Lewes.' Like other celebrities, Jack combined elements of robust individualism with eccentricity. Thus, when the same lady presented him with 'a sumptuous dog basket with a soft mattress', Jack spurned this luxury, preferring instead 'to sleep in the waste paper basket in the booking office' (*Amazing Dogs*, 89) - which, in dog terms, very probably smelled better.

    Another thing about great celebrities is the way that they often manage to turn potential disaster into one more element of their public persona (think, for example, of David Bowie and the curious appearance of his right eye after a schoolroom fight had damaged it). And it seems in some ways to have been a brush with death which shot Jack to still greater heights of fame. In January 1882 at least ten British papers reported on how, 'this well known dog has met with an accident'. After failing to return to his home at Lewes Station for about a fortnight, Jack had been brought back with a crushed leg. He had apparently been at Norwood Junction on the evening of Thursday 12 January, and, attracted by a dead bird on the line, had 'crossed the metals just as a fast train was running through. He missed his hold in jumping on the opposite platform, and fell under the engine. A surgeon has very successfully amputated the limb close to the shoulder, the operation being performed while the animal was under the influence of chloroform.' Although Jack managed to rub off his bandages, thereby causing a secondary haemorrhage, this was luckily discovered before it could prove fatal, and he was then closely watched.

Jack's fans were no doubt relieved to hear that 'no difficulty is anticipated as to Jack's future locomotion on three legs, although the radius of his operations will be necessarily more limited. Hitherto it has been from Paris to Scotland. The last previous appearance of Jack in Lewes was when he had just returned from a wedding, and he arrived gaily bedecked with ribbons in honour of the event' (*The Star*, 19 January 1882). By this time Jack had indeed been travelling as far afield as France and Scotland. The wedding where he was decked with ribbons, for example, had taken place in Berwick. His first foray north of the border may, however, have been due to a rare mistake. Bondeson, noting Jack's 'almost uncanny ability to always catch the right train', adds that he ended up in Edinburgh after somehow catching the wrong one in Croydon. Tellingly, by this time he was already sufficiently famous among the Scottish guards and porters to be 'fed and housed … for a week' before being put on a train back to Lewes. His trips to France, meanwhile, may have arisen because of his attachment to a military officer, who seems to have known Jack since the late 1870s, and with whom the dog (apparently thinking his uniform was that of a railway guard) would often travel in a first-class compartment over to the continent (*Amazing Dogs*, 87-88).

In July 1882 we hear of Jack being presented with yet one more silver collar by the judge, Sir Henry Hawkins, and in following months various dog shows featured him as a star guest, emphasising the strange status of our three-legged hero: these Victorian events were typically highly snobbish, and would normally have booted out mutilated strays pretty unceremoniously.

'Yesterday an addition was made to the Poultry and Dog Show at the Drill Shed by the arrival of "Railway Jack", the famous dog, who attracted a good deal of attention hopping about on his three legs. During the animal's stay his headquarters will be at the Golden Fleece.'
Portsmouth Evening News, 24 November 1883.

Southdown Fox Terrier Club Show.
'The 6th annual show of this club, under Kennel Club Rules, was held at the Aquarium, Brighton'. The quality of the exhibits was, we hear 'much higher than at any previous show' and 'a very interesting feature of the show was Railway Jack, who looked well, and was the recipient of many caresses.'
The County Gentleman, 15 November 1884.

Notice how this first report looks not unlike a little snippet from *Hello*! magazine: readers are informed where Railway Jack will be staying, rather in the manner of a columnist giving out the hotel of a movie star for those fans who wish to keep vigil outside. In a way, the second clip is even more revealing. It has very little to say, other than that Jack looks well, and is stroked by many admirers. The banality of this is striking: you could say exactly the same thing about any popular dog in any age or country – which brings us to a fascinating element of celebrities in general, animal or human. These people are famous for *being themselves*. Everything they do is a newsworthy event – as are their appearances, their clothes, and any physical peculiarities, from a black eye through weight gain or pregnancy. What is of course curious about Jack is that he was now famous for being himself without ever having aimed at it. In many ways, he was the reverse of the egotistical or reclusive celebrities of our times: he liked travelling on trains (and thus constantly appearing in public), he liked people, and he was more than happy to have them touch him.

By this time, however, Jack did have a kind of unofficial manager or agent. Originally, no one seems to have owned him (making us wonder if he first started travelling on trains to find the owner he had lost). But he naturally became attached to Mr F.G. Moore, the station-master at Lewes, and when Moore retired in 1884 he took Jack to live with him at his house in Mayfield. Moore also seems to have taken him about on trains a good deal, thus compensating for Jack's disability. In August 1885 Jack turned up at the Ryde dog show on the Isle of Wight, and at some point in these later years was presented to the Prince and Princess of Wales, as well as to the Prince and Princess Edward of Saxe-Weimar (also on Wight, though this time at the Cowes regatta). Even when he was not appearing in public, Jack was occasionally referred to in connection with other railway dogs, in Britain and America. His name in these cases acted as a kind of patent, with reporters referring to 'another Railway Jack' – a kind of minor version of the Original and Best. Nor was Jack forgotten when he died of old age in 1890. If an obituary is one clear index of fame, then Jack did as well as many human rivals here, with his death being reported in at least twenty British papers, from Scotland to Cornwall.

'A famous dog, which had more than once the honour of presentation to Royalty, died on Monday [27 October] at the house of his Master, Mr F.G. Moore of Mayfield, Sussex. Mr Moore was formerly station-master at Lewes, and his dog, Railway Jack, was known far and wide as a traveller. He began by taking the train to Brighton and Newhaven, and then extended his journeys to London, Dover and Canterbury, and afterwards went as far afield as Exeter, Edinburgh, and Glasgow – but always returned to Lewes. Once, at Eastbourne, the late Lady Brassey presented Jack to the Prince and Princess of Wales, and he was introduced to Prince and Princess Edward of Saxe-Weimar at Cowes. He was a great favourite everywhere, and had three fine collars given him, and a silver medal. Jack was nearly thirteen when he ended his notable career on Monday last.' *Sheffield Evening Telegraph*, 30 October 1890.

Are there any other similarities between Jack and the human celebrities of the past two hundred years? At least two come to mind. As saturated in celebrity culture as our own world is, we may not easily realise that such figures are only around two centuries old. Or so, at least, runs the argument. It has often been claimed that celebrities only came into being once sufficient means of mass communication and distribution were available to keep them in the public mind and eye. Hence two big candidates for the coveted title of First Ever Celebrity: Byron and Wilde. Both of these figures were highly flamboyant, talented, and unmistakable when they appeared in public. A new play by Wilde was a major event, and (allowing for differences of class, wealth and literacy) a new poem by Byron was a literary event not entirely unlike the publication of a new Harry Potter. Whilst Byron already had mass publishing to aid him, Wilde's age also had a well-established railway network, speeding up the distribution of both books and newspapers – to say nothing of other inventions such as photography and the telegraph. If we slot Jack in between these two figures, he fits rather neatly. It is obvious enough that he depended on the press for much of his fame. Moreover, whereas other celebrities were indebted to the steam trains which shuttled print across the world at ever faster rates, Jack was a celebrity who became famous just for having himself carried up and down the rails.

A second point about human celebrities is the strange attraction of their blankness or passivity. I say 'strange' because in many ways they are often highly distinctive and aggressive characters. Yet, at the same time, because their lives can so easily become remote, shrouded in rumour and scandal, it is also possible for their fans to project fantasies and dreams onto these mythic, semi-human figures. Like royalty, they rarely condescend to answer back. If this – even in the age of Twitter – is an important part of celebrity, then what could possibly be better than a media star who never says a word?

16. A Canine Triathlon.

'The following instance of canine sagacity is worthy of record. A dog bred in Hull, and which had never crossed the Humber, by some accident fell from a London trading vessel, on board of which he was, into the sea, off the coast of Lincolnshire, about six miles from shore. After swimming to land, he made his way across country to Barton, a distance of over 30 miles, and

walking into the ferryboat, was conveyed across the Humber to Hull, where he took up his abode at his old master's, who, as may be imagined, was not a little surprised at his return.'
Hereford Journal, 14 September 1808.

It would be interesting to know what breed of dog this was, given that its voyage seems to have involved intelligence and memory, along with that familiar homing instinct. We will presently meet a collie making a still more impressive trip by both land and water.

17. The In-Patient.

'Considerable interest was excited in Leicester yesterday by the publication of a remarkable, and indeed almost incredible "dog story" from the accident ward of the local infirmary. It is related that while a Bible woman was visiting the accident ward some days ago, and talking to one of the patients, a terrier dog made its way to her with difficulty from near one of the adjoining beds, and appealingly

HELD UP ONE OF ITS FOREPAWS.

She called the attention of one of the doctors to the animal, and it was then found that the limb was broken. The bones were set, and a bed made up for the canine sufferer in the ward, due instructions being given upon the patient's card as to his treatment and diet. The animal progressed favourably, and became a general favourite with both the patients and officials, until a day or two ago, when it was claimed by its owner, and taken away. How the terrier found its way to the infirmary is not known, but it

ENTERED THE INSTITUTION UNOBSERVED,

and curiously enough was found in the accident ward, where men were being treated for ailments similar to that with which the dog was afflicted. But it will be readily believed that the officials and patients regretted to part with so interesting a patient – one that proved so amenable to treatment and discipline.'
Sheffield Evening Telegraph, 25 March 1896.

As we will see, an impressive number of dogs pulled off this feat – and in one famous case the patient was 'taken to hospital' by two other hounds, who waited until he had been admitted. These incidents again suggest that dogs often observe what is happening around them pretty shrewdly – though we do not always realise this until they have to draw on such knowledge (Hmmm... Now where is it that humans go to get their paws mended? Ah, yes…).

18. Heroic Rescue.
'The following letter appears in the *Bath Journal*. The name of the heroic youth should be made known; his conduct deserves recompense.
"Sir – From the Reading Room of the Mechanics' Institution, the Grove, I, with others, was witness to an act of youthful intrepidity and affection which, had it happened in the palmy days of Rome, and the preservation of life for which he hazarded his own had been that of a fellow creature, instead of that of a poor dog, it would have obtained for its author the reward of a civic crown.

The circumstances are these. A drover's dog, driven by hunger to one of the slaughter-houses that lie at the back of Boatstall Lane, and upon the margin of the river, above the weirs, was detected by an enraged slaughterman, severely punished, and thrown into the river, which happens to be unusually high at this time. The poor animal, though much distressed, succeeded in reaching a part where the weir is much higher than at any other spot, and where it is always dry except in very extraordinary floods. Here the dog, terrified by the foaming waters that entirely surrounded him, lay down for 4 hours, from 12 to 4, without the least chance of escape, unless he plunged into the boiling cauldron below and swam to the opposite side of the river, which he did not seem to show the least inclination to do.

Whilst regarding the poor animal and commiserating its lot, we at once perceived a naked and venturous youth swimming from the slaughter-house side of the river to the elevated part of the weir with the intention of rescuing it from its prison; but how was this to be done by a naked lad? The courageous youth landed, took hold of the dog, which was very passive under his hands, unwound a cord that was round its neck to the length of about one yard and a half, took one end in his hand, the dog following, and stepped cautiously down on the weir, over which the water was pouring with great velocity, and where the water reached nearly to the height of his knees. The youth advanced carefully and slowly several yards, dragging the dog through the water by the cord, and whose head could be seen, but just above the water on the weir, on account of its depth. The stream proved too powerful for the dog, and he was carried down by its violence into the torrent below, and it was a matter of astonishment to the spectators how the youth could so coolly sustain his footing on the weir. The dog was for a moment overwhelmed and carried off to some distance by the force and turbulence of the stream, but he soon faced about in the direction of his liberator, and fruitlessly attempted to head it. However, at length he got into an eddy and succeeded in reaching the base of his former place of shelter, where he again met the dauntless youth, ready to conduct him to the top of it.

The energies of the lad seemed to be wholly engaged in the recovery of the dog, which completely blinded him to the imminent dangers that surrounded himself. Another attempt was made; the plan was to make a loop at the end of the cord still attached to the dog, through which he put his arm, and strained it up tightly to the top of it, as if he were now determined to share his fate with the dog's, whatever that might be. He then took the dog up in his arms and again stepped down cautiously on the weir and advanced upon it, though with some difficulty, some yards, when he, to the surprise of all, rashly plunged into the upper stream with his charge, with the intention to reach the slaughter-house side of the river, from whence he had first departed; but it was evident to all who were looking on, that the current was too mighty, and that it was madness to breast it. Both the lad and the dog, thus corded together, were, as expected, at once preciptated over the fall, and plunged into the chafed waters below.

Death seemed inevitable, and the scene was for a few moments terrifically exciting. They were lost in the surf, and when they appeared in the middle of the stream the lad was pushing the dog from his neck; he then struck out for the opposite shore, which he and the dog, still banded together, reached in safety, and where

were two companions ready to drag him on shore, and to cover him with a part of his apparel. The lad appeared about 17 years of age, and is a drover. Through the whole proceeding I never met with such a cool and determined courage in the course of a long life as was evinced on the above occasion, and exercised too in a cause that showed a high degree of good feeling, forming a noble contrast with that of the exasperated slaughter-man, who in his rage threw the poor animal into the river."'
24 Nov 1841. M.
North Wales Chronicle, 28 December 1841.

It is a shame that we do not know more about the man who witnessed this heroic exploit, and later committed it to paper. We can certainly imagine that he never forgot the incident, given the way he thrusts it before our eyes in all its breathless drama and detail. What we do know is that Mechanics' Institutes at this time acted as libraries and educational sites for working class people. This would therefore suggest that our author had an instinctive sympathy for the working class lad who risked his life for the stranded dog. Was it the boy's own animal? We will never know for sure. At any rate, it gave him a certain fame, and there is something very pleasing about being able to restore that to him, almost 180 years on. We can well believe that, even in the notoriously unequal and class-bound world of Victorian London, some genteel spectators or readers were touched by the daring of this quixotic lad. Animals, you see, bring people together.

    I would rather like to see a statue by the Thames, of this brave boy bearing the dog from the water. Readers' thoughts on this gratefully received.

19. You May Now Shoot the Bride.

'A strange event occurred a few days since in a commune near Coutance (Manche), in France. A young man employed on a farm had married his master's daughter, and in doing so had carried off the prize from several other suitors, and the nuptials were kept with all the rejoicings usual on such occasions. In the evening a large house dog, chained up in the yard, was heard barking most violently, and was at length set at liberty in order to quiet him. The moment the animal was let loose it ran into the house and up the stairs to the door of the room prepared for the married couple, against which he began scratching in a violent manner. On the door being opened by the persons who had followed the animal, the dog rushed under the bed, and immediately a loud cry was heard. On looking under a man, who had just been strangled by the dog, was found, having in his hands two loaded pistols. He was recognised as one of the defeated suitors of the bride, and doubtless meditated a sanguinary vengeance for his disappointment.'

The Penny Illustrated Paper, 1 March 1862.

20. A Dog Detective: II.

'A gentleman of property had a mastiff of great size, and altogether a fine intelligent animal. Though often let out to range about, he was in general chained up during the day in a wooden house, constructed for his comfort and shelter. On a certain day, when let out, he was observed to attach himself particularly to his master; and when the servant, as usual, came to tie him up, he clung so to his master's feet – showed such anger when they attempted to force him away, and altogether was so particular in his manner, that the gentleman desired him to be left as he was, and with him he continued the whole day; and when night came on, still he staid by him, and on going towards his bed-room, the dog resolutely, and for the first time in his life, went up along with him, and rushing into the room, took refuge under the bed, from whence neither blows nor caresses could draw him.

In the middle of the night, a man burst into the room, and dagger in hand, attempted to stab the sleeping gentleman; but the dog darted at the robber's neck, fastened his fangs in him, and so kept him down that his master had time to call for assistance and secure the villain, who turned out to be the coachman, and who afterwards confessed that, seeing his master receive a large sum of money, he and the groom had conspired together to rob and murder him – and that they had plotted their whole scheme leaning over the roof of the dog's house.'
Cleave's Penny Gazette, 17 October 1840.

I'd be very interested in what dog-owners think of these two stories. It is perhaps notable that the first has a definite location, whereas the second lacks one. There again, it does have enough particular detail to stop us from merely writing it off as an urban legend. Assuming it were true, this 1840 report presents another possible case of a dog spontaneously understanding what people say (rather than learning, for example, to understand commands through systematic training). Is this what our faithful mastiff did? Another possibility is that it simply sensed something dark and furtive about the men's tone of voice. Yet one other is that it literally smelled trouble – a possibility worth considering, given that in recent years dogs have, for example, been successfully trained to sniff out cancer in humans.

21. How he Brought the Good News from Paris to Perpignan.

'The following instance of fidelity and sagacity in a dog was some time back related by Dr. Pariset, Late President of the Academy of Medicine at Paris, at a meeting of *La Societé Protectrice des Animaux**: A young man of Perpignan was arrested on a charge of conspiracy, and taken by two gendarmes from that city to Paris. He had a dog, which, seeing its master carried off in this manner, knew that he was unhappy; and, in his looks showing sadness and grief, the dog followed the carriage in which his master was conveyed, but taking care not to show himself to him. When they arrived in Paris their carriage was driven to the prison of the Conciergerie. There the three travellers alighted, and the dog, not being able any longer to conceal himself, assuming an attitude of submission, of condolence and of fear, came crouching to his master, who, surprised and affected, replied to his caresses by his own, and obtained leave from the governor of the prison for the poor animal to remain with him.

Three months passed before the trial came on, and, on the day it took place, the young man was followed to the Hall of Justice by his dog, which lay down under a bench, where it remained during the trial. The young man was unanimously acquitted, and was most warmly congratulated by numerous friends who were present. Before leaving the court he inquired for his dog, but it was nowhere to be found. From the joy which followed the acquittal, the dog concluded that his master was out of danger and had nothing more to fear, and he immediately set out for Perpignan, travelling night and day, supporting itself by any nourishment which chance might offer, and by some moments of repose – repose too short, but yet too long for his impatience – poor nourishment, but rendered exquisite by the image of the happiness he was about to impart to the family of his master.

After a journey of more than a hundred hours he reached the city, and arrived at his master's house, where he barked loudly and scraped violently at the door, and when it was opened by the surprised family, the dog rushed in, his heart palpitating, his eyes sparkling with delight, running from side to side, leaping and uttering cries of joy; the movements of his whole frame seemed to say "Rejoicing be in the midst of you!" In reality, two days afterwards a letter arrived, acquainting the family with the happy result of the trial, and announcing the speedy return of him for whom they so long suffered the greatest anxiety. From Paris to Perpignan the distance is 240 leagues – 720 English miles.

As soon as the dog saw his master acquitted, which he knew from the joy of his friends, he must have reasoned in this manner, "My master is now in safety, and I am no longer necessary to him. Let me run home to those who are kept in a state of cruel suspense by the uncertainty of his fate, and show them by my joy that he is safe. They will then be as happy as I am."'

The Standard, 27 August 1847.

*The French SPA was formed in December 1845.

The conclusion of this account indeed seems as plausible as the other inferences made by the writer – showing us an impressive combination of perceptiveness and duty in this unnamed and faithful beast. It hardly needs emphasising that a round trip of 1440 miles ranks high in the annals of canine endurance. The question of navigation, admittedly, is a little more complex. Did the dog in this instance home as mysteriously as the Durham terrier and others? Or: had it managed to memorise the route, after following the coach? Even if the latter conclusion were true, that feat itself is fairly staggering. Keeping pace with the coach on the first leg would be one achievement, and remembering a route of that length would be another.

It is regrettable that we do not know what breed of dog this was. I for one would love to see the city of Perpignan erect a statue for this impressively shrewd and faithful animal. Again, any thoughts on this from readers – French or otherwise – are most welcome.

22. Ice and Fire.

The Troy Times, of January 8, relates the following incident:

'As two men were walking along the dock at the foot of Liberty Street, yesterday morning, about 10 o'clock, a large dog, belonging to Mr. Staude, tobacconist, on Congress Street, a cross of St Bernard and Newfoundland, accompanying them, discovered an object on the ice which attracted his attention, and going up to it he commenced howling. The men called him, but he refused to come, and persisted in his efforts to draw their attention. They finally went out to the dog, and discovered the body of a man partially covered with

snow. They found that he was still breathing, and took him up and carried him into Divine's saloon, on the dock, when Dr. Burton was immediately called in. On examination the doctor fouud a large wound on the right side of the head, the face and ears so frozen that one of the latter fell off; his hands and arms frozen half way up to his elbows, and his feet and legs frozen half way to his knees. He was removed to the Troy Hospital, where Dr. Burton has been unremitting in his efforts, but the patient still lies insensible, and but faint hopes are entertained of his recovery. The man's name is Lally. He is an Irishman, residing in West Troy, near the Arsenal. He left his home on Saturday evening to come to this side of the river, which is all that is positively known in regard to the affair; but from the nature of the wound on the head, foul play is suspected, as it would be impossible for him to receive such a wound from a fall on the ice.'
Troy Times, 8 January 1856.

'One of the most astonishing instances of the sagacity of the dog transpired this morning which ever came to our knowledge. The Messrs Staude, tobacconists, 35, Congress Street, closed their store last evening, leaving their favourite Newfoundland inside. This morning, on opening the store, the floor in the back room was found to be on fire, and the dog was labouring with his fore feet and mouth trying to subdue it. A pail of water which stood in the room had been poured down the hole. The faithful animal had so successfully combatted the fire as to prevent it spreading beyond a spot two or three feet square. How long the noble fellow had stood

sentinel and fought down the advancing flames can only be conjectured; it must have been several hours. His feet, legs and mouth were badly burned; and it is feared that he is seriously injured internally by inhaling the hot air. He refuses food, and is apparently in much pain. We trust the sagacious and faithful creature is not dangerously injured. This is the same dog which discovered the man Lally on the ice a few weeks since. He is worth his weight in gold, and may safely be pronounced the noblest of his race.'
The Times, 23 April 1856.

Sadly, I have not managed to learn more about the dog's recovery. If he survived, we can well imagine that he accomplished other exploits and rescues in later life. The detail about his knocking the pail of water down the hole is especially memorable. But so too, perhaps, is the probability that he smelled the wounded man on the ice, despite the intense cold which prevailed. Another possibility for a statue, perhaps, given how precisely located our hero is.

23. Canine Housekeeping.

'The *Lawrence American* tells a story illustrative of canine sagacity. A tradesman in this city, owner of a dog and cat, has been in the habit of letting the dog go to market and buy his own meat. The dog would bring the meat home and deposit it somewhere in the store, and when feeling the gnawings of hunger would go and get it. The cat acquired the habit of stealing its meat, and the dog would lie down near it, watch the thief, and when the cat came would drive her away. But at last he became tired of this business, carried the meat down to the cellar, and covered it up with sand.

One day the owner of the dog thought he would get the meat, bring it upstairs, and see what the dog would do. After taking a nap the dog went down to the cellar in search of his meat, and commenced digging as usual, but there was no meat to be found. He laid himself down a minute, as if in thought, and then rushed upstairs, and, espying the cat, "went for her" and chased her all round the store, as closely as a police officer in search of a thief. Can a dog reason?'
Sheffield Daily Telegraph, 1 October 1872.

24. Canine Devotion.
'A pious Catholic lady, who is accustomed to attend early Mass [in St Louis, USA] had her attention attracted by the singular conduct of a dog, who repeatedly met her at the corner of the street. He was not altogether a prepossessing specimen of caninity, being tawny, foxlike and scraggy, and his approaches somewhat annoying. He would follow her to the church, wagging his bushy tail, pricking up his little red ears, intelligence beaming in his eye, and significance in every movement, sometimes catching her dress in the most soliciting manner, pulling her gently, as if he would lead her in a certain direction, and towards some unapparent object. He would remain at the church door during service, and when it was concluded he would again put himself in company with the lady, and on her way home would repeat these singular manoeuvres. When they came to the accustomed corner, and the lady was passing away towards home, the dog would renew his solicitations with increased energy by pulling her more forcibly, moaning piteously. When he perceived

that she passed on without heeding his importunities, he would walk silently away with his head over his shoulders, and the same sad look fixed upon the lady.

The peculiar conduct having been repeated several days in succession, she finally concluded that she would follow the dog; accordingly, yesterday morning she yielded to his solicitations. The dog led the way into an alley, where were collected in contiguous misery several wretched hovels. To one of these the dog proceeded, and putting his nose against the dilapidated door, which was kept shut by a cord and weight, pushed it open and allowed his companion to enter.

Then met her sight a spectacle which would appall the most obdurate heart. There was a scene of misery such as rarely can exist in this region of benevolence and active charity. If ever disease and poverty held a complete ascendancy, this was an instance. There was a man some twenty five years of age, prostrate and helpless with a malignant fever; a wife, equally weak and helpless, with a child but a few days old, and two other children, twins, aged not more than a year. They had been without fire for several days, as well as destitute of food, excepting some bones and crusts which their faithful guardian had brought home, the remnants of which were scattered about the floor. A monkey was found dead in the room.

This state of things, as might be expected, awakened the philanthropic propensities of the lady, and she immediately set about relieving the misery brought to her view by the sagacious dog. She, at the earliest possible moment, procured the unfortunate persons proper food and secured for them the services of a physician. Under her care, and that of several other benevolent ladies whom she had interested in behalf of the family, they are in a comfortable condition, and the man and the woman will soon be restored to health. These persons are unable to speak a word of English, and from the circumstances of the dead monkey on the premises, are supposed to be Italians and organ-grinders.

The conduct of the dog during the whole transaction may be set down as one of the most remarkable instances of sagacity and instinct of that animal to be found on record. It may well be supposed that he is a peculiar favourite with the kind-hearted ladies above referred to, and he is soon to wear on his shaggy neck a silver collar, on which is engraved a certificate of his worth.'

The Cork Examiner, 8 May 1857, citing St Louis Leader.

The kind of animal experts who obsessively refer all such instances of seeming morality or benevolence to some secret piece of evolutionary self-interest would perhaps insist that the dog here was trying to save its family only because they fed it, and would not do so if they perished. But at the level of detail alone that theory is unconvincing. The dog was clearly pretty well able to scavenge food; indeed, if it was merely obsessed with its own survival, it might well have been expected to eat the dead monkey.

Rather than automatically assuming the worst of an animal where we would think the best of a human, we might instead wonder how many people actually knew of this family's situation, yet failed to come to their help. More subtly, it is also hard not to wonder if the whole situation appealed to the charitable lady more strongly, because of the dog's touching fidelity. Would the desperate family alone have necessarily provoked the same response from her?

25. Look for Trouble and Give me a Yelp.

'The *Border Post*, an Australian paper, relates: "A dairywoman residing on Gerogery Road, who is in the habit of frequenting the town of Albury with her produce, is invariably accompanied by a little black and tan terrier. About three weeks ago a large dog belonging to one of the local innkeepers worried the terrier, much to the disgust of its owner. During the holidays the dairywoman had occasion to visit the town, and on this occasion, the terrier was accompanied by the watchdog of the farm. The latter lay in ambush at the rear of the trunk of a large tree which spreads its foliage on the street. The terrier sauntered to the kennel of the enemy and commenced yelping, which brought the bully to his legs. A chase ensued, and on reaching the rendezvous of his companion the terrier abruptly turned round and showed fight. To be short, the two country dogs attacked the Albury bully, and that dog went home, carrying his tail behind him. It is thought that in future he would be more respectful in his demeanour to country dogs."'
Edinburgh Evening News, 27 March 1875.

26. Doggie Bag.

'A touching story of a dog is told in *Land and Water* by Mrs Isabel Burton, a lady who has done much to mitigate the sufferings needlessly inflicted on dumb animals. At the hotel near Trieste where Mrs Burton and her husband were staying was a well-bred setter, which when visitors were in the hotel, was put in the

stable to prevent him obtaining the scraps which would otherwise fall to the share of the servants, and the dog then considered himself on penance. Major Burton, with whom the dog had made friends, being unwell, remained in his room for some days, and of course the dog missed him. The poor dog is not too well fed, but one day he got a large piece of bread which would have been a great treat under ordinary circumstances. "He did not eat it", the lady says, "but saved it, came up and sat at our door. Somebody drove him away, but he returned later in the evening with his bit of bread, waited till the door was open, slipped in, went straight up to my husband, and laid it on his bed, thinking he was also in penance, and not allowed to eat. I need not say that his sagacity and unselfishness were rewarded with a good supper."'
Portsmouth Evening News, 5 August 1880.

Wife of the famous explorer Sir Richard Burton, Lady Isabel Burton was a notable character in her own right – a great traveller, accomplished writer, and passionate lover of animals. 'Her menagerie at Damascus' (notes Jason Thompson) 'was so varied that only with difficulty did she keep its members from devouring each other. At Trieste one of her chief interests was a local society for the prevention of cruelty to animals. Any coachman who flicked his horses with a whip was likely to receive a jab from her umbrella'.

27. A Dog Sends for the Doctor.

'A lady residing on Garnethill, who had been ill for some time, one night recently had been worse than usual, and had been moaning very much during the night. There was some conversation with her husband and family in the morning about sending for the doctor, who resides in St Vincent's Street, Glasgow, but it was not convenient for anyone to go at that time. The pet dog, who had been lying under the lady's bed during the night, heard the conversation, and evidently understanding that the doctor was wanted, immediately set off to the doctor's house, and as soon as the door of his consulting room was opened rushed into his presence, and by his signs and gestures made the doctor distinctly to understand that he wished him to accompany him. The doctor knew the dog, and, concluding that his patient on Garnethill was worse, resolved to comply with the evident wish of his canine friend, but could not go precisely at that moment. He therefore said to the dog, "Now, Floss, I will go with you, but you must lie there till I return."

The dog lay down at once in the spot pointed out, and though visited by the members of the doctor's family, nothing could induce him to move till the doctor returned, when Floss reminded him by his various gestures of his promise. The doctor then accompanied Floss to Garnethill, and found that his visit was really required. The dog is a Pomeranian, and a very sagacious animal, but never before exhibited such an instance of sagacity as this.'
Dundee Evening Telegraph, 16 April 1881.

Pomeranians – made popular in this age by the fact that Queen Victoria owned several – are certainly held to be intelligent, as well as sensitive to changes in their environment. Did Floss really understand the conversation about the doctor? The tale of the protective mastiff and the would-be murderers of course comes to mind here. Perhaps, on the other hand, our Pomeranian merely recalled such bed-ridden groanings as being associated with the doctor? Whatever Floss's cue, it was quite a feat to go and find the surgery, and it is also telling that she seemed to understand when the doctor explained the need to wait.

28. Collie Come Home.

'Many stories are related of the sagacity often displayed by cats and dogs on being removed from their native places, how they generally leave the land of their adoption rather suddenly, and are never more heard of till they turn up at their old quarters after a weary journey generally of some miles. A case has come under our notice, however, that outstrips them all to some extent, seeing that the creature – a collie puppy – had not been far travelled, neither by road, rail, not steamboat. In fact, the tourist's guide was quite unknown to it.

Whelped and brought up from its infancy under the cooling shades of the Lomond hill, in the ancient and once famous burgh of Falkland, and owned by a lineal descendant of King David – a shepherd lad – Collie, as we may call him, was destined to undergo a classical education in his early days, and for this purpose arrangements were made that he should be removed from plain fare to a home near the great seat of learning, namely St Andrews, where he would be under the eye of the mathematical teacher when engaged on the beautiful Links ...

For this purpose Collie was carefully entrusted to one of Her Majesty's servants – one sworn in to see that safe delivery was made of stock entrusted to his care.

Fernie, as the carrier is named, took Collie in charge on the afternoon of Saturday last, when the route to the Railway Junction was made by way of Newton, Freuchie, Rumdewan and Kettle. On arrival at Ladybank, he was safely given in charge to the Stationmaster there.

Collie had been supplied with a fine leather collar and belt before being sent from home, and in this condition, with an address in plain letters, he was taken along the platform to the passenger van of the 6.11pm train bound for the seat of learning. Here, however, some railway technicalities had to be gone through, and on the guard of the train seeing that Collie was supplied with a leather belt, he objected to take him in charge. Hence he was marched to the booking office for another three hours or more until an "iron chain" as provided by the rules of the Company, had been procured to adorn his neck. He was ultimately properly fitted out with a complete rig, when he was allowed to take his seat beside the guard.

All went well until the train arrived at Leuchars Junction. When the words "Change for St Andrews" were raised by a sturdy porter, Collie, up to time, was out on the platform as soon as the guard with only a few links of the chain attached to his collar. How he had devised to break it has not transpired, but here the best part of the sagacity of the dog commences. As soon as possible an attempt was made by all the officials to lay hold on Collie – "damages", no doubt, ringing in their ears at the loss of a dog. We are informed the train was delayed for some time – a high compliment on Collie – but he seemed determined not to be caught, and managed to evade all their manoeuvres.

Letters were then written, giving out the decree that "Collie" was lost. On inquiry being made as to how the sender would look at the matter on Monday, it transpired that Collie had arrived home at his old quarters just as the kirks were skailing* on Sunday afternoon, pretty footsore looking, with a few links still hanging on. It is believed that Collie must have travelled along the line, leaving Leuchars Junction after 10.30pm, and keeping on the track till he arrived at Ladybank Junction, where it is supposed he had left the track and taken to the turnpike road, as he was seen pacing along the road leading from Ladybank to Kettle at the Eden Bridge. We think eighteen miles, twelve of which was foreign ground to Collie, is not a bad tramp after all, and clearly shows the great sagacity of the canine species. The future history of this dog will no doubt be watched with some interest.'
Dundee Courier and Argus, 11 January 1882.
*Skail is a Scots' word for 'spill', here meaning that the churches were emptying after service.

Among other things, this colourful tale shows that dogs learned their homing skills early, given that Collie was merely a puppy.

29. Doggie Paddle.
'An incident illustrating the sagacity of a large black retriever dog occurred a few days ago near to Claxheugh Rock. The animal was accompanying Sergeant Johns and at the time of the occurrence both were on the south side of the river. On the north side two gentlemen induced a small terrier to take to the water. In one of his

expeditions the terrier swam too far out, and was carried away by the current. The little animal cried piteously, and the retriever on the opposite side of the river, who had watched the proceedings with evident interest, at a word from the sergeant, bounded into the water and swam to his unfortunate brother, secured him by the neck, and brought him ashore several hundred yards further down the river. The rescuer belongs to Mrs Wigham, of South Hylton.'
Sunderland Daily Echo, 18 March 1892.

30. Mr Doggie's War.
'A truly wonderful tale of a dog's wanderings in South Africa is forwarded by a correspondent. A stray retriever had attached itself to the 37th Yeomanry Company (Royal Bucks Hussars) during their training at High Wycombe. The Company grew fond of the dog, and took it with them on the Norman to Cape Town. They landed at Cape Town and were ordered to re-embark for East London, and in doing so they left the dog behind. The Company went 200 miles to Queenstown and 300 on to Kimberley, and they had two or three different camps. Eventually they arrived at Boshof, and on the 3rd night after their arrival, "Mr Doggie", as he was called, turned up quite fit!'
Daily Mail, 24 May 1900.

Taking this at face value, we seem here to have the most extraordinary case of canine navigation in our entire collection. Travelling by modern roads, the distance between Cape Town and Boshof is 626 miles north-east of the coast port. We know that the heroic hound of Perpignan did indeed beat this record, and at quite a pace. But Mr Doggie is supposed to have landed at Cape Town by ship, and then somehow reunited himself with the Bucks Hussars deep in the interior of a country in which he had never set paw. How could he have done it?

It is possible that the entire report was somehow chinese-whispered into existence. Yet it appears in several papers, and is oddly detailed: we have the dog's name and breed, the Company name, and their exact route. Moreover, we also have a surprising number of other cases in which dogs and cats have achieved similar feats. Sheldrake cites one from 1582, when a Swiss dog refound his master, Leonhard Zollikofer, after the latter moved to Paris, though the animal had never before been to this city. He also gives the famous instance of a terrier called Prince, which disappeared from London and found his owner in the trenches in France during World War One (this is true: much more of it in my next volume). Sheldrake's own database of cases runs to 42 such instances, 32 involving dogs, and 10 involving cats (*Dogs that Know*, 179-80).

Now, it seems unlikely that Mr Doggie could have stowed away unnoticed on the ship from Cape Town to East London, and even if he had, he would surely have been spotted once the Company disembarked. The best common-sense theory might be that our faithful retriever followed the trails of various British army units by sight, sound and (above all) smell – all the time carrying with him in his nostrils the distinctive olfactory mosaic (boot polish, starch, sweat, rifle grease, gunpowder, hair oil) which made up the scent signature of an Empire military force at this time. This may have been the case. But, as we will see, other instances of this extraordinary people-finding just could not have worked by smell alone.

No less staggering than the sheer practical achievement of Mr Doggie is his unshakable affection for the Royal Bucks Hussars in particular. Along the way, presumably beset by hunger, he could easily have sought shelter with any half-friendly unit, British or Boer. But Mr Doggie was so emotionally attached to the Royal Bucks regiment that he walked over 600 miles until he found them. That, surely, is more than just puppy love. Brief and relatively dry as the press report of the story is, even non-dog-owners can probably begin to imagine the first moments of reunion between dog and soldiers. I for one would give a lot to have seen that extraordinary scene of astonished recognition – one of those moments, no doubt, in which a dog wags not just its tail, but its whole body.

What sense did Mr Doggie have of the war itself? Whilst we can only guess at this, it is striking to find that for him, one of the severest British conflicts of the age is largely just an opportunity for friendship and fidelity.

31. Six Hours on the Sea.

'On the 29th ultimo, the Brazilian brig Victoria, bound from Mahanam to Queenstown for orders, became a total wreck during the late hurricane. For thirteen days she buffeted the billows, when at 8 o'clock at night on the above date she sprung a leak, and sunk about 150 miles off Galway, when the Captain and eleven of the crew were lost. John Keane, one of the seamen on board, a native of this town, was the only person saved. He furnished us with the following particulars of this dreadful catastrophe:

After struggling with the angry billows for about a quarter of an hour, he succeeded in clutching a piece of timber. A short interval had only elapsed when he felt something tugging his collar, upon which he hailed, as he thought, a comrade; but, not receiving any answer he felt with one hand, and found he was held by the captain's Newfoundland dog. The sagacious animal succeeded in placing his two fore paws across the plank, and, confronting Keane, held him by the collar, the latter as tightly holding the dog's paws, thus forming a cross-grip, each feeling [that] their deliverance from imminent peril depended on the other.

In this harrowing suspense and perilous situation they remained six hours. Keane's feelings, on being rescued by the Brigantine Stambone, can easier be imagined than described. He was safely landed at Queenstown* with his sagacious companion; and it is with regret we state, that on his way to Skibbereen he lost his faithful friend. Near Bandon the noble animal was attacked and chased by some dogs, and he fled across the country. Though Keane followed for a considerable time, he did not succeed in regaining his favourite.

From the above truthful narrative we trust he may yet recover this noble animal, for few there are who would have the inhumanity to retain him, as by doing so they would add to what Keane has already suffered. He is a very large Newfoundland, three feet high, with glossy, soft, black coat, and answering to the name of "Coburg". He had on a brass collar on which was engraved the name of the ship, and, Keane thinks, the name of the Captain. Should there be any clue as to his whereabouts we will be most happy to convey the intelligence to Keane, who, we are sure, will receive it with gratification and heartfelt joy.'

The Cork Examiner, 23 December 1863.

*Queenstown, named thus from 1849 after a visit from Victoria, has since 1920 been known as Cobh.

I have tried in vain to locate any further reports of Coburg – an animal who seems to have been as gentle as he was heroic. But he appears now to have vanished from the historic record, just as he vanished from Keane's sight, pursued by ignoble dogs who were – we must presume – jealous of his brass collar and his soft and glossy coat. Perhaps this is overly whimsical, yet… I cannot help but feel that, staring at Coburg in a state of sodden fear for a full six hours, Keane really got to *know* this dog… Another deserving case, surely, for a statue? And if so – in what form? The idea of one with both Keane and Coburg clutching the spar is rather tempting.

32. A Newfoundland to the Rescue – Again…

'On Wednesday last, two young men engaged a boat for a short excursion on the river Ribble, near Preston; and at about half past nine o'clock in the afternoon, when on their return, and near to Preston, they commenced the dangerous practice of trying which was strongest. Neither of them, it appears, could swim; and suddenly one of them fell backwards out of the boat and immediately sunk. Fortunately, a party on the shore perceived the accident, and almost at the same moment, when hearing the plunge a powerful Newfoundland dog sprung into the river, and reached the spot just as the body arose. On the cap of the sufferer presenting itself to view, it was seized by the dog, but it gave way, and the body sank a second time. The dog, however, finding he had missed his object, abandoned the cap, and, barking furiously, returned in time to get hold of the drowning man by the arm as he again rose to the surface. This hold he relinquished, and then seized the collar of the young man's coat and swam with him (keeping his head above water) till he reached the shore.

The person thus rescued was carried to Mrs Smith's, Ship Inn, when it was thought life was extinct; but upon the usual methods being resorted to, he began to show symptoms of reanimation, and though not out of danger from the effects of the submersion, it is hoped that he will recover. The name of the young man thus providentially saved by this noble animal is Richard Craiston, a native of Kendal. The owner of the dog is Mr S. Wild, a performer at a temporary theatre now at Preston.'
Westmorland Gazette, 16 June 1849.

It is probably a bit too much to hope that this particular Newfoundland was a descendant of the noble Carlo – an animal peculiarly used to watery rescues, night after theatrical night. Talking of descendants, however, we are prompted to wonder if the young Richard Craiston himself had a family some time after this affair – and, if so, do their current descendants realise that generations of this family perhaps owe their lives to our shaggy hero? Please do get in touch…

33. Bill the Firedog.

'The world has many a hero that it knows very little about, and as peace has its victories as well as war, so there is much heroism and chivalry that never heads a charge, or leads a forlorn hope, or is gazetted for its able service. Samuel Wood, No.11, in the service of the Royal Society of the Preservation of Life from Fire, has rendered the most efficient aid at many disastrous fires, and for efficient courage and cool determination is not surpassed in the force. He is a fine athletic fellow, as intelligent as he is daring … All kinds of rewards have been given him, and his exertions in Whitechapel have been so highly appreciated, that the inhabitants have given him £20, a Bible, and a silver watch ...

Wood is not a boastful man, and we are afraid does not do himself full justice in recounting his exploits. There is a becoming modesty about him, but he cannot help owning that he did save ten people in one night up in Colchester Street, and five another night in the same street ... and four in Blackchurch Lane ... But then Wood owns all this as a man who feels he has only done what he had to do. He mentions that he does not stay to think, but goes right ahead when an escape has to be effected; that he pulls his helmet over his eyes, and calls out as soon as he enters. He feels interested in the work, and likes it, and considers that the society and the public generally have done handsomely by him. As to his dog Bill, he regards him evidently in the light of a friend; he had him when he was a pup from a poor fellow who died in the service, and he and his Bill have been on excellent terms ever since.

The fire-escape man's dog takes after his master in courage and perseverance. He is of the terrier breed, six years old. An alarm of fire calls forth all his energy. He is the first to know that something is wrong – the first to exert himself in setting it right. He has not been trained to the work; "it is a gift", as his master says... On an alarm of fire Bill barks his loudest, dashes about in a frantic manner, till his master and the escape are on their way to it. He of course is there first, giving the police and the crowd to understand that Wood and his fire-escape are coming. When the escape is fixed and

Wood begins to ascend the ladder, Bill runs up the canvas; as soon as a window is opened Bill leaps in and dashes about to find the occupants, loudly barking for assistance as soon as he has accomplished his errand of mercy. His watchfulness and sagacity are never at fault, although on more than one occasion he has stood a fair chance of losing his life, and has sustained very severe injury.

Not long ago a collar was presented to Bill as a reward for his services; unfortunately for him he has since lost this token of public regard – a misfortune much to be regretted. The following verse was engraved on the collar:

> I am the fire-escape man's dog, my name is Bill.
> When "fire" is called, I am never still.
> I bark for my master, all danger brave,
> To bring the escape, human life to save.

Collared or collarless, Bill is always ready to lend a helping bark. May his life be long and his
services properly esteemed.'
Glasgow Herald, 7 April 1858.

Behind the heroic figures of Bill and Samuel Wood there lie some interesting pieces of forgotten history. The Society for the Protection of Life from Fire (SPLF) had been formed only in 1836. Before this, there were various small fire-fighting units in London, which themselves were banded into the London Fire Engine Establishment (LFEE) in 1833. So… why was the SPLF needed? The answer is pretty shameful. The LFEE and its earlier sub-units existed only to save property, not lives – and only *insured* property at that. The

SPLF was formed in order to try and save lives as well. Given the ugly social hierarchy which this implies, it is especially heartening to think of Bill hurtling about, indiscriminately rushing to the aid of both rich and poor.

The fire escape which Wood climbed up was a mobile ladder on wheels. By contrast, the canvas up which Bill rushed so impetuously seems to have been one of the period's internal fire escapes – a canvas chute or slide let down from within the building in time of emergency. Here we can again see the advantage of our daring fire-dog, who would be about the only useful creature (short of a monkey) able to go up rather than down this slide. Indeed, even terrified people inside burning buildings seem to have often been reluctant to trust themselves to the canvas escapes – despite an 1886 fire service exhibition which demonstrated one, allegedly creating 'much merriment' in the process (*The Standard*, 3 May 1886). Still – the chutes may have been more inviting (and practical) than the set of personal escape wings patented by one Pasquale Nigro in 1909.

34. Sometimes even a Newfoundland...

'A curious incident occurred the other afternoon at the bathing ground. A young gentleman came down to swim, accompanied by a large dog, a cross between the Newfoundland and the retriever breed. The man had no sooner entered the water than the dog jumped in after him, evidently with the object of rescuing him from the water. The dog got the man under water several times in its efforts to grasp him, and in doing so scratched him severely on his back. The struggle went on for some seconds, when the man succeeded in diving some feet from the dog. The animal swam round and round, and appeared as though it were about to dive for its master. Eventually the owner of the dog landed in a very

exhausted condition. He was unable, of course, to blame the dog, which clearly acted according to its instinct.'
The Western Times, Exeter, 2 August 1884.

Maybe this is what happens when you cross a great rescue dog with a retriever...

35. The Out Patient.

'At present there is an extraordinary out-patient at Chester Infirmary. One day last week a rough-looking, wiry-haired dog came limping into the waiting-room. Its lower lip was cut open and bleeding, and its leg was apparently badly injured. The poor animal, with really marvellous sagacity, lifted his stump to Dr Macpherson, who carefully bound it up, and stitched its lip. It remained til next day in the institution, where it was tenderly nursed. It then departed, but two days later turned up again, and presented its wounded leg and mouth for inspection. The bandages were carefully removed, and the officials were about to apply a second bandage, but the dog politely but firmly refused, and eloquently showed the uselessness of the process by putting down the injured foot. It again trotted off, wagging its tail in evident satisfaction at the kind treatment it had received.'
York Herald, 23 February 1885.

Most readers, I am sure, feel that you really cannot have too many stories about dogs wandering into hospitals and asking for treatment. The Victorians certainly thought so – for one of them actually produced an oil painting of one such incident. Just in case anyone feels otherwise, I would add that we have here the extra detail of the dog returning to get its bandages removed. This in turn confirms that the animal was a stray, with no owner to perform that task – an inference also supported by the fact that it was a 'rough-looking' dog, which had almost certainly been in a fight. Given this, it is touching to find that the Hippocratic oath, at least in Chester, was free from snobbery.

36. Arrested in the Name of the Paw.
'Mr Hiscock, hatter, of Friargate [Preston], has a large black Newfoundland dog, which for some time has often been left in sole charge of the shop. Mr Hiscock is now staying at Blackpool, and his wife when attending to some household duty upstairs heard a scuffling noise in the shop. On descending, she found that the dog had pinned a rough-looking fellow in a corner, having seized him by the breast, and though Mrs Hiscock called him off, he would not loose his hold of the man. She then said to the fellow, "You have been doing something wrong, or the dog would have obeyed me." 'No, ma'am, I haven't", said he; but she could not get the dog off him, until at last he pulled from his jacket pocket a cap he had taken from the counter. The man besought her not to prosecute him, and she let him go.'
Manchester Courier, 2 August 1884.

37. Second Chance on the River Spree.
'A Berlin paper describes an exciting scene which occurred the other day at the Lehrter-Bahnhol. A builder, accompanied by his little son, a child of three, went to pay a visit on board a boat that was lying at anchor in the Spree. The child, who was left alone on the deck, over-balanced itself, and fell overboard. The

stream, which is very rapid at that point, carried it away so swiftly that the spectators on the banks gave it up for lost. Just at that moment a medical student happened to be walking a little lower down the river with his dog, a huge St Bernard. The young man's attention was fortunately attracted by the child's coloured frock, which he pointed out to his dog, telling him to fetch it. The dog, anxious to obey his master's command, dashed into the water before the young man had time to remove its muzzle, but finding that it was hopeless to seize hold of the child's dress through it, the sagacious animal returned to its master to have it taken off. By this time the child was carried lower down the stream, but the dog, who was a powerful swimmer, overtook it, and brought it out alive amid the cheers of the persons who witnessed the scene.'
Huddersfield Daily Chronicle, 14 July 1890.

38. Rover's Leap.
'A fire broke out yesterday morning upon the premises of Messers Wake and Dean, school and church furniture manufacturers, in St George's Market, London Road, Southwark. It first appeared in a range of buildings used as workshops, stables, and stores. There was a large stock of timber both in buildings and in the open yard. The fire had probably been smouldering for hours, but at two o'clock yesterday morning a dull glare was noticed through the lower windows of the main building, and there was a sudden crash of glass, followed by a burst of flames and smoke.

Messers Wake and Dean's premises are closely surrounded by small private tenements crowded with occupants, and when some of these had noticed the outburst of the fire little time was lost in raising the alarm, and all the narrow streets around were thronged with half-dressed people. The progress which the fire made in a short time was rapid, and when a steamer and a horsed escape arrived, and the firemen were getting hydrants to work, the workshops, stables and stores, which extended nearly 30 yards in one direction, and 20 in another, were all involved, and the fire was raging amongst the masses of combustible materials. The heat which was thrown out from the blazing timber was terrific, and scorched the faces of the firemen as they essayed to attack the flames with the deliveries from steamers and hydrants. There was presently on the scene 13 steamers and nearly 100 men. The earliest arrivals amongst the firemen had had to burst open the gates of the open yard, and they were successful in rescuing two mules from the stables just before the fire blazed across to a big stack of timber in the yard.

At a quarter to three o'clock the fire was at its height, and presented a most threatening aspect. Great masses of timber were constantly crashing down, and several of the firemen had very narrow escapes. In the centre of a mass of highly valuable property, the flames were burning amidst the workshops and stores. The members of the brigade carried the lines of hose through the front buildings in the London Road, and up to the roofs of the surrounding dwelling houses, and threw tons upon tons of water on to the fire, but for a long time the mischief defied all their efforts.

An interesting episode in connection with the fire was the performance of a handsome retriever, who had

been chained to a staple in the yard, and had a very narrow escape of being roasted alive. By the exertion of wonderful strength, the poor creature succeeded in pulling the staple out of the ground, and then ran into one of the buildings, and then presently, driven out by the smoke, leaped from the top floor into the yard, the chain and staple still being attached to him. The animal, whose coat was scorched, then rushed to one of the pools of water and rolled over and over in it ... The firemen had to continue pumping water on the ruins all day yesterday, and the duty was not left until last night.'
The Standard, 15 March 1899.

39. Rescued by a Miner.
'A humane act by a collier named Herbert Weston was recognised at the Cheadle Police Court yesterday week, when the magistrates, on behalf of the Royal Society for the Prevention of Cruelty to Animals, presented him with the certificate of the Society and a reward in money, for saving the life of a dog under extraordinary circumstances. The animal had for three days been heard howling at the bottom of a disused pit shaft, 160 yards deep, and at the bottom of which was a great depth of water. On the third day Weston was lowered at the end of a rope, and after a perilous adventure he brought the animal to the surface alive.'
Grantham Journal, 25 March 1882.

40. Follow that Dog...
'The following anecdote is an instance of that sagacity and attachment which so justly contribute to make the

dog our favourite. Those valleys, or glens, as they are called by the natives, which intersect the Grampian mountains, are chiefly inhabited by shepherds. The pastures, over which each flock is permitted to range, extend many miles in every direction. The Shepherd … [has to] make daily excursions to the different extremities of his pastures in succession, and to turn back, by means of his dog, any stragglers that may be approaching the boundaries of his neighbours.

In one of these excursions, a shepherd happened to carry along with him one of his children, an infant about three years old. This is an usual practice among the Highlanders, who accustom their children from the earliest infancy to endure the rigours of the climate. After traversing his pastures for some time, attended by his dog, the shepherd found himself under the necessity of ascending a summit at some distance, to have a more extensive view of his range. As the ascent was too fatiguing for the child, he left him on a small plain at the bottom, with strict injunctions not to stir from it till his return.

Scarcely, however, had he gained the summit, when the horizon was suddenly darkened by one of those impenetrable mists, which frequently descend so rapidly amidst these mountains, as, in the space of a few minutes, almost to turn day to night. The anxious father instantly hastened back to find his child; but, owing to the unusual darkness, and his own trepidation, he unfortunately missed his way in the descent. After a fruitless research of many hours amongst the dangerous morasses and cataracts, with which these mountains abound, he was at length overtaken by night. Still wandering on without knowing whither, he at length came to the verge of the mist; and by the light of the moon, discovered that he had reached the bottom of his valley, and was now within a short distance of his cottage. To renew the search that night, was equally fruitless and dangerous. He was therefore obliged to return to his cottage, having lost both his child, and his dog, who had attended him faithfully for years.

Next morning by daybreak, the shepherd, accompanied by a band of his neighbours, set out in search of his child; but, after a day spent in fruitless fatigue, he was at last compelled by the approach of night to descend from the mountain. On returning to his cottage, he found that the dog, which he had lost the day before, had been home, and on receiving a piece of cake, had instantly gone off again. For several successive days the shepherd renewed the search for his child, and still on returning home at evening disappointed to his cottage, he found that the dog had been home, and on receiving his usual allowance of cake, had instantly disappeared.

Struck with this singular circumstance, he remained at home one day; and when the dog as usual departed with his piece of cake, he resolved to follow him, and find out the cause of his strange procedure. The dog led the way to a cataract, at some distance from the spot where the shepherd had left his child. The banks of the cataract, almost joined at the top, yet separated by an abyss of immense depth, presented that appearance which so often astonishes and appals the travellers that frequent the Grampian mountains; and indicates that these stupendous chasms were not the silent work of time, but the sudden effect of some violent convulsion of the earth.

Down one of these rugged and almost perpendicular descents, the dog began, without hesitation, to make his way, and at last disappeared into a cave, the mouth of which was almost upon a level with the torrent. The shepherd with difficulty followed; but on entering the cave, what were his emotions when he beheld his infant eating with much satisfaction the cake which the dog had just brought him; while the faithful animal stood by with the utmost complacence! From the situation in which the child was found, it appears that he had wandered to the brink of the precipice, and then either fallen or scrambled down till he reached the cave; which the dread of the torrent had afterwards prevented him from quitting. The dog, by means of his scent had traced him to the spot; and afterwards prevented him from starving by giving up to him his own daily allowance. He appears never to have quitted the child by night or day, except when it was necessary to get his food; and then he was always seen running at full speed to and from the cottage.'
Chester Chronicle, 28 January 1803.

41. Your Humble Serpent.

'Lady Combermere's mother (Lady Cotton) had a terrier named Viper, whose memory was so retentive that it was only necessary to repeat to him once the name of any of the numerous visitors at Combermere, and he never afterwards forgot it. Mrs A came on a visit there on a Saturday. Lady Cotton took the dog up in her arms

and, going up to Mrs A, said, "Viper, this is Mrs A." She then took him to another newly arrived lady and said, "Viper, this is Mrs B", and no further notice was taken. Next morning when they went to church, Viper was of the party. Lady Cotton put a prayer book in his mouth, and told him to take it to Mrs A, which he did, and he then carried one to Mrs B, at his mistress's order.'
North Wales Chronicle, 15 September 1835.

42. Turco Takes a Bow.

'Real horses were perhaps first brought upon the British stage in 1668, when Mr Pepys witnessed ... Shirley's comedy of *Hyde Park* at the King's Theatre, and pronounced the work to be but of "very moderate" quality, its animal attractions notwithstanding ... the new canine melodrama, entitled *The Dogs of St Bernard*, produced at the Mirror Theatre ... is of "very moderate" worth; nor indeed can much more be observed of the dogs ... Of four dogs figuring in the new play three indeed are but supernumeraries, entrusted with no histrionic duties, but simply required to cross the stage in the charge of certain attendants garbed as monks of St Bernard. The fourth dog, who answers ... to the name of Turco, affects the airs of a skilled and learned performer, but without apparent warrant. An inconvenient obesity hinders his agility, his command of his part is very imperfect, and of his efforts generally, it must be said that they are remarkable rather for the failure than the success attending them. Turco's chief feat consists in ambling down a not very steep incline, and holding in his mouth the while the sawdust-stuffed effigy of an infant supposed to be rescued from the

snowy perils of Mount St Bernard. This scene was but tolerably performed, for Turco manifested occasional forgetfulness of his duties and now and then shook and worried his charge as though it had been a rat ... *The Dogs of St Bernard* was [however] received with unbounded applause, and the fact that Turco could perform the ordinary feat of "giving a paw" after repeated invitation thereto, seemed to be generally regarded as an interesting addition to natural history, and therefore deserving of extraordinary recognition.'
Pall Mall Gazette, 26 August 1875.

If Turco would probably not have distinguished himself rescuing a child from an artificial lake, we should also be thankful that he was never asked to save a baby from a burning building.

43. A St Bernard as Nanny.

'In the district of Samland, near Konigsberg, a dog has just saved the lives of two children of a landed proprietor ... Two youngsters – a boy of ten and a girl of eleven – were playing on the brink of a deep piece of water, and while trying to reach a piece of wood overbalanced themselves and fell into the water. The dog began to bark but created little attention. The animal then sprang into the stream and swam to the children. Seizing the clothes of one with his teeth, he brought it to shore, and plunging again succeeded in bringing the other likewise. Then Jordan – for so the dog was called – ran to the manor-house and howled. Something seeming to be amiss, the dog was followed to the scene. The children were on the shore senseless. When they regained consciousness the dog began to lick their faces and hands, and pranced about with the utmost delight. The next day the boy, apparently none the worse, clambered up on the back of the faithful Mount St Bernard, but the dog now took an opposite direction to the water. Jordan is to be rewarded with a brand-new collar, with the date of the rescue engraved upon it, and will be rewarded with a life-long pension from the family for his sagacity.' *Blackburn Standard*, 20 Aug 1892.

By the sound of it, Jordan's happiness at saving the children was probably reward enough for him. In some ways his delighted prancings are more interesting than his shrewd avoidance of the water the following day. Again, this is the kind of apparently genuine animal emotion which so many scientists in the area have been oddly determined to deny or ignore. Given the very famous dog-nanny which wowed readers and theatre-goers a few years later in *Peter Pan*, one wonders if J.M. Barrie ever saw this story.

44. A Welsh Singing Dog.
'Mr John Davies, postmaster, was summoned [by the Merthyr Tydfil magistrates] for keeping a dangerous dog not under proper control. Mr Powell, the complainant, alleged that the dog sprang upon him in the street near the Post Office, and bit his leg. For the defence it was urged that the dog was perfectly harmless if left alone, and that complainant had provoked the animal on several occasions.

Among the witnesses called to testify to the dog's character was Mr William Morgan, High Constable of Merthyr, who said it was one of the best-conducted dogs in Dowlais.

- The Stipendiary Magistrate: You could consider that

high praise?

- Mr Morgan: Very high praise indeed. The only peculiarity that I have seen in the dog is that it is a singing dog.

- Magistrate: What does it sing?

- Mr Morgan: You can very often hear it on the doorstep singing the accompaniment to a brass band.

- Magistrate: You mean howling?

- Mr Morgan: No, sir, singing. They say the musical people are exceedingly well-disposed to it.

The Bench came to the conclusion, after hearing the evidence, that the dog was not dangerous, and the summons was therefore dismissed.'

Portsmouth Evening News, 24 September 1891.

45. The Out-Patient Immortalised.

'The porter of King's College Hospital relates an incident which goes well to show that dogs are acquainted with the skill of nineteenth-century surgery, and are glad to come under treatment when the circumstances are critical. He heard (writes a London correspondent) the bark of a dog while engaged in the hall, and went outside to drive the disturbing animal away. To his surprise he saw three dogs on the front steps, and two of them departed on seeing him, as if their mission had been fulfilled. The third dog, a collie, was evidently weak, and could not go away. It was lying in a pool of blood flowing from a wounded foreleg. There was a cut three inches long, and blood was running freely from an artery.

A medical man came in at that moment, and he bathed the wound and applied a bandage. The dog's life

was saved. The porter made inquiries where the dog had come from by tracing the blood stains, and he discovered that they led round the back, underneath a hoarding, to Yates' Court, where the dog had been cut with a piece of glass, and had bled profusely. After receiving the wound, the dog had crawled under the hoarding and round to the front of the hospital, and thanks to his sagacity and the surgical attention it procured him, he is still able to wag his tail.'
Edinburgh Evening News, 3 August 1887.

As promised, here is our wounded dog being taken to hospital by two of its chums… Not only that, but within months the incident had been reproduced in oils… Our artist, James Yates Carrington, takes up this part of the story, explaining how he and the secretary of King's College Hospital, Mosse Macdonald, traced the dogs' route by following the trail of blood and finding a piece of glass. While the two men were studying the scene of the accident,

'Mr Hutt, the bookseller, came out and informed us that his terrier was one of the actors in the drama, and thus No.1 was secured. The second terrier belonged to his brother. The patient was [Bob], the property of a drover, who, in driving his cattle was frequently in the vicinity of the hospital. You see the three dogs were evidently in the habit of meeting one another, for two lived close by the hospital, and the third often passed it. They were playing together on the Sunday morning. The collie cut his foot, and his little friends induced him to follow them to the out-patients' door of the hospital … The conclusion I came to was that the terrier had constantly seen patients carried in that way … I got the drover to lend me the collie, and was also able to borrow the terriers. The collie was the most intelligent dog sitter I ever had. Jack, one of the terriers, did not at all approve of studio life, for on the fourth morning after his arrival here my servant informed me at breakfast that he had vanished. Little thinking that Jack, who lived four miles away, and had never been up in St John's Wood before, had been cute enough to find his way through Marylebone and Holborn, I wired his master, and received the reply that Jack arrived safely at 6.30am, barking for admission in time for breakfast.'

By now, readers will hardly be as surprised as Carrington was about the terrier's homing ability – though they might be interested to know that the painter's use of the word 'cute' was a short-form of 'acute', this in fact being where our modern 'cute' originally came from. Now, we need not trust all Carrington's theories about the dogs' behaviour and habits. He was, after all, pretty obsessed with animals, and painted an impressive number of dog pictures in his short life (1857-1892), including my cover image, *The Orphans*. But we do have to admire his laborious realism. Not only did he go to some effort to get the three original dogs as life models, but he also (as he added in the *Illustrated London News*) went to the butcher's for some blood 'and dabbled the collie's paw into it'. The animal would, however, 'persist in licking it off, and with evident relish'.

A black and white copy of Carrington's *The Out-Patient* appeared in the *Illustrated London News*, which explained that Pears Soap had bought the painting. Having previously been shown at the Royal Academy, it could now be seen by anyone able to present a visiting card, and with the leisure to get along to Pears' Gallery in New Oxford Street (where their efforts would also be rewarded with a view of Millais's famous *Bubbles*). But... where did *The Out-*

Patient go? It was said to have hung for many years in King's College Hospital, but (despite the very kind efforts of King's College Archivist Jessica Borge) at the present time no one seems to know its whereabouts. Pears Soap – now apparently the oldest continuous brand-name in the world – is sadly very hard to contact. If any readers have clues as to the fate of this lost masterpiece I would love to hear them.

46. 'A Return, Please'.

'The other day Mr Alexander F. Nicholl, cattle salesman, Coatbridge, sold at his auction mart there a fine collie dog which had recently been transferred from Forfar. The collie was bought by a Coatbridge butcher, and shipped at Glasgow to a friend at Buncrana, in the north of Ireland. The latter duly acknowledged receipt of the dog, but in a day or two wired to Coatbridge that it had gone missing. About the same time the dog entered the shop of the Coatbridge butcher who had despatched him, having of his own accord crossed the channel again for Scotland in one of the steamers. The animal was, however, again despatched to his new master at Buncrana, but evidently had no taste for Irish soil, as he was in a day or two thereafter again found at the butcher's in Coatbridge. It is remarkable that the collie should have twice boarded the right boat at the crowded pier at Londonderry, and shown a greater partiality for Coatbridge than for his old habitation in the north.'
Dundee Courier and Argus, 11 June 1888.

Given the perks of being a dog in a butcher's shop, it is perhaps not so remarkable that our collie stopped here, without heading on back to Forfar. What certainly is striking is the way that he twice managed to get on the correct boat from Ireland. This would seem to involve skills of memory and judgement, rather than just the compass-like homing instinct seen in so many other dogs.

47. A French Greyfriars Bobby.

'We have frequently recorded the fidelity and attachment of the canine race, and now extract the following, [from] a writer strolling over the fields several days after a severe battle had been fought in Spain, between the Duke of Wellington and Marshall Soult: "The enemy, it was evident, had not taken the trouble to bury even their own dead; for of the carcasses around me as many, indeed more, were arrayed in French than in English uniforms. No doubt they had furnished food for the wolves, kites, and wild dogs of the thickets; for the flesh of most of them was torn, and the eyes of almost all were dug out; yet there was one body, the body of a French soldier, quite untouched; and how it chanced to be so, the reader may judge for himself…

About the middle of the line covered by my chain of sentries, was a small straggling village containing a single street, about twenty cottages, and as many gardens. In the street of that village lay about half a dozen carcasses, more than half devoured by birds and beasts of prey; whilst in several of the gardens were other little clusters similarly circumstanced. At the bottom of one of these gardens a Frenchman lay upon his face perfectly entire, and close beside the body sat a dog. The poor brute, seeing us approach, began to howl in a very melancholy manner, at the same time resisting every effort, not on my part only, but on the part of another officer who accompanied me, to draw him from the spot. We succeeded, indeed, in coaxing him as far as the upper part of the garden; for, though large and lank, he was quite gentle. But he left us there, returned to his post beside the body, and lifting up his nose into the air, howled piteously.

There are few things in my life that I regret more than not having secured that dog; for it cannot, I think, be doubted, that he was watching beside his dead master; and that he defended him from the teeth and talons which made a prey of all around him. But I had, at the time, other thoughts in my mind; and circumstances prevented my paying a second visit to the place where I found him.'
The Westmorland Gazette, 27 August 1825.

We have seen enough dogs at funerals to understand that this dog's behaviour was far from unusual. As the officer suspected, in this particular case the dog was probably also keen to protect its master from scavengers. Perhaps the animal was not as yet certain of his owner's death: if he still smelt much as he had in life, then this may have given the dog some hope. Viewed from another angle, this tale underlines the universal nature of bereavement. Even those of us who know for certain that someone will never come back find it very hard to let them go.

48. 'Father!'

'Mansion House. On Saturday a strong instance of brute attachment was exhibited in the justice-room, before the Lord Mayor, in a case in which a dog of King Charles's breed was a subject of dispute. A person named Alloway stated that he had lost the dog, which went by the name of Fan, some months ago from his shop, and that a few days since, seeing the dog pass by with the defendant, who was a dog-fancier, he thought the best thing he could do was to seize the animal, which knew him perfectly well, and insisted upon detaining it as his property. The seizure was at once resisted by the defendant, and the matter was ultimately referred to the Lord Mayor.

His Lordship was obliged to examine several witnesses, who were brought forward by both parties to prove that Fan was the property of both, and these witnesses swore so resolutely that his Lordship began to suppose that the dog must ... possess the capability of being in two places at one and the same time. It appeared that Fan had, since the complainant said he had lost her, grown from puppyhood into bitch-hood, and it was attempted upon the part of the defendant to show that the marks of canine infancy disappeared as the animal advanced to the years of discretion; while, on the other side, it was contended that the distinguished characteristics of the pup became more strongly developed by time.

The Lord Mayor, during the course of the long investigation, during which Fan was seated on the table, occupied in alternately noticing the two claimants to her person with affection, gave an opinion, founded upon various little indescribable circumstances, that the complainant [Alloway] was the legitimate owner. His Lordship, however, expressed a wish that he had some opportunity of testing the judgement of the merry little subject of dispute herself, to whose authority he was more disposed to look for assistance in forming a correct estimate of the merits of the question than to that of any of the bipeds by whom he was surrounded.

Mr Hobler having, during the examination, noticed that the complainant mentioned that he had received Fan from a gentleman who resided in the borough, named Newsom, and who had been a most affectionate master, proposed that that person should be sent for.

The Complainant: She was quite a pup when Mr Newsom gave her to me, but I dare say, though she can't know him, that he well recollects her.

The Lord Mayor immediately desired that Fan's first master should be sent for; and a messenger was accordingly despatched to the borough. Mr Newsom, upon looking at the dog, whose back was turned to him, told the Lord Mayor that he had no doubt at all upon the subject. He then described the marks upon the breast, feet and face of Fan, which at once set at rest all doubt, if any existed, of the identity of the animal. At this moment the defendant was fondling Fan, and the little good-humoured creature seemed to divide her affections equally between the claimants, turning from one to the other, as if to conciliate both.

The Lord Mayor: Perhaps she would know you, Mr Newsom?

No, my Lord, I don't think she would, as she was so young when I parted with her to the complainant, to whom I gave her when she had the distemper, upon condition that he would give me one of her first pups. Besides, her name is changed, I used to call her name Primrose.

The instant the little creature heard the name of Primrose, she started from the hands of the defendant, and springing towards Mr Newsom, actually flung her paws round his neck, licked his face, and howled with delight.

"What d'you say to that, Mr Defendant?" said the Lord Mayor, "Don't you think Fan knows her first master best?"

"Oh, my Lord, she'd go to anybody! Here, Fan, Fan, Fan!" Amidst the laughter of the whole office, the defendant continued in vain to call her Fan and "pretty bitch", and to snap his fingers and chirrup to her. Primrose had, after a long absence, met her first love, and she could not part with him for any other suitor.

The Lord Mayor: I thought I'd get some help from Fan herself, and I am much gratified at the unerring testimony which she has given. Mr Alloway, take her home, she is yours, and you ought to be fond of her.

Defendant: But,- My Lord--'

The Lord Mayor: What do you want more? You don't suppose the dog tells a lie, do you?

Defendant: I'm blest if she ain't as great a liar as her master, and no mistake. (loud laughter)

The Lord Mayor: I wish you had taken a lesson from her; if you had done so you'd have saved us all this trouble. This is a most valuable animal.

Defendant: Begging your pardon my Lord, I don't think she's anything of the kind. I can tell you I take her for a different character, for I'm sure she's a d—ed bitch!'

Northern Star, 11 August 1838.

Among other things, this tale offers us a strong argument for the powers of canine memory. It must have been at least a year since the dog left Newsom, and by the sound of it ('she was so young when I parted with her') quite a bit longer. We might also wonder if for some reason the animal was more attached to the name 'Primrose' than she was to 'Fan': it was not only her first, but produced by far the strongest reaction from her.

49. Purvis the Collecting Dog.

'In today's *Glasgow Herald* appears a paragraph from the cashier of the Royal Infirmary, who acknowledges receipt of the sum of £4, being a donation from "the dog Purvis". This animal, we may explain, is a brown retriever belonging to Mr James Ferguson, wine and spirit merchant in the city. Purvis is a wonderful dog of his kind, and he has been so thoroughly trained by his owner that he responds to orders given him either in Gaelic or English; indeed, we are told that he seems best pleased when addressed in the former language. The animal is a great favourite with all his master's customers, who delight to see him put through his performances. At the word of command he will fetch coals from the cellar, close doors, pull bell ropes, brush boots with his paws, and when the name of Professor Blackie is mentioned he mounts a chair and sits with patience till he is decorated with a white paper choker, and spectacles are placed across his nose.

Purvis has always had an eye to coppers, which he has a knack of extracting from the pockets of customers when they permit him, and exchanging them for biscuits or baps at the nearest pastry shop. Some time ago it occurred to his master that instead of allowing him to spend his gratuities on luxuries, it would be better to save up the coppers and gather a respectable sum in aid of the funds of the Royal

Infirmary. A cash box was accordingly procured, and Purvis received instructions to collect for the Infirmary. This the animal has taken delight in doing, and instead of going to the pastry shop the coppers were dropped into the box, to the infinite amusement of the donors. In this way, within a brief period, the coin accumulated to the sum of £4, which Mr Ferguson has handed over to the cashier of the Institute.' *Dundee Evening Telegraph,* 20 February 1879.

As readers may know, collecting dogs could be seen all across Britain until around sixty years ago. I will be giving more of their stories in my second volume. But it is worth reminding ourselves briefly why it was a good idea to give your collecting dog a box. In the 1860s Brighton Bob was sent around this same town to collect money for Christian missions abroad. Being, however, more an advocate of free enterprise than Victorian charity, Bob would secure the coins in his mouth, before trotting off to the bakery to spend them on biscuits.

    Purvis, meanwhile, was still going strong over two years later. In August 1881 Mr Ferguson was summoned to the police court, because he had allowed Purvis to run about collecting in Hope Street without a muzzle. Having noted that the animal had collected over £13 for the Infirmary, the magistrate let Ferguson off without a fine (*Portsmouth Evening News,* 22 August 1881). John Stuart Blackie (1809-1895) was a Scottish scholar. At the time of Purvis's impersonations Blackie was professor of Greek at Edinburgh University.

50. Fetch!

'A short time since, writes Mr Harrison to the *Animal World*, I called on a farmer in my parish to ask him a few questions of business. On my entrance to his house, his housekeeper said "he was out, but if I particularly wished to see him, she would send for him." "Oh, never mind," said I, "I will call again. Don't send for him." "Perhaps I had better," said she; then writing a note, she tied it on the collar of a spaniel dog, and bid it "go and find his master". "Will the dog find him?" said I. "Yes, though he is miles away. One day he was gone two hours before he found him, as he was gone into a house; but he got to him, and delivered the letter by running up to him." After waiting about a quarter of an hour, back came the dog, closely followed by Mr E with the note in his hand.'
Dundee Evening Telegraph, 20 August 1881.

Presumably these discoveries were accomplished by the dog following his master's scent trail. A friend of mine who owns a golden retriever was one day walking it home after work when the dog stopped dead on the pavement outside Marks and Spencers, sat down, and refused to budge. After much pulling and coaxing my friend got her on the move again. Later, she told her boyfriend about this strange incident. He thought for a moment and then asked: 'What time was this?' When she told him, he said: 'I was in Marks and Spencers.' The dog had clearly been following his scent, and stopped when it did. Such are the secret lives of pets, unknown to us save by such rare accidents.

51. Lady Without a Lapdog.

'A curious case comes up for trial, in a court of second instance, in Russia, next week … The plaintiff, a lady, took a strong fancy to a tiny lapdog a few months ago, which she declared was the prettiest and funniest little creature she had ever set her eyes upon. The dealer, however, damped her enthusiasm by asking an exorbitant price for the animal, whose nimbleness and vivacity were certainly marvellous. A day or two later the lady called again, determined to pay the extravagant price, but her offer was refused and the price raised. She paid the money and returned home with the coveted prize.

All her friends admired her new acquisition, but both she and they agreed that it was somewhat queer that the animal should be continually slinking away into dark corners, and generally fighting shy of the light, while she had no more success in trying to tame it than if she had tried her hand at a jaguar. The general conduct of the lapdog was highly mysterious, but it was a mystery possessed of a certain charm which rather added to its value than otherwise.

She fed the animal with the best of everything, and one day, after it had partaken of a hearty meal, its mistress thought she heard an explosion. Looking round, she missed her lapdog, but in its place beheld an enormous rat standing upon the lapdog's skin, in which it had been cunningly sewn up by the dishonest dealer. The case will now be heard by the court of second instance in connection with the question of the amount of damages claimed by the plaintiff. The dealer alleges

that he was deceived himself, having purchased the animal for a lapdog.'
Cambridge Independent Press, 4 November 1892.

52. Madame Hager and the Amazing Minos.

'"Minos" is like a Skye of the long-haired, silky kind, only that he turns his little feathered fore-paws out in an odd way, which reminds one of the hands of certain lecturers when they are emphatic; his large brown eyes are inquiring, serious, and closely attentive; his little black nose twitches with a variety of expressions very curious to observe, as the several problems of his arithmetical examination are presented to him; and to see him lift his head with a sharp air of questioning, and slightly shake it when he has been answered to his satisfaction, is the prettiest and quaintest sight possible. He was deposited on a large table by his mistress, and mildly regarded so many of the company as were within easy reach, but he betrayed no vulgar curiosity, while he waited until Madame Hager's preparations were complete. She conversed with him cheerfully, as she arranged a number of cards bearing the numerals 1, 2, 3, and so on, and several double figures.

With a gentle shake of one paw, the little creature began his "exercises." He picked out a dozen cards in succession, named by various persons among the audience, the number being distinctly repeated to him by his mistress, and then she asked any one present to name a sum in addition which "Minos," who had just brought the card marked 6 in his mouth to her, should work. A lady said, "Let him add 12 to it." "Ajoute douze,

Minos, cherche, apporte!" He gave his mistress a long look, twitched his nose, ambled gently over the spread cards, without displacing them, and presently returned, carrying in his mouth the card marked 18.

Several experiments of the same kind were suggested, and in every instance "Minos" made the calculation correctly. Then came exercises in subtraction, during which his gravity, con- sideration, and frequent reference by questioning looks to Madame Hager were very pretty to see. He never once failed to bring her the correct card, though some puzzling numbers were proposed
to him (if, indeed, there be any question of degree in so phenomenal a performance), and only once did he "give it up," on which occasion he had all the sympathies of the audience with him.

This was when a gentleman requested him to find "the half of 27." "Minos" paused, looked at his mistress, shook his right paw, twitched his right ear, and walked straight across the table to a card with 0 upon it, and laid it before Madame Hager. He was modestly conscious of the applause elicited by this brilliant failure, but not elated; indeed, throughout the entertainment, although quite free from the oppressed and misanthropic weariness characteristic of almost all "performing" animals, and particularly noticeable in bears, he had a humorous air of restrained cleverness,—an "we could an' if we would" expression, especially pleasant at little confidential moments between his mistress and himself, when he nibbled tiny shreds of pink sweetmeat, and was told that he had been "paresseux" yesterday, but was "charmant" on the present occasion. He would sometimes sit up, with his funny forepaws turned out in front of him, and survey the audience with a benignant gaze, as of a dog who said, "Good people, you are amused because you do not understand me, and my kind. We know all about you, but you know little about us. You might learn a great deal from the mere fact that a little creature like myself exists."

He conversed with his mistress freely, in short barks, in winks, in twitches, perfectly to their mutual satisfaction, and was penitently sensible that he had slightly committed himself by lying down before company, in an idle moment, during the substitution of photographs for the numbered cards. Madame Hager explained that "Minos" was susceptible to the drowsy influence of the weather, and had been going out a good deal. From that moment he assumed a delightful briskness, and he entered into the game of picking out the photographs which were named in succession with much spirit, turning his soft brown head about in eager expectation of the next order, and exchanging looks with his mistress which people present said were "quite human."

Every one wanted to know "how it was done," few were contented to receive Madame Hager's assurance that the feat is entirely one of memory, when "Minos" picks out an individual among the royal and princely personages of Europe (he even crosses the Line in favour of the Seyyid of Zanzibar) at the request of any member of the audience. A favourite theory was that Madame Hager conveyed an indication to him by changes of voice in repeating the name after the chance nominator. But even if it were so, that would be a more surprising exercise of memory, because it would require its employment on countless inflexions of one voice, and the connection of them with the pictures, of which he is said to recognise four hundred. He picked out twenty-five without any difficulty, and when the titles of the Queen of England and the Princess of Wales were changed to "the august mama" and the "august wife" of the Prince of Wales (who is a special patron of "Minos"; indeed, he came to London at the express invitation of His Royal Highness), he found the portraits just as readily. The spectacle was a charming one, not only because of the extraordinary sagacity and memory of the little performer, but because of something exquisitely gentle, trustful, and loving in his look and movements which went to people's hearts.

When he had found every photograph that was asked for, a pack of playing-cards was produced, a handkerchief was thrown over the dog's head, and three persons among the audience were asked to select cards, which were afterwards replaced in the pack, unseen by Madame Hager—a detail of no real importance, because she could not teach the dog anything in the time or unobserved,—and the whole distributed over the surface of the table. "Il est un peu sorcier," said Madame Hager, as she withdrew the handkerchief. The brown eyes and black nose turned up again, and "Minos" started on the first of the three perquisitions, which were all successful.

It may be as well to mention that of the three persons who selected the cards two are well known to the present writer, and the third is a distinguished lady, a compatriot of "Minos," but who had the pleasure of meeting him on this occasion for the first time. To such of our readers as already know or shall divine how this feat is performed, it will furnish a proof of the marvellously fine and exceptional organisation of "Minos"; such as do not know, or cannot guess, must "burst in ignorance," for our information has been received from Minos himself, and is strictly private and confidential. His distinguished compatriot was requested to write a word in their common language on a sheet of paper, to be shown to "Minos." She, with the neat politeness of her nation, wrote "esprit," and "Minos," having attentively inspected the writing, brought the letters e, s, p, r, i, t, in their proper succession, and arranged them on a book. This achievement terminated the performance, and then the little dog, with unabated gravity and gentleness, received the personal congratulations of the audience, who afterwards had the pleasure of seeing him running about on a croquet-lawn, sniffing at the balls, inspecting the mallets, and inspiring all observers with the conviction that he could croquet everybody, if he only gave his very superior mind to it.

"So many people," says Madame Hager, "ask me, What is your secret? I have no secret, except that I love dogs, and they love me. Minos never leaves me; I tell him everything I think and feel, all joys and all troubles; he knows my thoughts; we are only two, in England, and I never hurt him by keeping silence. He never rehearses; it is needless. He has no fear of any one or anything, for he never had a harsh word spoken or a finger raised to him in his life. There's no secret, except

the truth that men will not see; that you can do anything with a dog, if you only make him the friend and companion he wants to be."'
Manchester Times, 7 August 1875 (abridged from *The Spectator*).

It certainly sounds as if Minos had more skill and judgement than an animal merely trained to pick out a card dabbed with aniseed. (This was allegedly one trick used by Sieur Scaglioni with his famed performing dog Munito in the early part of the century – although it only came to light after the shrewd observations of one audience member, no less than Charles Dickens (*Amazing Dogs*, 30)). However Minos learned all this, one thing seems very clear. As the reporter emphasises so strongly, Minos evidently *enjoyed* his performances. Perhaps because of the attention, perhaps because he liked to please Madame Hager; or perhaps just because he liked being clever.

    Arguably one of the shrewdest impressions of our unnamed journalist was their sense of Minos thinking to himself, "Good people, you are amused because you do not understand me, and my kind. We know all about you, but you know little about us". However articulate Minos' sense of this may have been, the basic point surely holds good. At one level, we can only approximate the emotions or consciousness of a dog in this or any other situation. At another, we know that dogs can achieve prodigious homing feats, but have no idea how they do it.

    It is, finally, worth pausing a moment over the very basic question: how did Minos do all this? Whilst the simplest explanation would see his achievements as feats of understanding and memory, we would have to be impressed at this level of intelligence in itself. There is, though, one other possibility. In the words of the eminent dog-trainer Barbara Woodhouse: "'You should always bear in mind that the dog picks up your thoughts by an acute telepathic sense ... I have great difficulty in this matter in giving the owners commands in class, for the dog obeys my thoughts before my mouth has had time to give the owner the command"'. Sheldrake, who cites this, found that in the US and the UK an average of 45% of dog owners and 32% of cat owners noted some degree of telepathy in their pets.

Anyone interested in this should take a look at *Dogs That Know...* where a number of detailed cases suggest that dogs (and cats) know this because they somehow sense the *intention* of the person who has just decided to return home. Sheldrake also discusses the early twentieth century experiments of the Russian neurologist Vladimir Bekhterev (1857-1927). Bekhterev claimed some success in getting dogs to perform tasks by visualising the task in his mind and staring at the animal, which presently complied with his thoughts. He also concluded that this could be achieved when the dog could not see the human agent. In a further twist on this last point, we find Sheldrake getting broadly similar reports from the owners of guide dogs – blind people who could not influence their animals by eye contact. Interestingly, several owners felt that this ability 'depended on the closeness of their relationship with the dog' – something which nicely matches Madame Hager's closing words (*Dogs that Know*, 106-7, 110-12).

53. Friends.

'Thirty years ago (a writer in *The Spectator* says) I was living in St George's Square, Pimlico, and near me – in Denbigh Street, at a distance of about ten minutes walk – resided a well-known journalist, Mr Percy Gregg. He had a little black and tan dog, for which I found a home when his master was about to leave London. It was reported to me that "Jimmie" always left my house after breakfast. At first some alarm was felt that he would stray; but as he invariably returned after an hour's stroll, I took him to be one of those "vagrom" animals who cannot live without a prowl in the streets, and I felt no anxiety. But I ascertained that whenever he went away he carried off a bone or something edible with him. I watched him one or two mornings, and saw him squeeze through the area railings, on each occasion carrying a big bone, which he had great difficulty in steering through the iron bars. Being curious about the destination of the food, I made up my mind to follow him.

I tracked him to an empty house, next to that in which his former owner had lived. In a cellar in the area there lived a half-starved, ownerless terrier, who, I suppose, had once been a friend of Jimmie's, and whom my dog in his days of prosperity never forgot. Regularly the good little fellow trotted off to the empty cellar, and divided his morning's meal with his poor friend. The story is told of the great Napoleon riding over one of his battle-fields – I don't know whether it was Wagram or Austerlitz – and pointing to a faithful dog watching the body of his dead master, with the words, "That dog teaches us all a lesson of humanity!" So did Jimmie.'
Dover Express, 17 January 1896.

It has often been said that dogs treat their owners rather in the way that a wild animal treats the Alpha Male in their pack. If this is true (and I am not sure that it precludes friendship, even if it is) then it is especially striking to find Jimmie so devoted to a canine friend – one from which, apparently, he can gain no practical advantage. Another little lesson from the secret lives of pets – dogs can have friends…

Cats

Almost forty years ago my mother and I went on an exciting evening drive one winter's night. In an unofficial cat sanctuary a few miles from our home (basically, a kind lady's sitting room) we beheld various animals, climbing up the curtains or perched atop cupboards. More shy and sedate was a black kitten hidden beneath the table with its legs folded under its body. One small donation later he was tucked inside my half-zipped jacket as we drove him home to my brother, Chris, whose Christmas present he would be. Sooty (as he was presently christened) survived two family dogs, and was with us for the next ten years.

My second attempt at keeping a cat was less successful. My friendly student neighbours had a black and white one called Ziggy, of whom I first learned when they knocked one night after it had got locked into the next-door garage. When the students moved across the road the new landlord would not allow cats, and so I adopted Ziggy, complete with all his food and toys and cat-carrier. As instructed, I kept him in for some time, until he became used to his new home. But at about 5 one morning, when he was unusually frolicsome around my bedclothes, I rashly let him out for the first time. He did not return. Occupying a house without cat-flap, back garden, or back door, I was hard pressed to spot him, or to catch him if I thought I had. For about a fortnight after alerting the students and handing out leaflets I kept a sharp eye out for black and white cats as I cycled around the neighbourhood. The first thing I learned was that black and white cats seemed, frustratingly, to be the default breed of the area – all looking slightly like Ziggy until closer inspection.

I had almost given up all hope of finding him again when one sunny evening I took a random detour into a nearby cul de sac. And... there was Ziggy. I locked my bike, picked him up, and began walking back to the main road, from which it was just five more minutes to my house. But, as we neared the busy traffic, Ziggy grew nervous, kicking and scratching until he had landed back on the pavement. After three attempts at this, with my shirt now in ribbons, I realised that walking was not going to be an option.

At this moment a couple and their young daughter came to my rescue as they were getting into their car – kindly agreeing, when I explained my predicament, to give Ziggy and I a lift around the corner and down the road. The daughter was good with cats, and Ziggy fell into a surprising calm in her embrace. Back at my front door I thanked them, opened up the house, and let Ziggy back in. I then headed over the road to tell Amber, one of his former owners, the good news. Very pleased at this she came in; looked at Ziggy; stopped; looked at me and, after an ominous pause, said: 'That's not Ziggy.'

Blast. Prudently waiting until dusk had fallen I dropped the pseudo-Ziggy into the upended cat carrier, walked him back the way we had come, and released him at his old home. What I had not realised at the time was that I could probably have just let him out of my door and left him to find his own way back.

Cats are the warm weight on your lap; the soft texture of a silent room; the romantic loner; the airy defiance of gravity; the liquid ripple of fur and muscle atop a wall or through the bushes. Some will tell you that cats, in their sleek grace and quiet wisdom, are always essentially feminine, as opposed to the boisterous rowdiness of the masculine dog. For a long time, general and expert opinion seemed to hold that dogs were more intelligent than cats, with brain size relative to body size usually being cited in support of this belief. I have often wondered if this is true. Were people confusing intelligence with the more typical dog trait of *displaying* intelligence, or using it for human benefit? Having a good home, plenty of food, no duties, and a measure of independence might all seem pretty smart, overall. Recently, some Japanese scientists have been challenging the older view. A study of 49 domestic cats allegedly showed them to be 'as good as dogs at certain memory tests, suggesting they may be just as smart'. The subjects could, for example, 'recall memories of pleasant experiences, such as eating a favourite snack'. Not exactly rocket science, but arguably proves my point about self-serving intelligence.[5]

As we will see, cats also rival (and arguably outdo) dogs when it comes to feats of homing and sheer four footed endurance. Our first, however, travels by coach – and is on its way to a young and influential animal lover, by the name of Queen Victoria.

54. Present of a Kitten to her Majesty.

'A few months ago an old woman named Baker, living at Scredington, near Sleaford [in Lincolnshire], sent a kitten to the Queen. It was placed in a basket, furnished with white clothes for it to lie on, with an abundant supply of bread and butter for its sustenance during its long journey; the basket also contained a letter, setting forth how, some time before her Majesty was crowned the old woman had been informed in her midnight visions that her favourite tabby would have three kittens on the day of the Coronation, and had been commanded to send one of the litter to the Queen. The day arrived, and wondrous to tell, the cat did bring forth three kittens. The old woman, not at all surprised at the event, selected the finest of the feline trio, upon the head of which her fancy had impressed a crown, and securing it in a hamper as above related, she despatched it by coach, having appended to it the following direction: "To the Queen, in Lunnun or elsewhere: to be taken great care of." Nothing was heard of pussy's journey, and the newspapers contained no account of her arrival at the palace to satisfy the old woman, who, indeed, had almost despaired of the cat having reached her destination; when a few days ago a letter bearing the royal arms was received by the old lady. It was from the Queen! and contained the important information of the young kit's having safely arrived, and that she had become a very fine cat; and in proof of the letter being genuine, two Bank of England £5 notes were enclosed.

The letter and the notes were unintelligible to the old woman, who cannot read, but, on her being informed of the meaning thereof, she could not restrain her expressions of gratitude to her Majesty, who had thus been the means of affording an accession of comfort to one who, though fantastic in her notions, is not an undeserving object. She immediately laid in a stock of tea, and bought two pigs, putting the remainder of the money in the savings' bank. Her Majesty's generosity will, therefore, in all probability, be productive of comfort to the old woman to her dying day.

Though the good dame was confident that the migration of puss would produce a useful result, her husband was incredulous, and much he feared that the act of his wife would be considered an insult towards her Majesty. The old people were weeding on the farm of

Mr Robert Spanby, when the letter arrived, and its contents, to them a little fortune, not only rejoiced the hearts of both by the sudden acquisition of wealth, but relieved the old man's mind of the dread of expected punishment. The old lady, too, had been subjected to the jeers of her neighbours for what they thought a foolish whim, but the arrival of the money turned the tables, and caused the old people to be envied by them.'
The Westmorland Gazette, 29 June 1839.

Given that the kitten seems to have been despatched very soon after Victoria's coronation (28 June 1838) we are prompted to wonder about its adventures across almost twelve months. How long did its journey take? The distance from London to Lincoln is 145 miles, and by this period a stagecoach could cover twelve miles per hour. Puss's journey seems to have taken a lot longer than just two or three days, and it may well be that her larder of bread and butter was emptied before she reached London. Amongst various striking details in this story, it is interesting that our whimsical old lady is unable to recognise a five pound note. Above all, however, what chimes most resoundingly through this tale is our opening motto. If this is the most impressive instance of an animal bringing two unlikely people together, it is in fact not the only one which involved Queen Victoria. We will meet her and her family again presently, taking their seats for the performance of a singing mouse.

55. Two Railway Cats.
'Stories of dogs and their journeys by train have been related. The London District Railway, however, has a cat which visits the various stations up and down the line by the same means. The Echo relates that on Saturday morning the cat was awaiting the 6.34am train from

Hammersmith at the Sloane Square station. As the train drew up the animal dodged the feet of the passengers, and sprang into a third class "smoker". There it curled itself up beneath the seat, although attempts were made to coax it from its retirement by other occupants of the compartment. At Victoria the cat jumped out of the train, and, with tail erect and mewing loudly, trotted off to the luggage entrance. Had this animal the faculty of distinguishing the station at which it desires to alight?'
Dundee Evening Telegraph, 9 December 1895.

'Some years ago a dark tabby was in the habit of "working" the Somerset and Dorset line between Burnham and Wimborne ... It was the custom of the cat, on the arrival of a train at a station, to leap from the engine and to disappear amongst the passengers and luggage; but, on a premonitory whistle from the locomotive, the cat would hurriedly return and take its accustomed place with the driver. At the end of the day master and cat went to their home at Wells. Like many another "servant of the Company" the animal was destined to be "killed upon the railway"'.
Dundee Evening Telegraph, 28 November 1890.

Although much less famous, the habits of our Wells commuter make it not unlike Railway Jack. It seems to travel on trains for pleasure, and always goes home to the same place every night. It may be that we nowadays hear less about cats boarding trains because both stations and carriages have become less accessible. There again, this has not stopped a brown and white tabby regularly travelling on Tokyo's Seibu Ikebukuro metro line. Coming to public attention in 2016, the cat (which sits placidly on a seat and sometimes sleeps) was thought by some passengers to have been making its commute since 2013.

In recent times a few cats have been seen taking daily bus journeys. Casper, in Plymouth, became famous in 2009 for hopping on the bus each morning for an 11 mile round trip, and Dodger, a Bridport ginger tabby, was doing the same in 2011. Whilst Casper's owner, Susan Finden, thought he was attracted to buses because he liked people, Dodger's guardian, Mrs Fee Jeanes, thought that he liked the bus because it was warm. A sample of three is probably too small for firm conclusions – but what is it, precisely, about west country cats and public transport?

56. A Water Cat.

'Last Saturday morning about noon a cat was observed on the shoal of rocks just underneath the upper walk of the Castle Walk. The tide was rising and the rock on which the animal was mewing piteously was just awash with the rising tide. As a boat containing a fisherman was only a hundred yards or so away the latter was hailed, and accordingly he pulled to the cat's assistance. When, however, close to the rock the cat instead of jumping into the boat sprang into the sea and commenced swimming vigorously towards the land. This the animal safely reached, having swum to the slip opposite the London Brewery, a distance of about 200 yards. How the cat got on the rocks where it was first observed is a mystery, as at no stage of the late neap tides are they connected with the shore.'
The Star, 14 August 1894.

57. Signor Capelli and His Amazing Learned Cats.

'In preceding and darker ages, ponies, pigs, sparrows,

and dogs, have had their day of fame, elephants have displayed considerable wisdom, monkeys happy talents in the arts, and mice ingenuity in mechanics; but never till now have we witnessed "the greatest wonder in England" of them all – the exploits of learned cats ... Their restoration to rational functions is the best proof we have yet met with of the progress of education and the march of mind.

The schoolmaster who has come from abroad with the cats ... is a Signor Capelli; and on Monday he introduces his pupils to the public, at their academy in Regent Street, next door to the Argyll Room: as patrons of literature and talents of every kind, we have been indulged with a private interview.

The *corps dramaticus* whom we saw yesterday, consists of four red and white cats, mother, sons and daughter; and one lady of colour, namely a jet black and maternal looking negress. Of the former, three are French by birth, and one Italian; the latter is French. ... we had only time to witness a few instances of their intelligence and abilities, such as ringing bells, working a machine to grind rice, hammering on an anvil, and drawing a bucket up and down from a well, which last is amazingly well done.'

Westmorland Gazette, 28 February 1829.

The *Leeds Intelligencer* also marvelled at how 'the young ones could jump through an iron ring ... and the elders turn a spit' whilst 'Mamma puts a set of church bells in motion', noting that one 'sensible individual refuses to turn the spit until she gets a slice of meat herself'; and adding that 'it is not the least amusing part of the exhibition to observe the watchful eyes of the whole brood following

[Signor Capelli] in a few legerdemain tricks, which he plays off to vary the entertainment'. Advertisements for their performances showed that the cats were still going strong in February 1832.

In recent years the unofficial title of 'smartest cat in the world' has often been bestowed on a Persian cat named Cuty Boy. This animal was bought in Dubai in 1998 by Hema Chandra – who, after finding it initially very reclusive, took to carrying it around and talking to it a great deal. Interestingly, Chandra did not seem to be the sort of person who habitually claimed immense powers or intelligence for all of her pets. She remarked that she had grown up with cats in Kerala, India, but had never come across anything like this until now. Cuty Boy was supposed to have a command of eight languages, and be able to answer various questions by giving signs for 'yes' or 'no'. Echoing Minos, Cuty Boy was also allegedly an impressive mathematician. Sahadevan Panicker, a mathematician at the Gulf Modern School in Dubai, tested the cat for ten minutes and pronounced him 'extraordinary'.

Like myself, readers may be reluctant to accept this animal's ability with square roots. It has been suggested that the cat was in fact merely responding to unconscious cues from his owner – that is, stopping his nose-bumping count at the point subliminally hinted to him. This would match the famed 'counting horse', Clever Hans, trained by German farmer Wilhelm von Osten in the late nineteenth century – an animal which knew to cease its hoof-tappings when, for example, von Osten gave a slight involuntary bend forward. Like Minos and Capelli's cats, it seems that Cuty Boy had a very strong bond with his owner, and corresponding sensitivity when with her.

58. Death of a Prime Mouser.

'For the past 14 years a cat known in the neighbourhood as Tom had taken up its abode in the sentry box opposite the Premier's official residence in

Downing Street. It was a general favourite and had been frequently noticed and petted by the late Lord Beaconsfield, Mr Gladstone, the late Mr W.H. Smith, Lord Salisbury and the late Earl of Iddesleigh. On Friday, to the general grief of the inhabitants in the vicinity, it was set upon by two bull terriers, and after a brave fight, was killed.'
Gloucester Citizen, 23 January 1892.

Tom bears some comparison with the now famous Larry, Chief Mouser to the Cabinet Office – part of Larry's fame indeed being some impressive scraps with Palmerston, the cat which moved into the Foreign Office in April 2016. A key difference is that Larry was adopted by Downing Street staff, whereas Tom seems to have adopted Downing Street. Given how very little in common Disraeli (Lord Beaconsfield) had with Gladstone, we can again here see an animal bringing some unlikely people together.

58. A Cat Goes Home (I): Leeds to Surrey.
'A remarkable story, for the truth of which several responsible persons vouch, is reported from Godalming, Surrey, of a cat which was sent from that town by train to Leeds, and which reappeared at its old home at Godalming six weeks later. The cat, which is now in the possession of Mrs E. Jones, 6, Rose Terrace ... belonged to her son, James Jones, who with his family left Godalming shortly before Christmas in order to take up residence at 22, Harold View, Burley Fields, Leeds. The cat, a peculiarly marked black and white one, the chief favourite of the infant son, was conveyed to its destination in a closed basket.

Within five days Mr Jones wrote to his mother at

Godalming informing her that the cat had strayed … A few days ago Mrs Jones's attention was called by several friends to a cat which was mewing piteously outside her son's house at Godalming, which was then vacant. She at once identified the cat as her son's, and wrote informing him of the discovery. In addition to this a photograph of the cat was taken by Mr W. Collard of Town End, Godalming, and forwarded to Mr Jones, at Leeds, who, in acknowledging it, wrote, "I received the photo of Old Tim quite safely. It is the very image of him."

It is interesting to recall a similar case which happened a few years ago, and which was vouched for and verified beyond doubt. In this case the cat walked from Forest Hill to Lincoln, more than 100 miles, had to cross two rivers, and endure the severest cold throughout its long journey. It arrived in a very emaciated condition.'

Yorkshire Evening Post, 12 February 1897.

59. A Cat Goes Home (II): London to Lincoln.

'Dr W. O'Neill, of Lincoln, describes the following incident in the history of a cat: the animal was born and reared in one of two semi-detached houses on a hill overlooking the well known racecourse, the Carholme, of Lincoln. This house was occupied by a military medical gentleman and his family for six or seven years, and the cat was so great a favourite that last December, when the gentleman removed to Forest Hill, London, the cat was taken to the new home by one of the family. It was put in a comfortable basket and conveyed to its destination by train. For about a month the cat seemed to be contented and happy, but it was noticed that it ate largely and slept much. Towards the end of the month, however, the cat disappeared, and, after a fruitless search for it, pussy was given up as irretrievably lost. This event took place in the beginning of the severe frost and snowstorm, and before the storm was over

THE CAT TURNED UP

at its old home in Lincoln, where, one morning, the gentleman who occupies the other half of the detached villa was aroused by the loud mewings and noise made by the cat to gain admittance to its old, but now empty, home. The gentleman, who knew pussy well, gave it a kind reception, and with him it now passes a couple of hours daily, and spends the rest of the time roaming at will over its old haunts. It is computed that the animal performed the journey in about eight days, travelling at the rate of over seventeen miles per day; and, although the cat was travel stained and rather thin in flesh, still it was in fairly good condition when it reached Lincoln. When one takes into consideration the distance between Forest Hill and Lincoln, nearly 140 miles, the intense severity of the weather, and the thousand obstacles which the poor creature must have encountered on its way across London and down to Lincoln, the journey is a marvel for so small and weak an animal to have accomplished. But the most wonderful thing of all is what might be called the geographical knowledge possessed by the cat, which enabled it to steer a straight course to Lincoln, although it had been taken to Forest Hill blindfolded. This journey displays the great love the cat had for its old home, and verifies the old opinion that cats are more attached to places than to

people.'
Hull Daily Mail, 13 February 1894.

Readers have perhaps noticed that this second cat may well have completed its London-Lincoln marathon more quickly than the kitten which travelled from Lincoln to London by coach. Its feat would certainly have been impressive at any time of year, let alone during severe winter snowstorms. The reporter's concluding words seem generally recognised among cat owners. A friend of mine who moved house a few months ago quickly had a cat-flap fitted so that the family cat should not get lost around its new home. Ironically, however, the cat-flap merely facilitated the cat's repeated and determined escapes. Three times it returned to its old house, around a mile away – after which my friend decided that its choice was too clear to ignore. The animal now lives back there in the shed on rats, mice and birds, and occasional food supplements brought in by its original family. As we will see in a moment, however, some cats also have a powerful attachment to their owners.

The Lincoln cat's journey has been outdone in recent times – albeit in better weather. On New Year's Eve 2012 Holly, a four year old tortoiseshell which had been lost on a trip to Daytona Beach, Florida, by Jacob and Bonnie Richter, was found a mile from their home in West Palm Beach. It had (reported Pam Belluck of the *New York Times*) travelled around 200 miles in just under two months. This case showed that scientists are still utterly baffled by how cats achieve their homing feats. John Bradshaw, of the University of Bristol's Anthrozoology Insititute, tried to explain the adventure away by conjecturing that it was a different cat (it was not, as Holly was micro-chipped). Rather more open-mindedly, John Bekoff, an animal expert from the University of Colorado, stated: "I really believe these stories, but they're just hard to explain … I have no data for this." Cambridge University biologist Patrick Bateson thought cats' ability to smell across long distances might be relevant; but it is hard to see how this would lead a cat precisely home, rather than merely into the right county.

In 1978 Howie, a three year old Persian cat belonging to Kirsten Hicks and family, in Australia, was left with relatives whilst his owners took an overseas holiday. On their return they found that he had gone. A year later, Howie turned up at their home in Adelaide, dirty, sore and bleeding. He had walked a thousand miles from the Gold Coast of Queensland.

But Howie's trek is in fact not the longest cat adventure ever described, nor even the oddest. Imagine, for example, a cat which finds its owners after they have moved to a new location, which it has *never previously known*. Enter Sugar, a half-Persian, cream coloured cat living with a family in Anderson, California. Animal expert Paulette Cooper described how, when Sugar's owners decided, in 1951, on a move to Oklahoma, they gave Sugar to a neighbour, owing to the cat's dislike of car journeys. Fourteen months later in Oklahoma, a cat identical to Sugar leaped onto the shoulders of its former owner.

Now, it would be one thing to know that (as the family soon learned) Sugar had indeed gone missing from her California foster-home just two weeks after the move. Even so, the cat could have attempted to find them and failed. And there certainly have been cases of people 'reunited' with their pets, only to find later that the new cat is some smooth-furred imposter. After all, if you *want* to believe that badly… However: whilst initially doubtful that this could be her cat, Sugar's owner presently found that the animal had the identical hip defect which had afflicted Sugar. The cat had apparently walked 1500 miles, navigating only by some bizarre sense-memory of its owners, rather than any possible attachment to place.[6]

To put this another way: do people have a kind of sensory

fingerprint, or personal GPS, which certain animals can unfalteringly track? If so, how long does it take a cat or dog to develop or lock in this ability? Returning to the scientific failure to understand this extraordinary animal compass, we cannot help but suspect that this is not just because it is very difficult to experiment on animals in these situations. Is it also because scientists cannot see how something so useful to cats and dogs could also be useful to humans? In reality, of course, many remarkable scientific discoveries are made by accident, or in the course of exploratory, Blue Skies research. Personally, I think there could be interesting secrets and real benefits to be gained from rigorous study of the Universal CatNav (or Global Pussitioning System). Although no scientist myself, I already have the feeling that this feline knack has little to do with intelligence: Cuty Boy aside, Persians are thought to rate pretty badly on that scale.

One last detail shows that Sheldrake, so shamefully marginalised by the scientific mainstream, is again ahead of other scientists in this area. Commenting on Holly's US marathon, New York animal behaviourist Peter Borchelt asserted that, 'nobody's going to do an experiment and take a bunch of cats in different directions and see which ones get home'. Well, maybe not a bunch of cats… but Sheldrake cites experiments which in fact occurred in America in the early twentieth century. One day the zoologist F.H. Herrick took his cat in a bag to his university office in Cleveland, Ohio, only to have the animal make a dash for freedom the moment it was unzipped (no prizes for spotting the proverb here). Puzzled by its having returned home that same night, Herrick experimentally repeated this initial accident, 'taking the cat in a closed container and releasing it at distances from one to three miles from his home'. He found that 'the cat could home under a variety of conditions and from any point of the compass' (*Dogs that Know*, 144). Notice one interesting irony here. Herrick was a professional zoologist. But his discovery and cat research were not prompted by his professional work. If he had not been a cat-owner as well, he would probably never have taken any interest in an ability which thousands of non-academic cat-lovers must have been observing across hundreds of years.

60. A Cat that gets Drunk.
'In a Strand tavern, well known amongst members of the theatrical profession, is to be seen a cat which is habitually in an intoxicated condition. For some time past this specimen of the feline race has accustomed itself to watch the filling of the wine decanters in the bar, and to lap up any of the liquid which might have been spilled. As it frequently happens that a considerable quantity of wine is lost during the day, pussy has indulged in her pernicious habit to such an extent that towards evening she cannot walk without staggering. The favourite beverage of this extraordinary animal is port wine, but if that is unobtainable pussy satisfies her craving with sips of whisky, or any other beverage that comes her way.'
Western Mail, 12 August 1899.

As we will see below, a drunken cat was a lot less trouble than a drunken baboon.

61. Red in Tooth and Paw.
'On the 14th instant as a snake of the viper species was lying basking itself in the sun, in an orchard, belonging to Mr Noble Jackson, Whallenrigg, near Broughton-in-Furness, it was pounced upon by a cat. The viper, on finding itself thus rudely attacked, erected itself in an attitude of defence, and commenced hissing, and

darting its forked tongue in every direction, bidding defiance to its feline assailant. Puss, nothing daunted, returned to the charge with redoubled fury, when a fierce encounter took place, puss appearing to be perfectly aware of what kind of an antagonist she had to contend with, by displaying the greatest caution and adroitness in repelling the attacks of the viper with her fore-feet. After a protracted struggle, the viper judged it prudent to make a retreat, on which Mrs Puss, taking her advantage, seized the reptile by the neck with her teeth, and bore it off in triumph to a kitten which she was suckling. The viper measured 25 inches in length.'
Blackburn Standard, 9 August 1848.

62. A Pet's Pet.
'Last week, while a shoemaker in the south side of Edinburgh was engaged in cleaning a cage in which he kept a lark, he left the door of the cage open, of which the bird took advantage, and flew away by a window at which its owner was then standing. The lark being a favourite, its loss was much lamented. But it may be imagined what was the surprise of the house, when in about an hour and a half the cat belonging to the same person made its appearance with the lark in its mouth, which it held by the wings over the back, in such a manner that the bird had received not the least injury. The cat, after dropping it on the floor, looked up to those who were observing her, and mewed, as if to attract attention to the capture. The lark now occupies its wiry prison, with the same noisy cheerfulness as before its singular adventure.'
Morning Post, 6 December 1822.

63. Feeding Time.
'Dr Frost, in *Nature*, gives an instance of wonderful sagacity in a cat. During the past winter Dr Frost's servants used to throw the breakfast-table crumbs out into the garden to the birds, and the cat, with a cunning worthy of a diplomatist always went and hid under the bushes before the crumbs were thrown, in order that, while the birds were making a meal of the crumbs she might emerge and make a meal of the birds. But, by-and-by, the practice of throwing out the crumbs was discontinued, and pussy, seeing that her preserve would be spoilt unless something was done, got the crumbs (where Dr Frost does not say) and scattered them on the ground herself.'
Edinburgh Evening News, 7 April 1879.

64. Nocturne in C.
'A few evenings ago, and at a late hour, a family residing not far from Dingwall [in the Scottish Highlands] were startled by hearing the piano in the parlour immediately above the apartment in which they were then seated, suddenly strike up a lively tune. As there was no person there at the time, the younger members of the family became very much frightened, attributing the performance, of course, to some supernatural agency – or, as one of them tremblingly expressed it, "a ghost". They believed this the more readily, having heard the same thing on previous occasions, though they had not sufficient courage to make any attempt to solve the mystery. Indeed, for some time past the more timid of the household considered that apartment as haunted,

and would not enter it alone after nightfall.

On this occasion, however, the head of the family was present, and seizing a lighted candle he hurried upstairs, followed at a respectful distance by his better half. On entering the parlour they were much surprised to see a favourite cat standing on her hind legs upon the stool in front of the piano, vigorously beating the keys with her paws, running over one after another with wonderful precision and with amazing rapidity, and with such force that each note could be distinctly heard in every part of the house. Miss Puss did not cease playing when discovered, but continued thumping away for some time, to the no small amusement of the onlookers and evidently to her own very great delight.'
Dundee Courier and Argus, 5 February 1870.

It has been argued convincingly that animals get enjoyment out of doing things they are good at (with Minos being just one case in point). Here we seem to have an example of a cat enjoying something which (we can assume) it was probably *not* very good at. Do dogs occasionally try this too? There is certainly a painting of such a canine maestro – by none other than Yates Carrington, our great Victorian animal artist.

65. A Mummy Cat.

'In taking down an old building in Paisley, the labourers found the remains of a large cat between the [roof panels] and the wall, which seems to have been immured where it was found when the house was being erected in 1781. It is quite dry and the skin whole, but so close to the bones that it would seem the animal died from starvation, and not from want of air in

consequence of being buried alive. It retains its whiskers, teeth, and claws in good condition, notwithstanding its long entombment'.
Liverpool Mercury, 28 June 1859.

66. The Station Kitten's Debut.
'Quite a crowd of people were entertained at Moorgate Station yesterday morning by a diminutive kitten, evidently making its debut in mouse-playing. Each time the mouse escaped through the ring [of people], the crowd scattered with alacrity; when the kitten marched solemnly back with the recaptured mouse the circle reformed, and the performance went on again. It might have been repeated *ad infinitum* but for the fact that the crowd grew too great for the patience of the railway officials.'
Daily Mail, 9 September 1899.

67. The Royal Marines' Kitten.
'Among the minor incidents of the army manouevres there is one well worth recording. During one of the field days of the Northern army, before the declaration of hostilities, a tiny, good looking kitten was picked up on the downland south of Salisbury by a subaltern in one of the two battalions of Royal Marine Light Infantry forming part of that force. The kitten was brought back to camp and entertained in the officers' mess tent with that lavish hospitality which is a tradition of the Marines on shore. A bed was found for it in an empty soda-water box, and the mess kitchen received orders to see that it lacked nothing. The kitten has now become a sort of diminutive regimental pet, going about

everywhere "on paw", and spending its evenings reposing on the broad scarlet-clad chests of the sunburned giants in command of the Marine battalion on Salisbury Plain. It seems to thrive in its new environment, and there's talk of its even taking part in the march-past on Boscombe Down on Thursday morning.'
Daily Mail, 9 September 1898.

68. Of Wings And Whiskers.

'Sir - ... A pair of swallows have built for the last few years on a cross-beam in an empty room in an outbuilding here, and I have kept the moveable side of the window open each spring that they might have their ingress and egress to and from their nest from the early dawn of day to the late dusk of evening; and, to make assurance doubly sure I drove a nail each year betimes into the sill to prevent the slide being shot back by anyone to its place. But this year, unfortunately, I forgot to do so in good time ... and so, though I then looked for their return, they did not come back to their old domicile.

 As it turned out, however, they were equally well employed elsewhere. Near the other end of the same building is the stable, the windows to it being wooden sliding ones ... If the door of the stable had been constantly open night and day the birds would naturally have flown in through it to their own nest; but as this was not always the case they took their way in through one or other of the interstices being made by the one half of the window being drawn aside ... When I happened to hear of this I watched a few times to see how they went in and out .... It was at one and the same time the simplest and the most difficult thing you can imagine. Each bird in turn – no doubt they were both of them then feeding their young – flew up to about the middle of the window, and poising itself for a moment in the air close outside went in with folded wings without an effort.

When I have said this I have said all, excepting, indeed, to mention the fact that the wings of the swallow in flight expand to the width of one foot two inches, and that the breadth of the opening in the window, which I measured carefully with a hand rule, is less than two inches and a quarter.

I watched them afterwards more than once, and on one occasion one of the pair alighted on the windowsill ... from which it could, if it liked, have stepped through the lattice to the inside; but instead of doing so it flew up a couple of feet, or thereabouts, and then flitted through as deftly as before.

From the bird to the cat is, I am sorry to say, too often an easy transition. The same window was the scene of a still more wonderful performance. We had a splendid large Persian cat, sent to us to some years ago from Lincolnshire ... Some two or three years ago, she used sometimes to be put into the stable for the sake of warmth in the winter; but more than once after I had sent her out for the purpose she put in an appearance as before. This was the case ... repeatedly, and I could only conclude that she had been set down outside without being carried as far as the stable. I was, however, assured that it was not so, but that she had been duly shut in, and had made her own way out.

And so it was, though at first I could scarcely believe it; and being told what her modus operandi was, as observed several times, I then went to see it for myself, and afterwards we had the performance gone through more than once for other friends to see by shutting her into the stable in the middle of the day … we had not to wait long, for in a few minutes we saw the slide pushed sideways, and then her head – and it was a very large one – put out, sideways also, and then she leapt down to the ground.

The height of the window from the floor is just five feet and three quarters, and though she probably made use of a rather flat and low corn bin as a stepping or jumping stone, yet she did the same from the other window, where there was not one, but only the bare wall. The ledge on which she had to stand while thus pushing the bars on one side – and there are seven of them, besides the top and bottom ones – was only two inches wide, and, moreover, all steeply slanted down by an additional edging nailed onto the narrow flat top piece.

It seems impossible to conceive that this could have been done in consequence of having observed the window being thus opened by someone or other, but the other alternative is almost as inexplicable, how she came to reason it out for herself. For myself, I can only say that "such knowledge is too wonderful for me" …
I am, sir, your very obedient servant, F.O. Morris.
Nunburnholme Rectory, Hayton, York, Sept 23.'
The Times, 25 September 1885.

In another incarnation this animal might well have found itself on stage with the wonderful learned cats of Signor Capelli. But our rural puss is of course in one way more impressive – as she seems to have figured out this highly demanding procedure for herself, without any training.

69. Healing Instincts.

'Sir – A perusal of the interesting letter of the Rev. F.O. Morris ... has forcibly recalled to my mind an incident which occurred some twelve years since with a cat in my own family ... We had a small but prettily-shaped chinchilla cat, which was a favourite and would sit on its hind legs and beg like a dog at meals, and at the words "first position" would hold up its right fore paw erect before taking the morsel of food presented to it. We once missed this cat for two days, which, being a very unusual circumstance, we gave it up for lost. One morning, however, it came crawling, or rather dragging itself, up the garden walk in a most piteous condition, and with its body terribly swollen and its eyes glassy. It crawled into a sunny corner – it was full summer – and to my caresses it responded by feebly pressing its head against my hand. I concluded that it had been poisoned by someone who had sought to protect the floral at the expense of the animal world, and I conceived the best thing to do in its painfully wretched state was to put it out of its misery.

    I went into the house, loaded a pistol, and returned to the cat, which I found feebly scratching a trench in the soft mould, in which after a short time, she deposited herself. Having a vague notion that I had heard or read somewhere of earth baths among some of the Indian or African tribes, I at once concluded that nature was prompting this remedy to the animal. There was, however, the misgiving that she might be digging her own grave. But be which way it might, I thought it best to assist the poor creature, so I made the trench deeper, which appeared to satisfy her as she took to it quickly, nor did she object to the mould being packed around her so as to leave but a small portion of the body exposed. Thus I left her, and on my return home late in the evening I found that she had crawled into the house, presumably for food, which in the form of milk, had been given to and taken by her, and had crawled back again, and had almost wholly buried herself. I left the cat for the night, and in the morning its appearance presented a remarkable contrast to that of the previous day. It slowly but surely recovered from its illness, whatever it was, and was with us for several years afterwards.

I am, sir, your obedient servant, P.F.N.

Clapham, 26 September.' *The Times*, 29 September 1885.

70. Fur Dodger.

'Upon the arrival of one of the Midland expresses at Kettering a day or two ago a cat was discovered sitting on the axle of the carriage. It must have occupied that position all the journey, as the train did not stop between St Pancras and Kettering.'

Hull Daily Mail, 8 June 1894.

Perched there for more than an hour on a journey of over 80 miles, this cat seems to have been a very cool customer.

71. Kitty Come Home.

'Numerous instances are recorded of remarkable sagacity being displayed by the canine species in travelling long distances to discover the abodes of their masters or former friends, but very few similar cases are related of the domestic cat. The following recent incident, however, is vouched for by several individuals. In May last a family residing in the south of Ayrshire removed to near Lochend, Edinburgh, one of them a young woman, leaving behind her a cat which she had been at some pains to rear. A friend with whom the animal was left wrote twice to Edinburgh soon after the family's departure, the first time stating that it had refused to take any food since its mistress left, and the second time intimating that it had gone away. Nothing more was heard till the end of July, when a poor cat, spent almost to a skeleton, was observed approaching the house at Lochend, exactly like the cat left behind, which answered at once to the name by which the latter had been known. For several days it scarcely looked up, but by and bye showed its recollection of some of its former tricks, and soon convinced the whole family that it was the poor animal that had been left in Ayrshire. How it had travelled and how it had been guided remains a mystery to them, all the more difficult to solve, [given] that part of their journey here was made by water.'

Morning Post, 6 September 1856.

72. Fur and Feathers.

'A Liverpool gentleman, who visits Oldham occasionally, states that a curious incident occurred at a gentleman's house in that town. A cat belonging to the house had recently given birth to three kittens, two of which it was found necessary to drown, and the mother was left only with one. About the same time two chickens, just hatched, were placed in a basket on a table, and covered with a piece of flannel. Shortly after they were put there one of the chickens was missed, and for a long time could not be found, but ultimately to the surprise of everyone, it was discovered snugly nestled with the remaining kitten in the soft fur of the cat, and chirping with evident satisfaction.

It was removed to its basket and a watch set upon the cat, which, after a while, was seen to go to the basket, gently lift out the chicken by the down and feathers at the back of the neck, jump off the table, and carry it away to where the kitten was, without hurting it in the least. This instance of ultra-natural affection is the more remarkable because on ordinary occasions the cat is a savage one, and has a very bad reputation for destroying chickens, pigeons, and other birds in the neighbourhood.'

Edinburgh Evening News, 1 June 1876.

It would be interesting to know if this kitten, in later life, was unusually kind to birds… What we do know (thanks to Masson and McCarthy) is that a much later example of unlikely adoption stands as a kind of karmic comparison to the Victorian case. 'Lucy, a chimpanzee reared by humans, was given a kitten to allay her loneliness'. On her first two encounters with the puss, Lucy was alarmed and violent. But, 'at their third meeting she was calmer. As she wandered about, the kitten followed her, and after half an hour Lucy picked it up [and] kissed it and hugged it. Subsequently she groomed and cradled the kitten, carried it constantly [and] made nests for it ... Lucy either carried it in one hand or urged it to ride on her back' (*When Elephants Weep*, 111). As we will see in my second volume of animal stories, there are an impressive number of twists on the cat/chicken adoption scenario.

73. Special Delivery.

'A lady residing in Glasgow had a handsome cat sent to her from Edinburgh; it was conveyed to her in a close basket, and in a carriage. She was carefully watched for two months, but having produced a pair of young ones at the end of that time, she was left to her own discretion, which she very soon employed in disappearing with both her kittens. The lady in Glasgow wrote to her friend in Edinburgh deploring her loss, and the cat was supposed to have formed some new attachment, with as little reflection as men and women sometimes do. About a fortnight, however, after her disappearance from Glasgow, her well known mew was heard at the street door of her old mistress, and there she was, with both her kittens, they in the best state, but she very thin. It is clear that she could only carry one kitten at a time. The distance from Glasgow to Edinburgh is forty miles, so that if she brought one kitten part of the way, and then went back for the other, and thus conveyed them alternately, she must have travelled 120 miles at least. Her prudence must likewise have suggested the necessity of journeying in the night, with other precautions for the safety of her young.'
North Wales Chronicle, 15 September 1835.

Whilst this story looks genuine, I wonder if the author's

interpretation is right… You could imagine the cat going back for the second kitten; but – would it still be there? Could she have carried one on her back, and one in her mouth? I would like to know what readers (and especially cat-owners) think about the mechanics of this motherly adventure.

74. The Minister and His Cat.
'The inhabitants of a well known border town are greatly exercised about a funeral that has recently taken place in their midst. It seems that one of the clergymen of the town had a large black and white cat, of which he was exceedingly fond. Pussy reciprocated the affection, and though troubled to an incompatible extent with obesity would go out for a walk with her master, when the weather was suitable. Lately the process of fatty degeneration went too far and the favourite died, with the result that the house-hold was thrown into mourning.

For three days pussy, whose remains were placed with loving care in a beautiful brass-bound oaken coffin, with inner linings of silk and wood, lay in state in the drawing-room. At the termination of this period, the reverend gentleman, hiring a cab, drove to the station and took train for the north, bearing with him the oak coffin and the precious remains. Where the funeral took place seems to be somewhat of a mystery – at least there are conflicting accounts – but of one thing the people seem to be certain. The ceremonial respect which had been accorded to the deceased was maintained to the last, and the burial service, or part of it, was recited at pussy's grave.' *Edinburgh Evening News*, 9 March 1897.

'The Lord so loveth this his feline servant that he has seen fit to whisk her off to heaven…'

75. Long-eared Kittens.
'On 23rd of last month a cat, belonging to Mr Thomas Park, residing in Upper Cheese Lane, had a litter of four kittens; and three days after, a doe had four young rabbits. At the expiration of three days the doe died: the rabbits, by way of experiment, were then put with the kittens, and the old cat has continued to nourish the whole to the present time: any curious person may see by applying as above.'
The Bristol Mercury, 17 June 1837.

76. Stage Fright.
'On Saturday evening, during the performance of *The Lady of Lyons*, at the Prince's Theatre, a singular interruption took place, which fairly upset the gravity of the house. Just before the crisis in the fifth act, when Pauline is about to sign the marriage contract, and Claude Melnotte is preparing to assert his prior claim, the property-man's cat made its appearance on the scene, and frisked across the stage in a highly grotesque manner. Of course the apparition was in ridiculous contrast to the "dandy pathos" – to borrow Tennyson's phrase – of the author of *Money*, and a general titter passed around the house.

After a momentary stoppage of the play, the business of the scene was just being resumed when the animal suddenly appeared at the opposite wing, this time with an outstretched tail, and exhibiting other symptoms of alarm. After scampering twice or thrice across the stage, and probably finding all the places of exit occupied by "supers" intent upon its capture, it looked for safety on the other side of the footlights, and without letting "I dare not" wait upon "I would", cleared the orchestra and stalls at a bound, and alighted on the shoulder of an elderly lady in the third or fourth row of the pit, to whom it quietly surrendered.' *Grantham Journal,* 14 September 1872.

One suspects that Edward Bulwer-Lytton (d.1873), the author of this play, would probably have seen the funny side, had he been in the audience. Bulwer-Lytton was one of those characters who seemed to be everywhere in their heyday (compare Robert Fraser in sixties London) though largely forgotten in later times. He was a politician, close friend of Disraeli, and a prolific writer.

He left us the phrase 'the pen is mightier than the sword' and the name Bovril: the latter comes from his remarkable science-fiction novel, *The Coming Race* (1871), in which 'vril' is a mysterious energy force (with 'bov' deriving from 'bovine'). He was said to have referred to Queen Victoria as 'the missus' – a nickname less than pleasing to her Majesty when she inadvertently learned of it. Finding him remarkably precocious as a boy, his mother (notes biographer Andrew Brown) decided it was time to send him to school when he asked her, at around age eight: 'Pray, Mamma, are you not sometimes overcome by the sense of your own identity?'

77. Sailor and Kitten.

'In connection with the wreck at Blackpool, it is worth noting that when the tide left the Sirene high and dry on Monday one of the Norwegian sailors re-entered what remained of the vessel to secure his kit, and not only did so, but rescued a ship's pet. He left the wreck

fondling a kitten. The onlooking crowd cheered this incident, recognising in it one of those touches of nature which makes strangers kin.'
Dundee Evening Telegraph, 13 October 1892.

78. The Kitten's First Mouse.

'Mrs Lynn Linton, writing from Malvern … says: "Is the following experience more general than I know of? To me it was unique. I have a kitten, not yet fully grown. Last week she caught her first mouse, with which she played in orthodox feline fashion. Suddenly the mouse disappeared down her throat – alive, unbroken, unmasticated, fur, tail, bones, flesh, and palpitating heart, all undisturbed. The kitten was in great distress, and cried more like a child than an animal. I took her up and she looked at me and left off crying, but when I put her down she stretched herself under the kitchen table, her body pressed close to the ground, and all four paws wide out. She shivered strongly but was silent. My cook, whose especial property she is, took her up and put her inside the kitchen fender, where she lay for hours in an almost death-like state, her eyes glazed, she herself absolutely powerless, like a bit of cottonwool, [rather] than a creature with bones and muscles. After some time, when I was free, I went into the kitchen, and took her in my arms, calling her by her name. She opened her eyes and knew me – it was a very human look – then shut them again. We put her on the table, but she could not stand, though she lapped a little milk, then went back to her lethargy. By the next morning she had digested her furry elephant, and was alright.

Is this is a common mistake for a kitten to make with

her first mouse?"'
Daily Mail, 8 March 1898.

79. An Out-Patient.
'A correspondent writes as follows to the Echo: "Allow me to give you an instance of feline sagacity that will more than match that of the dog as reported in your columns. Puss hailed from Brighton, and suffered last year from a severe tumour inside the fleshy part of the leg. When apparently ready for the knife, she walked into a chemist's shop in Queen's Road, laid on the table, and spread herself out to show her trouble. No struggle, no scratch followed the operation, and she returned every day under like circumstances until cured. What human being could have done more?"'
Edinburgh Evening News, 15 December 1884.

Like myself, readers are probably surprised to find a cat achieving the relatively common canine feat of taking itself to the doctor. (As cat-owners will probably know, these animals seem to have an uncanny knack of anticipating a planned trip to the vet, and disappearing accordingly.) Also notable is the way that it goes back so regularly until completely cured.

80. Knight and Kitten.
'In this week's issue of "The Bazaar" there appears the following advertisement:

> Kind home wanted (country or suburbs) for black she kitten, very affectionate, followed me New Year's Eve, so will bring good luck for year, living in an upper flat I cannot keep her. I will pay

moderate carriage. Write to Sir F.L. Robinson, 9, Kensington Court Mansions.

The little story of the homeless kitten and the good knight began on New Year's Eve, when Sir Frederick Robinson, making his way through Kensington Court, heard the plaintive mewing of the tiny waif. To the first appeal he made no response, and kept his way homewards, but persistent supplication from the mite that came trotting along trustfully at his heels at length brought Sir Frederick to the compassionate contemplation of the very small and very wistful black kitten. Then the knight looked hard at the kitten, and the kitten looked softly at the knight, and one piteous cry from the little outcast completed the conquest. Sir Frederick Lacy Robinson, KCB, picked up the waif and carried her home.

The temporary nature of the kitten's residence at no.9, Kensington Court Mansions, is explained in Sir Frederick Robinson's advertisement, but it is pleasant to know that the little wanderer has at last found permanent home and happiness. There were many replies to the advertisement, and the kitten has been well placed, and is already a cherished addition to a family circle. It will be interesting to learn whether Sir Frederick Robinson's prophecy as to a year of good luck for those who have adopted the castaway is fulfilled.'
Daily Mail, 27 January 1900.

The already sharp contrast between our two principal actors is strengthened when we learn that Robinson (around 60 at this point) was the deputy Chairman of the Inland Revenue. It may also be relevant that Robinson was not born with a silver spoon in his mouth: on his retirment two years later he was described as 'a rare example of promotion from the ranks', having begun 'his career as a junior clerk'. Given that Robinson must have met Victoria when he was knighted, we thus return indirectly to our opening: from the kitten which pawed its way into the Palace a year after Victoria's coronation, to one which scampered into the home of one of her knights, around twelve months before her death.

Mice

In Douglas Adams' improbable classic, *The Hitch-Hiker's Guide to the Galaxy*, mice are revealed to be leading an impressive double life. Mistakenly believed by humans to be merely small squeaking animals frequently used for scientific experiments, they are in reality responsible for the creation of the Earth, and two in particular are keen to extract Arthur Dent's brain as part of their own intergalactic research programme.

In many other ways, we seem to have an oddly dualistic relation with mice, the world's commonest mammal (there are 130 types of house mouse alone). For much of history people who kept cats did so solely as mouse-catchers (for which reason cats were not fed), and in present-day Britain there is a multi-million pound industry devoted to trapping or killing mice. And yet, at a convenient distance mice proliferate in miniature cuteness upon Christmas cards, in cartoons and films, and as caged pets, whilst one still stands as perhaps the most famous icon of that great purveyor of American magic, Walt Disney.

Has any other creature provoked such an impressive range of reactions, from protective tenderness to unreasoning terror? In my second student house in Leeds, mice were wont to run, not up the clock, but nimbly up a length of wood which someone had thoughtfully left propped by the cooker. From here their famed agility took them to the grill pan, where they had midnight feasts, chewing up the fat-soaked foil on which bacon had been cooked. By some cruel and improbable twist, they were first actually seen (rather than inferred) at the very top of the house, in the bedroom of the one person most terrified of them. Why a medical student of all people should be reduced to gibbering palsy by mice is hard to say, but he is in good company, as a tale of mouse and tiger will presently reveal. With Dominic perched safely on his bed, and Bob – a hardy Engineering student – poised over the mousehole with baseball bat, the scene has often returned to memory in the years since I left this male bachelor paradise. Anyone who is currently wavering between lethal and humane mouse-traps may want to suspend their decision until they have read the saga of the singing mice below.

81. The Prisoner and His Mouse.

'A singular case came before the Central Criminal Court on Friday. John Edwards was indicted for attempting to wound William Hewetson with intent to do him grievous bodily harm, and secondly he was charged with a common assault. Mr Montagu Williams, in opening the case to the jury, said the prisoner was indicted for attempting to wound one of the warders of Coldbath Fields Prison, where ... the prisoner was undergoing a sentence of two years' imprisonment for uttering counterfeit coin. The prisoner had been confined in a cell, and he appeared to have formed a friendship with a mouse, of which he was very fond. The prison authorities, however, thought it their duty ... to take the mouse away from him, and to kill it. The prisoner went out into the corridor to see what had become of his friend, and when he found the authorities had taken it away, he naturally enough did not like it, and he refused to return to his cell. The prisoner was forced back, and seeing an open knife, he snatched it up and ran after an officer, but instead of striking him he struck the back part of the cell door.

… It appeared that the prisoner readily gave up the knife when he was asked for it, and it appeared also that he was subsequently charged with attempting to commit suicide by hanging himself, but the magistrate refused to entertain the charge. The prosecutor admitted that he was out of the cell before the prisoner struck the door, upon which, moreover, there was no mark, and it was shown that the prisoner was very excited after having been deprived of his mouse. The mouse had got into his cell by the ventilator. He caught it and tamed it. Subsequently he became much attached to it, taking it up his sleeve into the exercise yard, making his fellow prisoners laugh, and it required two warders to get it away from him.

Mr Justice Hawkins: Does it require two prison warders to take away a mouse? (laughter)

The witness replied that the prisoner would not relinquish it.

Mr Justice Hawkins: He only stuck to his friend. (laughter)

Mr Montagu Williams: Yes, and his friend stuck to him, which is not always the case. (laughter)

Mr Justice Hawkins, in summing up, said there did not appear to be any doubt that the prisoner had formed a strong attachment for the little animal that had come to his cell, and that he was very angry when he was deprived of the society of a little animal which stood to him almost in the relation of a friend. It would, however, be impossible by the gaol regulations for a prisoner, to be permitted to make such an animal … a source of

amusement. If one was allowed to have a mouse, another would have a guinea pig, another a rabbit, and so on. The question, however, in the present inquiry was whether the prisoner ought to be convicted of attempting to stab the warder, and it appeared to him that … if any such attempt had been made, it was done while a stout iron door was between the prisoner and the warder, and it was difficult to see how any injury could be inflicted under such circumstances. The Jury immediately returned a verdict of not guilty.'
Gloucester Citizen, 26 November 1881.

This is not the only tale of a prisoner and a pet mouse: in 1979 Long Island inmate George Balboa attempted to file a murder investigation after guards discovered and destroyed the whiskered companion in his cell (*Eeek*!, 112). The 1881 story also reminded me of a more famous prison cat. Sir Henry Wyatt (father of the poet Sir Thomas Wyatt) was imprisoned by King Richard III, c.1483-4, and kept cold and hungry during his confinement. Legend has it that presently a cat began to visit him. It not only helped keep him warm, but also occasionally brought him a dead pigeon. Whilst the jailer was not permitted to supply Wyatt with extra food, he agreed that he could cook any pigeons which the cat brought. Given the tortures inflicted on Wyatt at Richard's orders, it indeed seems likely that Wyatt would have starved to death, if not for this charitable puss. Named 'Acater' (as in caterer) the animal later featured in two pictures of Wyatt.

82. A Broken Nest Egg.

'A workman employed at a housebuilding at 15, Avenue Versailles, was disagreeably surprised last week to find that a sum of 2000 francs in bank notes which he had hidden in a cellar for safety had disappeared. The pocket-book which had contained the notes was there, lying open, but there were no signs of the notes. On searching well, however, some small fragments of paper were seen lying about, and the master builder, M. Picard, who had come forward at once, thought that the mice might be the thieves. Following the direction of the fragments, he had the flooring taken up of a room above used as an office, and in which a fire had been lighted, and there near the stove was found a mouse's nest lined with the precious paper, nibbled into small pieces. These were collected and taken to the Bank of France, where the notes will be reconstituted if possible; and if the numbers can be ascertained, other notes will be given by the Bank in exchange for those nibbled by the mice.'

Portsmouth Evening News, 13 March 1883.

I can't pretend that I wouldn't be a touch put out if this happened to me. And yet… in a world where the inflated value of money and mortgages has brought such chaos, it is rather touching to find banknotes being put to such a straightforward practical use. I have yet to learn if modern mice find the new, almost universally-hated British five pound notes to be suitable bedding material. Perhaps, given the inclusion of animal fat, they would at least make a tasty meal.

83. The Mouse's Jewellery.
'Several months ago a lady of Boston took off a number of rings from her fingers and laid them upon her dressing-table. After washing her hands she returned to the room to replace her rings, when, to her astonishment, one of them – a diamond ring – was

missing. She was certain that she took the ring from her finger, and equally certain that no one could have entered the room without her knowledge during the five minutes she had been in the bath-room. A most rigid search was instituted, but the missing ring – valued at $200 – was not found.

A few weeks later the lady was much annoyed by mice. Almost nightly they held their revels. They not only destroyed her sleep, but choice laces were mutilated. The lady procured a trap, one of the old-fashioned kind, and having baited it with a tempting bit of cheese, placed it near the scene of depredations. On the following morning she had three fine silky mice of various sizes. One of them was so peculiarly constructed that it attracted her attention, as it appeared to have a string tied around its body. The servant girl was instructed to drown the captives and reset the trap, and she was about to throw the dead mice into the dirt barrel, when her eye was attracted by a sparkle from what proved to be the lost diamond ring, which was not perceptible when the mouse was alive, but which came to light after the severe soaking which the mouse received. It is supposed that in his haste to get away he ran his head through the ring, and subsequent struggles only forced it over his forelegs, where it remained.'
Dundee Evening Telegraph, 24 March 1883.

84. A Singing Mouse at Buckingham Palace.
'This heading, strange as it appears, is not a fiction … We give the following account, furnished us by an intelligent correspondent: "I have much pleasure in

endeavouring to give you some account of a musical phenomenon which I have just beheld and heard ... This wonder is in the shape of a 'singing mouse!' Let it not raise the smile of incredulity, for sing it does in verity. The little creature is the common house mouse, of the masculine gender. When I heard him he was in full song – having all the notes of a full grown canary. The imitation in the sostenuto passages and cadences of that bird was perfect. I feel assured that no deception was practised, for by the aid of a powerful glass, which I purposely borrowed, I could observe the tremulousness of the throat; and I asked the proprietor to retire from the room for a moment, which he did, in order that I might convince myself that I was not being made the dupe of ventriloquism. I then placed my ear close to him, and the effect was still the same. No human being could make his *piano* passages.

One circumstance places this beyond doubt; for sometimes parties have to wait a considerable time before he will pipe. An instance of this kind happened recently at the palace, where he was taken for the little Prince of Wales and the princesses to hear him. But I was informed that he fully made up for this silence by afterwards singing more lustily than he ever did before. He requires to be attentively observed, and by so doing you catch his variety. When quite still his notes are surpassingly distinct, and have all that peculiarity of the notes of the canary when he is singing himself to sleep. When he was in motion I tried the effect of sound upon him, by vibrating a tuning fork upon the table. This, although repeated several times, neither deterred him from singing, nor in the slightest degree alarmed him. If

I may hazard a conjecture, his pitch is more than an octave above that of the bird he imitates. It is very difficult to guess how this faculty got into him; for supposing that he listened to the canary from his hiding place, the larynx is not formed for such a purpose …

Its history is somewhat interesting. The wife of the man to whom it belongs (they were poor people, but are now on the high road to competence) occupied the second flat of a mean house in Red Cross Square … at a tailor's. One night, not being able to sleep for what she conceived the gentle singing of her bird, she removed the cage; but the singing remained, and not coming from the quarter in which the poor innocent canary was placed, it both puzzled her and excited her curiosity for the rest of the night. The noise was of a flitting kind, like Hamlet's ghost, sometimes here, sometimes there. She, however, felt convinced that it came from the wainscot, and she was right. A trap was set, and two nights afterward the syren was caught, which is likely to prove a golden egg to this knight of the goose.' *The Times*, 31 August 1843.

Have you ever heard a mouse sing? Aside from brushes with Disney and Bagpuss, 'no', you will probably answer. And yet, there are pretty good odds that a mouse has sung in your presence. Many of us have lived in at least one home visited by mice. As we have just seen, even 10 Downing Street has rarely been free from vermin – a situation which may only have worsened in recent years, despite the efforts of Larry, Chief Mouser to the Cabinet Office. It seems that in fact certain male mice are frequently singing; but at about two octaves higher than the kind of pitch audible to most human ears.

After one seemingly bizarre find in an 1843 paper, the story of singing mice presently led me from Buckingham Palace to the home of William Morris and his children (Kenilscott in Gloucester), to mice trilling into microphones at the BBC and the NBC, with these efforts captivating radio listeners during the International Mouse Singing Contest of May 1937. It ran right on down to our own times, as mouse music warbled through the laboratories of Cambridge, America and Japan, to say nothing of the Amazon rainforests. All in all, the surprising mass of data which tumbled down on my head in my travels through the mousehole made me ever more convinced of how rash it can be to ignore even one improbable tale.

Leaving the singing mice of 1930s recording studios to my next volume, let us make a necessarily brief tour of our century's whiskered recitals, before glancing at more modern scientific theories about their performances. As promised, the singing mouse of Red Cross Square gives us one more example of animals bringing unlikely people together, in view of its command performance before the Prince of Wales and princesses. (We can presume that Victoria's Lincolnshire cat was kept well out of the way on this occasion.) It also presents a charmingly ironic parable of how two poverty-stricken people were one night visited by a fairy godmother with a tail, and were thus probably able to escape an area cited in Parliament as one of the worst slum districts in the capital.

Just under a year later a further press report on the subject runs as follows:

'The mouse, whose wonderful vocalism lately occasioned so much surprise in London, may now perform a concert with kindred artists; two *prima donnas*, of the like rare talent, having been discovered at Watchet, in Somerset. They were shown in Taunton by a Mrs Griffiths, who has charge of the harmonious pair, to whom they had been entrusted by Thomas

Prest, in whose house they were found. A number of respectable persons of the neighbourhood have put their names to a testimonial, in eulogy of the sleek candidates for popular fame, who, although they will sometimes capriciously refuse to perform, are not generally reluctant to exert their vocal powers, and seldom fail in so doing with surprising effect on the audience. The tones are soft and low, but occasionally elevated, so as to resemble those of the canary, and sometimes the note of a woodlark' (*North Devon Journal*, 13 June 1844).

Whilst numerous similar reports are heard down to the close of the century, and from all across Britain, this early one caused me to wonder… The odds were that mice must have been singing their tiny hearts out in homes rich and poor well before people read of that vocal celebrity of 1843. But… did it take official news of a verified, *bona fide* mouse vocalist to make others realise that the curiously pleasant chirpings behind their walls were *actually* singing mice? To put it another way: can we always hear something, when we don't know what it is?

Those hosting singing mice often initially assumed that it was their pet canary, or a wild bird which had flown in and become trapped somewhere. Meanwhile, in spring 1851 a couple living in a cottage in Derby suffered some terror upon hearing mouse melodies for several nights running. The cottages in their row were all shortly due to be sold, and they presently concluded this midnight vocalist to be "the ghost of the gentleman who was formerly the proprietor of the cottages, and who had assumed the voice of a singing-bird, to mark his unwillingness that the property should be sold." Thanks to the growing number of press reports on other singing mice, however, neighbours were able to offer an alternative explanation, and they 'presently found Mr Mouse behind a pitcher, "singing like a nightingale"' (*Woolmer's Exeter and Plymouth Gazette*, 3 May

1851). Writing to *The Times* much later, a Mr Barker recalled occupying a Dartmouth house graced with singing mice in 1890. At the time he and his family had been similarly baffled, and on making inquiries 'we were asked by our old landlady not to mention it, or "it would be said that the house was 'whisht'"' – or haunted (*The Times*, 3 May 1937). To compound this problem, it was repeatedly said that mice would sing more frequently at night than during the day.

This was the case with one found in a Cork home in 1845, reported to be 'more melodious at night than by day' and audible through the entire house (*The Cork Examiner*, 8 August 1845). One caught by John Watkins of Brecon in 1849 could perfectly imitate lark, linnet and nightingale (*Illustrated London News*, 21 April 1849); but by contrast a specimen captured in Maxwelltown, Scotland in 1851 responded by eating the sheet music it was placed on, and thereafter falling silent (*Liverpool Mercury*, 28 November 1851). As late as 1869 some still considered singing mice to be purely mythical creatures. We can imagine that this perception changed when Frank Buckland's nature journal *Land and Water* weighed in with a new find in 1877. If nothing else, this one was certainly memorable:

'A few days ago I was invited by a medical friend to visit him at his house, and hear two musical mice sing a duet ... I gladly availed myself of the opportunity, and duly arrived half an hour before the commencement of the concert. My friend explained to me that every evening two little mice came out from behind the skirting-board in his dining room and sang for their supper of cheese, biscuit, and other muskine delicacies, which he took care to place on the carpet always for them at the same hour. One of them had received the name of "Nicodemus" – an allusion, I suppose, to a certain furtive visit by night* – and the other was known as "The Chirper" ...

True to time, just as the clock struck eight, and whilst we were conversing, there came from a corner of the fireplace "chirp, chirp, chirp", the same note being repeated several times at the rate of about thrice in a second, and gradually becoming louder ... after some hesitation a little brown mouse came out upon the carpet, leisurely sniffed about for its accustomed meal, came close to my chair, looked wistfully up to my face, and I was introduced to "The Chirper". As a critic, I am bound to say that "The Chirper's" performance was of second-rate quality; but ... the principal artist was yet to appear. We had not to wait long. At the conclusion of The Chirper's ineffective solo, a prolonged trill was faintly heard from behind the scenes, followed by others ... and ultimately Nicodemus, the soprano, came forth before the audience, perfectly self-possessed, and showing no signs of stage-fear. The song to which the little creature gave utterance again and again in our full view was as sweet and varied as the warbling of any bird. It most resembled that of the canary, but the melody of the nightingale was occasionally introduced. Every note was clear and distinct, but withal so soft, so gentle, so tender and *pianissimo* that I can only compare it to the voice of a bird, muffled by being heard through a down pillow.

In the room was a canary, whose cage was suspended in one of the windows. He had settled to roost, and his head was under his wing, but at the sound of Nicodemus's serenade he awoke, and listening attentively, and fantastically leaning alternately to right and left, peeped curiously down to the floor. I learned that mouse and bird were intimately acquainted, and the former frequently visited his feathered friend and stayed to supper ... Nicodemus now climbed up the drawn curtains, entered the bird's cage and partook of the seed – the canary showing no symptoms of disturbance, but merely from his perch peering down on his visitor in a ludicrously quaint and odd manner ... The two little songsters having done their best to please us, were rewarded with all that mice could wish for ... and after selecting the portions they severally preferred, gracefully retired'.[7]

*The name 'Nicodemus' alludes to the New Testament character who made a visit by night to help Joseph of Arimathea entomb Christ.

Those who are rather taken with the idea of mouse duets (and perhaps secretly visualising whole orderly rodent choirs, complete with starched white ruffs) may be interested to learn that this was indeed part of the transatlantic contest of 1937, whilst a duet between mouse and canary was reported from (where else?) Nashville, Tennessee the following year. As our witness of 1877 was Henry Lee, resident naturalist at the Brighton Aquarium, we can assume that his authority went some way to demythicising the singing mice of the Victorian age. Thinking about it, given that children's hearing is a good deal better than that of most adults, we must suspect that for a long time many kids of the day were chided for telling silly stories about these creatures, trilling away beyond the hearing-range of their parents.

    Toward the close of Victoria's reign mouse music seems to have more widely credited – at least if we are to believe 'Lady

Charlotte', the correspondent of the *Daily Mail*, who in 1896 claimed to have found an establishment selling them as an alternative to song-birds.

'In the window of a certain bird-fancier's shop in North London is a sign which reads: "Singing mice a speciality". "Yes", said the fancier, in answer to a query, "they are a variety. In fact, I am the only man in London who keeps them. They are the most profitable stock I ever had, and I get good prices for them. Sometimes I charge a couple of guineas apiece when they are scarcer than usual." The fancier brought one of his mice and put it on the counter. It was an ordinary piebald tame mouse, and it commenced a sort of piping symphony which was not exactly a song, but was really musical, and seemed out of place in so small an animal … "Teach them? No, I don't teach them. There's a special strain of mice that can sing like that. I am the only person who knows anything about singing mice. Some folks say it is a kind of lung complaint that makes them sing, but I believe it's a natural gift; all my mice are healthy enough. Some people" (he added) "have extraordinary ideas of what the mice can do. One gentleman, a violin player, brought back a couple he'd bought of me, because he said they didn't sing in tune. A week or two an old lady came to me and asked for a mouse that could sing 'God Save the Queen'. She offered me £10 for such a mouse, but I hadn't one, so she went away disgusted"'.
Daily Mail, 14 July 1896.

Our retailer should, of course, have offered a mouse descended from the one which sang *for* the Queen… However much we trust all of our Lady journalist's report, the detail about the lung complaint rings true. Time and again those discussing singing mice claimed that some inflammation of their throats or other affliction was what caused them to sing. Indeed, the naturalist Frank Buckland (of whom much more below) asserted that he had personally dissected various singing mice, and found this to be the case during his post-mortems. Having initially wondered if this was not a rather grudgingly scientific attitude to the mouse's talents, I presently began to suspect that it might be broadly true.

For… within just the last few years, science has finally begun to take singing mice seriously. In the process, it became clear that mice were singing at very high frequencies, so that their songs had to be specially recorded or manipulated to be audible to human ears. This would seem to indicate that the various singing mice of the past which people did hear must have had something about them which caused them to drop a couple of octaves. This itself further suggests that, pleasing as they were to humans, these oddities may have been much less appealing to their own kind, who preferred high-pitched or ultrasonic melodies. All of which prompts the question: why do mice sing? It has been argued that ones studied in the cloud forests of Central America do so as a means of communication, and that others do so to establish their territory. Thirdly, we have the male mice which sing to females as part of the mating process – with the latter responding in quite definite ways to various mouse serenades played back through loudspeakers.

As we will see in our closing pages, there appears to be a certain nice symmetry between an animal's size and its preference for high or low pitch – the latter being appealing, for example, to elephants. I had wondered at first if the typically inaudible mouse-song was designed to offer a safeguard against predators – until I realised that the upper hearing-range of a cat beats even that of dogs, at around 60khz, as opposed to 40 (or 20 for most humans). Across the near century between Red Cross Square and the BBC, people repeatedly argued for and against the idea that mice learned their songs by imitation. At a glance, the occasional instance of a singing mouse which shared a room with a canary is not convincing; after all, something wired in for the purposes of mating would surely not be so accidental. But, among various findings from a recent Duke University study (led by neurobiologist Erich Jarvis) was the theory that mice might actually be able to learn new songs, and that males who could do this were more effective in gaining the attention of females.

Among other things, mouse song sharply focuses a question running through this whole book. Do animals *enjoy* what they are good at? Some readers may find the answer to this so obvious as to make the question hardly worth asking. Yet we must remind ourselves how many animal experts have been at pains to attribute seeming pleasure to purely automatic, evolutionary instincts. As Joseph Wood Krutch refreshingly puts it, 'Whoever listens to a bird song and says, "I do not believe there is any joy in it" has not proved anything about birds. But he has revealed a good deal about himself' (*When Elephants Weep*, 202). Now, it seems pretty certain that the singing mice recently studied by scientists are engaging in courtship behaviour (for example, they sing more when they smell female pheromones), something obviously of evolutionary significance.

But… stepping back a moment into the human world, we can hardly deny that men or women dancing are enjoying themselves, even if they are also potentially advertising themselves to possible mates. For an example of an animal which seemed to be riotously delighted with its vocal skills, we could hardly do better than Hespie, the singing mouse of Florida. First captured here, Hespie was presently given to the minister and amateur naturalist, Reverend Samuel Lockwood, who in 1871 was living in Freehold, New Jersey.

Lockwood and his family spent a great deal of time watching and listening to Hespie as she frolicked in a cage with a mouse wheel. Before long they had grown so accustomed to two of her best songs that they gave them names ('The Wheel Song' and 'The Grand Role') and scored them in standard musical notation.

Lockwood tells of how, on one particular occasion Hespie seemed in especially high spirits, having just had a good sleep and a meal. Running and jumping about, she now began The Grand Role, leapt onto the wheel, set it racing, and switched into The Wheel Song, repeating it several times before executing some extraordinary variations on The Grand Role. (Sceptical readers may want to bear in mind that Lockwood was fairly musical himself, noting for example that Hespie always sang in the key of B major.) This exuberant burst of physical energy, play and sheer virtuosity lasted for a full nine minutes. Hespie almost literally never paused for breath, taking at most a second's break from her singing, and overall pulling off a 'feat [which] would be impossible to a professional singer'. It certainly sounds to me as if this animal was enjoying itself. And we should add that, as it was a female, there was no obvious evolutionary benefit to be gained from its operatic performance. Having no musical ability myself, I sent Lockwood's article and scores to my musician friend Matthew Nisbet. Nicely attuned to vocal range after playing recently at the Glyndebourne Opera Festival, he confirmed that the scores looked like notations of bird song, adding that Lockwood's comments reminded him of what he had heard about the improvisational qualities of whalesong. 'A somewhat fanciful comparison with today's musician', he concluded, 'might be somewhere between a performance of a free jazz improvisation and a Theme and Variations.'

Viewing the strange and colourful careers of our mousey troubadours across more than 170 years, it is again hard not to be struck by the strange relations between life and science. What was once the stuff of myth or whimsy now underpins cutting edge research into the origins of speech, the problems of autism, and much more. So… why did it take so long? Despite the immense public celebrity of singing mice in the 1930s, the isolated experiments carried out at this time by Professor Lee R. Dice of Michigan were soon to be forgotten. There is something peculiarly ironic about this long delay, given how many mice across so many decades have lived and died in research laboratories, whilst generations of white-coated observers turned a deaf ear to the songs with which their subjects cheered their clinical prisons.

Did the singing mice of press and radio somehow inspire those of Disney's 1950 Cinderella, or those chirruping around Britain's best-loved floppy cat, Bagpuss? Although it seems unlikely that this kids' stuff influenced scientists, it is rather pleasing to find a recent Cambridge University study of singing mice referring their high-pitched flutings to The Clangers.

85. Mouse and Tiger.

'Captain Basil Hall recounts a curious anecdote of a fine tiger kept at the British Residency who ate a sheep every day for dinner. "But what annoyed him far more than poking him up with a stick, or tantalizing him with shins of beef or legs of mutton was introducing a mouse into his cage. No fine lady ever exhibited more terror at the sight of a spider than this magnificent royal tiger betrayed on seeing a mouse. Our mischievous plan was to tie the little animal by a string to the end of a long pole, and thrust it to the tiger's nose. The moment he saw it he leaped to the opposite side, and when the mouse was made to run near him, he jammed himself into a corner and stood trembling and roaring in such an ecstacy of fear, we were sometimes obliged to desist

from mere pity to the brute."'
Morning Post, 28 May 1833.

86. Pentmouse Apartment.

'In a potato field, at Woodslee, in the possession of George Scott Elliot, of Larriston, a long, slender pole, of some eight or nine feet in length, had been inserted in the ground some time during the summer, in order to frighten away the rooks – to the upper extremity of which a piece of whip-cord, about two feet in length, was attached, from which was suspended by the neck a common black quart bottle: no bad representation of the human form divine. A few days ago, while the tenants of Mr Elliot were employed in digging up the potatoes, and had come to the neighbourhood of the forementioned pole, to the amazement of all the bottle was seen to commence a rotary motion, and increased its velocity to such a degree, that its evolutions were almost imperceptible. The rustics gazed upon it with amazement, for the day being exceedingly cool and temperate, the cause of such an extraordinary commotion ... could not be accounted for, on any rational and Christian-like grounds.

After circulating round for a few minutes it made a sudden halt, and faint sounds of dolorous lamentations were heard to issue from its lengthened neck. One of the rustics, bolder than the others, hinted at the noble resolution of tearing it down, and examining the invisible agency working within it; and, backed by three or four of his companions, with trembling hands he wrenched away the pole, and along with it came the dreaded enemy. On a closer inspection nothing was to be seen; but, on breaking off the neck of the bottle ... a poor mouse, with an amiable family of eight children, was exposed to the extended eyes of the gaping spectators. The little animals seemed to mourn the snug and aerial altitude from which they had been taken ... The mother of this *high-bred* family had fitted up her house in the most warm and comfortable manner, and when we consider the immense labour she must have endured in carrying up the pole, and then down the string into the bottle, all the articles with which her domicile was lined, we are struck with wonder at the wisdom of the meanest of God's creatures, and that almost human knowledge which they sometimes exhibit.'

Westmorland Gazette, 24 November 1832.

Birds

Whenever I have paused on a country walk to wonder about the name of a bird, moss or flower I have always thought, 'Well - Christopher would know'. This gently remarkable friend was the kind of person who would stop suddenly in a wood and alert you to the sound of a bird you had not quite noticed – then explaining, not only which bird it was, but also that it happened to sound almost the same as another bird which in fact looked completely different... This is not, I must confess, a chapter about the everyday magic of birds seen or heard (something which can delight even those as ignorant as myself). Nor does it attempt to do justice to the yet greater magic of navigation, achieved across thousands of miles each year by swallows, nightingales and geese.

What follows is a mixture of the surprising and the improbable. It is dominated by parrots – in part just because these highly intelligent, affectionate and long-lived birds are so remarkable, and in part because I was startled at how badly they have been misrepresented in the popular imagination. If, after reading these stories, you feel much less inclined to use terms like 'parrot-fashion' or 'parroting' I will feel I have done something worthwhile.

87. A Political Commentator.

'A well known centenarian has just died in Paris. His name was Lenoir, and he was 103 years old. Lenoir was a parrot, and a parrot gifted with really remarkable

talent. It was born in the reign of Louis XVI, and has consequently witnessed the rise and fall of a large number of governments. It has never quitted the house where it first saw the light, having been handed down by will to the different owners of the house. It belonged to no less than ten different families, and its political notions were consequently somewhat confused. Lenoir was a capital talker, and knew a number of phrases, which it often brought out very *mal a propos*. Since the reign of Charles X there was a good deal of difficulty in getting the bird to learn anything new. However, a servant with radical sympathies taught him in a few weeks to say "Vive Gambetta!" This it occasionally varied with "A bas Robespierre!" which it had been accustomed to say during the Reign of Terror. The last words of this remarkable bird were, it appears, "Grâce pour Marie Antoinette." It is certainly wonderful, under the circumstances, how Lenoir succeeded in escaping the guillotine.'
Dundee Evening Telegraph, 21 May 1886.

Léon Gambetta was a key figure in the formation of the Third French Republic. As this began in 1870, during the Franco-Prussian War, we can see that Lenoir was still able to learn new tricks, even at the ripe old age of 87. Given some of the wacky balloon stunts we will encounter below, it is interesting to note that during the siege of Paris by the Prussians, Gambetta succeeded in escaping in a balloon – what we might see as the nineteenth century equivalent of emergency evac by helicopter.

88. Our Bird the Raven.

'The following account of a talking raven [is] given by a very little girl, named Mary E. Thompson ... The writer lives at Hayesdale Lodge, Patterdale. "We know our bird is a raven. When we got it at the first it made a croak like a raven. There are a great many ravens about here, and we hear them croaking nearly every day. We have had her about one year and eight months. She is a great pet, and flies about our house and fields. One misty day she lost herself, and we did not find her for five days. Mr Martindale saw her flying a great height up and about two miles from home, and called her, and she came to him. She was very pleased when she got home again. Next morning she called 'Poll not go away, Poll not go away' ...

We have a large tub in which she washes herself. When the water gets dirty, she calls out, 'Dirty water, Poll wants a wash.' As soon as we give her some clean water, she dives in over-head. She has a bell put up where she sleeps, and when she wants to be out, she rings it very hard and says, 'Poor Poll, Poll wants to be out.' She has a large pouch under her tongue. She can catch the stones as fast as anyone can throw them. She will steel everything she can get hold of, nicer the artical the better. She plays with our dog and cat, sometimes in a very rough way. There are many more things she can say and do which I cannot write about."'

The Star, 22 January 1891.

Hayesdale Lodge, which still exists, is now an outdoor adventure centre.

89. A Patriotic Parrot.

'A beautiful grey parrot arrived at the castle on Wednesday afternoon, which has been purchased by Prince Albert for fifty pounds, from Mr Shepherd, of the City Road. The Prince saw it yesterday at Buckingham Palace, where it was taken, by command of his Royal Highness, by Mr Shepherd. It is three years of age, and has been in this country about fifteen months. It is perfect master of upwards of 800 words in the English language, and can speak several sentences in French. It sings, with great apparent feeling, the first verse of "The flag that braved a thousand years", and likewise sings, with considerable humour, the first verse of "Jim Crow", and afterwards whistles and jumps it in a most ludicrous manner. If Poll sees a person about to take a glass of wine, it will hold up its right claw, and lustily sing out, "her Majesty Queen Victoria's good health"; occasionally varying the toast to "The health of his Royal Highness Prince Albert", and "the Princess Royal's good health, and God bless her!" "Pretty Poll" Has been placed under the immediate care of the Baroness Lehzen.'

Morning Post, 25 December 1840.

90. Remarkable Robbery by a Raven.

'A few days ago a gentleman residing in Ward Terrace, Hendon, was informed by a passer-by that a raven had flown into his bedroom, the window of which was open. The gentleman scarcely crediting the story, went upstairs, and found sure enough, "a stately raven of the saintly days of yore" perched upon his dressing table

and pecking away at a cravat, from which he speedily drew forth a golden breast-pin, and made towards the open casement. The gentleman sprang towards the imupdent and ingenious thief; but the bird was too quick for him, and it flew away towards New Hendon, with the glittering pin in its mouth. Had the bird not been observed in its felonious act, the servants in the house would undoubtedly have been blamed for the robbery.'
The Huddersfield Chronicle, 29 August 1863.

91. A Parrot in the Witness Box.

'The following extraordinary case has lately been decided at the College Green Police Office, Dublin. Mr Jones H. Davis, Anglesea Street, summoned Mr Moore, of the Quay, for detaining a parrot, his property ...

Mr Hitchcock [to the complainant]: "... did you lose a parrot, and when?"

Complainant: "Yes, your worship, I lost a parrot, and a very good one too."

Mr Fullam [for the defendant]: The parrot is here, or at least outside the court.

Complainant: Then bring in the bird, and I'll engage I'll soon prove my case by his evidence.

...

Mr Hitchock: Well, go on, and let us hear your evidence at any rate.

Mr Davis said, on Sunday evening, 28th April last, he lost the bird, and did not see it after that til Friday evening last. (Here an immense cage, covered in cloth, was carried into the board room amid a shout of laughter.)

Witness: I will give up the whole matter if the parrot will not prove my case. He is my principal witness.

Mr Fullam: And do you swear, sir, that Mr Moore stole him?

Witness: No, certainly not, for I don't think he did; but it may have been stolen by some person, and sold to Mr Moore … The bird is now in Court, and let me take him on my finger and ask him two or three questions, and if he don't answer to my satisfaction and that of all present, I will give up the case.

Mr Fullam: Do you intend to have him sworn? If you do, I'd like to know on what book, as it is very likely he is a Heathen or a Turk.

… in the middle of which the parrot commenced whistling, "Take your time, Miss Lucy" amid a scene of the most boisterous mirth.

Mr Fullam: Let him be examined by you, and then I have a right to cross-examine him … What words did you teach him?

Here the cage was uncovered and the parrot stared about the board room for some time, until Mr Davis stepped over to him and said, "Come old fellow, give me a kiss." The bird, which is a very pretty one, thrust its neck out of the twisted gyres, and kissed Mr Davis with great apparent fondness … A fat young fellow here came forward, and said that the bird would do the same to anyone in the room, and therefore it was no proof that he belonged to Mr Davis.

Mr Davis said that he would not kiss any one but himself, and cautioned the lad not to try the experiment; but the advice was unheeded, and the boy, stepping over to the cage, asked for a *buss* also. The bird looked at him for a moment, bristled up its feathers, stretched out its neck, and seized the boy by the lip, out of which it nearly took a mouthful before it could be loosened, and the shouts of the lad mingled with the laughter had a very excellent effect indeed.

Mr Davis requested any other gentleman that pleased to ask the parrot for a kiss, but the invitation was politely declined by the whole of the company. He again begged the favour of a salute from the bird, which was granted ... and then he appealed to the bench and the audience if the kind bird was not his property.

Mr Hitchcock said the evidence was very strong in his favour certainly; but Mr Fullam said his client was by no means satisfied with the proof adduced on that point.

Mr Davis: Very well (taking the bird out of the cage on the forefinger of his right hand), I will ask him a few questions now, and I think I will settle the matter. Tell me, old fellow, what does the dog say? The answer was a *bow wow wow*, so loud and musical that one would imagine the Kildare hounds had run a fox into the board room. When the laughter which followed had ceased, Mr Davis again asked, Well, what does the cat say? The parrot gave a sly glance round the room, and then commenced purring a little, after which he set up mewing.

Mr Davis asked, was there any more proof necessary? and Mr Hitchcock said the evidence was quite conclusive, and he would order the bird to be returned to its original owner, Mr Davis. Mr Fullam said Mr Moore was a most respectable person, and he could bring proof that he bought the parrot in July last, for

£1, 13 shillings.

Mr Hitchcock said that might be true, but it was quite clear the bird belonged to Mr Davis, and he must therefore, make an order for its restoration.

Mr Moore: And am I to be done out of my property in this manner?

Mr Davis: You admit that you bought the bird after the police notice was served on you (showing a printed notice)?

Mr Hitchcock: You bought the bird after you read the notice, and I will not allow you anything for its support. The parties then left the office, the parrot whistling, "There's nae luck about the house".
Morning Post, 8 January 1845.

As terms like 'parrot-fashion' or 'merely parroting' show, for most of history people have been reluctant to accept that all the things parrots say really *mean* much to the bird in question. Probably still more scorned or denied have been attempts to show that parrots, like dogs, can have strong emotional attachments to their owners. When viewed open-mindedly, the above case gives good evidence for the intelligence and feelings of parrots. Aside from the kiss, notice how the bird's whistling 'Take your time, Miss Lucy' suggests, first, that it understands what is going on, and second, that it is faintly bored and sardonic about these tiresome human proceedings.

Well over a hundred years later, scientist Irene M. Pepperberg found that attempting to study parrot intelligence and emotion was still a very good way to get marginalised, if not shunned, by the scientific establishment. Yet by the time that Alex, her African grey parrot, died prematurely in 2007, the obituaries for the bird which appeared everywhere from the *New York Times* to *The Economist* showed that she had proved them wrong with a vengeance. Among many other startling findings, Pepperberg's life with, and study of Alex since the 1970s had indeed shown that he appeared to grow bored when asked the same question repeatedly during scientific tests (wouldn't you?), and that he could also display something like sarcasm. On one occasion, when he was denied a nut, he creatively stopped saying 'want nut' and instead spelled out the word: 'Nuh – uh – tuh'. As for affection? Almost the last words spoken by Alex to Pepperberg one evening in September 2007 were: 'You be good. I love you.'

92. Alarm Call.

'Mrs Watt was this morning at Port Glasgow foiled in her second attempt at suicide, by the parrot in the house calling out, "Come on, John, she's going over the window again." John was just in time to prevent the rash act. On Friday she tried the same thing, but the husband caught hold of her by the foot, but through exhaustion, had to let go. She fell to the ground and was severely injured.'
Edinburgh Evening News, 10 July 1878.

93. A Hungry Baby.

'Many years ago, when a respected friend of ours was in Australia, an acquaintance asked him to take charge of a baby emu on the voyage home, and he, being a guileless and unsuspecting man, consented. The creature arrived at the ship in a small box like a portmanteau, and was released therefrom on the deck. Forthwith occurred such an alarming extension of leg and neck that clearly human art could not again pack it into the box, nor, indeed, was the hopeless task essayed. During the voyage the emu grew in girth and

stature, it picked up and devoured most of the loose ironwork on the ship, it swallowed our friend's forty guinea gold watch, whose unnatural fate would have baffled Gaboriau himself to trace had not the last inch of the long chain been seen glittering at the beak's tip, and generally it so absorbed nutriment from all sources that our innocent friend had to hire at Blackwall a van to convey the gigantic bird to its new home at Kew.'
Financial Times, 26 June 1891.

Émile Gaboriau was a French writer of detective fiction, whose first work in this genre appeared in 1865.

94. A Parrot's Grief.

'The notion that parrots talk mechanically and without understanding is somewhat shaken by the following story, published in the New York Journal: "Broken-hearted at the death of his mistress, a blue-headed Brazilian poll parrot, with red spots on his wings and tail, wandered away from the home of Mrs Mary Walsh, no. 1976 Lexington Avenue, yeterday, and she has asked the police to find him. The bird belonged to Mrs Walsh's daughter, who died on April 28, after a lingering illness. After the funeral, he roamed about the house calling for 'Lovie', which was the name by which the girl had been known. Day after day he searched in every nook and corner for her, and at last, Mrs Walsh believes, he has gone out to continue his search in strange places."'
Daily Telegraph, 15 August 1899.

95. A Pious Parrot.

'Mrs Mackay, the "Bonanza Queen", has during her absence provided the public of London with a gratuitous entertainment of a most diverting nature. At her open window in Buckingham Palace Gate is a wonderful green parrot, which attracts hundreds of people every day to hear him talk. The crowd on Sunday was so great that the policeman had to request the people to "move on". "Move on" echoes the parrot, to the intense delight of the mob. "Polly, what is o'clock?" asks a man. The parrot, pretending to look at the clock, cries out in answer, "Half past five" – and he was right. I asked him how his mistress was. "Coming over soon, all right", replied the marvellous bird. "How old are you, Polly?" "Don't know. How old are you?" ... Asked what day of the week it was, the wretch hopped about, screaming, "Sunday; go to prayers. *Ora pro nobis*", and fell into a paroxysm of laughter that was quite contagious.' *Dundee Courier*, 20 September 1889.

Mrs Mackay was a wealthy American socialite, wife of the millionaire Mr John W. Mackay.

96. The Ostrich Takes Flight.

'Strange, indeed, are the events which the progress of discovery brings about ... Railways, steam-ships, and balloons have opened our minds to the reception of any wonder ... The nineteenth century beats every other age hollow ... but we shrewdly suspect that if the first half of the age has made men open their eyes, the second half will keep them wide awake.

A balloon ascent was not long since a great and crying wonder ... It was reserved for Monsieur Poitevin to start a new species of attraction ... Most persons have heard of the various ascents of M. Poitevin on horseback, and subsequently as Don Quixote and Sancho Panza on a real live jackass ... Vast crowds congregated on every occasion ... Last week Madame Poitevin made an ascent ... mounted on horseback, in a riding habit ... after this any novelty seemed hopeless, when M. Poitevin hit upon a new scheme.

For some time three ostriches from the desert have been exhibiting at the Hippodrome. M. Poitevin proposed to go on one of these birds, which offer was accepted. Yesterday (Friday) the queer-looking animal was attached to the balloon, and the aeronaut, with some difficulty fixed upon his back. The ostrich kicked, poked his head about, and made divers attempts at resistance; but in vain, and at four o'clock yesterday the whole of Paris was witness to the strange exhibition of a man sailing over their vast city mounted on an African bird ... The balloon went slowly over the town, and descended at St Denis, the whole material, man, balloon and ostrich, being returned to the Hippodrome [by] 11 o'clock at night.'
Berkshire Chronicle, 12 October 1850.

Believe it or not, this was not the craziest animal stunt pulled by the daring aeronauts, Monsieur and Madame Poitevin. Ascents were also made on pony- and horse-back, and lavish costumes tended to be *de rigeur*, with Sancho Panza and Don Quixote being two examples, and Poitevin dressed as an arab for his ostrich ride. Whilst fairly substantial harnesses were used for these exploits, this kind of stunt was certainly not without its hazards. When Poitevin and his unhappy ostrich ascended over Paris, his daring must have been heightened in many minds by the recent death of his British rival, George Burcher Gale (b.1794).

Gale's biographers, James Burnley and Julian Lock, relate how our British balloonist made his first successful ascent from the Rosemary Branch tavern at Peckham on 7 April 1847. Come 8 September 1850 he undertook his 114th flight from Vincennes in Bordeaux, 'seated on the back of a pony suspended from the car. He descended at Auguilles, and the pony was released, but owing either to Gale's "imperfect knowledge of the French language" or (the less charitable have suggested) to his intoxication, his rope holders mistakenly let go, and he was carried out of sight', still clinging to the underside of the balloon. '.His body was found several miles away on the morning of the 9 September, with 'limbs all broken' … He left seven children and a widow, who was also an active balloonist'.

97. A Parrot as Biographer.

'A gentleman of fortune named Aveline, residing at Camberwell, has now in his possession a most extraordinary parrot, to which he attaches great value, and for which he would take no sum of money that liberal curiosity might offer. It is not that he thinks the bird gifted with reason denied to the rest of his race, but memory most retentive and correct, it certainly possesses. Add to that, it is supposed to be forty or fifty years old, may have had many masters, and has certainly witnessed many scenes, the actors in which little imagined that their speeches would be reported at a distant day, *verbatim,* by the unheeded prisoner who was the involuntary witness of their "sayings and doings".

Yet such is the fact; and as many of the conversations which the unconscious utterer repeats from day to day must certainly have occurred more than a year ago, it is not certain that the lapse of time at all effaces what the creature has once learned, and that therefore what took place ten, twenty, or thirty years ago may, for aught that is at present known to the contrary, come as trippingly off the parrot's tongue as that which it only heard yesterday.

The bird was bought on the 12th July 1842, having been advertised in *The Times* newspaper. From the 12th of July to the 31st December she only repeated common sentences. From the 1st of January 1843 every new sentence has been daily put down. Her style was thought to improve in March last; but about the 22nd April there was a marked difference between what she uttered and what had previously been heard from her.

Many parts of the Church Catechism, the Marriage Service, the Baptismal Service, the Lord's Prayer, in French and English, have been at various times correctly repeated; but what may be regarded as more curious, are the dialogues she furnishes, and, as we are informed, with varieties of intonation not unlike to those heard at a theatre in what is called "a patter song". We quote one of them. The Mr and Mrs Wimbleton, as well as the other parties named, are at present wholly unknown to Mr Aveline.

"Here's a letter from Mr Wimbleton. 'Mr and Mrs Wimbleton present their compliments to Mr and Mrs Robinson, and beg their acceptance of a glass chandelier, which they request they will see if it is perfect.' Tell the man to bring it into the dining room, and to be very careful. (Mind that none of you touch this parrot.) Bless me, this is a fifty guinea concern! How very handsome and liberal of Mr Wimbleton! Yes, it is alright. Here is a half crown for you." "Thank you, sir."

"Do you think it would be more polite to write, or to go and thank Mr Wimbleton?" "Oh, I think we had better write." "Mr and Mrs Robinson present their very best compliments to Mr and Mrs Wimbleton, and beg them to accept their warmest thanks for their very elegant present of a glass chandelier; and according to their request have examined it, and found every iota perfect." "Don't you think it will do?" 'Very well; I suppose as well as you can do it." "Well, if you think you can do it better, try." "It was only my fun, Julia. Get the sealing wax. – To Mrs Wimbleton, No.12 Castle Street, Portman Square."

This occurred on the 19th of last month. On the 20th the creature mentioned the Wimbletons again, and then brought forward a junior member of the family, who is thus introduced:

"Here is a letter from Georgy: I do think it is his writing. Oh dear! there is a black seal; what's the matter now? However, he begins in high glee. 'My dear papa and mamma, I have the pleasure to announce to you that we break up next Saturday, the 20th instant. I shall be delighted to find myself once more at home again, and have the pleasure of kissing you all. I hope you will find that I have made progress in every branch of my studies; and at any time when I find myself at all idle, I think how grieved you would be, and also try to think what pleasure it would give you that I have got good marks. I will keep you in suspense no longer, but may say the reason why I put a black seal was because I have got no red wax, and Dick Nelson, who is in mourning, lent me some. I must now conclude, in love to brothers and sisters. Believe me your dutiful son, George Henry Wimbleton.' "Do you think there will be any occasion, to write a letter to George?" "Perhaps so; just a line or two." "Can't you write, Maria?" "No, Mamma."'

The following amusing anecdote is given by Polly, of Miss Julia Robinson:-
"Do you know, Fanny, when I was at a drawing-room, my garter dropped off while I was dancing with a gentleman; and the gentleman said, 'You have dropped one of your keepsakes, Miss Julia Robinson'; and I felt the colour rush into my face. So picked it up and put it into my pocket, for I could not leave the room just then, because we were in the middle of a dance; and before it was finished my stocking dropped over my shoe, and I thought I should have dropped too. To my great disappointment, when I got upstairs, I found the clasp was off and gone. I did not know what to do, for I could not go downstairs, as my stockings was down; so I rang the bell, and asked the servant to sew my stocking to my petticoat.'

The following singular conversation was lately repeated.
'What a beautiful sermon Mr Dale preached last Sunday! It was in the 12th chapter of Matthew, and the 40th verse, "For as Jonah was three days and three nights in the whale's belly, so shall the Son of Man be three days and three nights in the heart of the earth."'

The text was found correctly repeated, word for word, when compared with the Bible.

The parrot has evidently been, and indeed is now, the property of a medical man. Her recollections of the sweets of an *accoucheur's* [male midwife's] life are rich. We give them by way of finale.

"'Who's there?' 'Mrs Jones wants you, if you please, sir.' 'Very well, I'll come directly. What a bother it is! I don't believe it; I have not been in bed half an hour, and I went to see her the very last thing. She is so fidgety, and the nurse is as bad. I declare I'll have *"accoucheur"* scrubbed off my door if they go on in that manner. Well, I've been, and Mrs Jones no more wants me than you do, my dear; I'm sure she's in no need of me for these five or six hours. I'll make them pay for it prettily, calling me out of my bed when there is no occasion.'"

The bird, it may not be improper to mention, will not talk before strangers, nor even in a common way in the presence of Mr Aveline. Two highly intelligent young ladies, the eldest 12 years of age, are her confidants. Their character, as well as the nature of the conversations reported by the parrot, forbid suspicion of any trick. Besides, they have brought to their father remarks of his own, made when they were absent. He would be well content that the capacity of the creature should be tested by two gentlemen talking in her presence by themselves. Were this done, he is confident that in the following week he could give them an exact account of what passed, obtained from the "feathered reporter." The dialogues are given out piecemeal and slowly, with sometimes long pauses between the sentences.' *Hereford Journal*, 10 Jan 1844.

Some parts of this long report are, I realise, less interesting than others. But I decided to reprint the whole thing just to show how staggering this bird's memory was. It seems to have acted like some kind of feathered tape-recorder, being remarkably observant, although much less interactive than other parrots. It also evidently had its own personality, given its special fondness for the two young girls. We can well imagine that, had they known what it would do with their private dialogues, the parrot's previous owners would have been far less keen to sell it – unless, of course, it had already embarrassed them by repeating secrets which one part of the household wanted kept from another. For this it evidently did in Mr Aveline's own home.

98. A Child Seized by an Eagle.

'A New York paper says: "A child was captured by an eagle near Meigsville, Tennessee, on Christmas Eve, and carried about two miles … He was a bright little fellow, just old enough to be learning to walk. When no one was in the house he managed to roll out of his trundle-bed and crawl into the front yard. A great grey eagle came swooping down and fastened its immense talons in the clothing of the little boy, then rose up with much difficulty and sailed off across the adjacent woods, just skimming the tops of the trees. Its course lay towards the Cumberland River. A servant girl saw the eagle, and gave chase. She dashed into the tangled wood, and tried to keep a straight line, thinking the bird would do the same. The patch of wood was fully a mile and a half through, but the girl made the run to the other edge of it without feeling fatigue.

Beyond the wood, and between it and the

Cumberland River, lay a patch of cleared ground, partly marshy and partly cornfield, full of old stumps. When the girl left the wood, and had a clear view, she saw the eagle in the air. He seemed inclined to alight with his burden somewhere in the neighbourhood of the river. This gave her new courage. It happened that there was a man hunting in the neighbouring marshes, and, just at the moment when the eagle reached the ground with his burden, a shot went off so dangerously near him, that he mounted into the air again, but this time without the boy.

  The pursuing girl began a vigorous shouting as she ran, which attracted the hunter's attention, who, seeing the eagle quite near him, and a lady rushing down the slope with streaming hair and garments, and wildly shouting, concluded at once that there was something strange, and perhaps dreadful, in his immediate vicinity. He also set up a vigorous hallooing, and proceeded to reload his gun. The eagle soon became aware of the formidable opposition he would meet, hovered over the spot a moment, and then wheeled around in one grand sweep across the river, and then disappeared behind the shelving rock which forms the opposite bank. When the girl came down to the hunter she fell stiff, and was not able even to indicate what was the matter. The rough gallant then heard the scream of a child, and soon found a fine, healthy, rosy boy, with torn clothes, but otherwise uninjured, endeavouring to rise upon his little feet.'
Glasgow Herald, 1 February 1869.

Did this child suffer nightmares about the incident in later life, or was he too small to remember much? Looking at the jaunty way he attempts to pick himself up moments after his escape, I am reminded of the lovely scene in Edward St Aubyn's novel *Lost For Words*, recalling the earliest childhood memory of the character Penny Feathers. Happily playing with her treasured doll's house one day during World War Two, whilst a kitten sat by the fire, she had been startled by a horrible screeching noise - the sound of a bomb crashing through doll's house, floor, and finally into their cellar, where it lay unexploded. As Aubyn remarks, in those days, rather than being subjected to intensive counselling, you dusted yourself off, carried on, and thought yourself very lucky that the bomb had not exploded. In another world, Penny and our unnamed infant might well have been happy playmates.

99. True Reminiscences of a Parrot.

'When I first went to live in the house where it was, I heard it say, "Who are you? What's your name?" The mistress said, "This is Agnes"; upon which the parrot said, "So you are Agnes; ho! ho!" The next morning when I was upstairs, I thought I heard the Mistress call out, "Clear away, Agnes." And on going down I saw no one, and the parrot said, "What a fool you are! Ha! ha!"

It was quite a nuisance sometimes, as it would tell anything it saw. One day when the children, of whom I had the care, were playing with the baker's boy, and seizing buns from his basket, my hair was pulled down in the scuffle, and the parrot when he saw his master began, "Pretty Polly", etc. The master, who had guessed he had something to tell, said, "What's the matter, Polly?" and the bird replied, "Ha ha; the baker pulled Agnes's hair down!"

One evening, a young man who was engaged to be

married to one of the maids kissed her on leaving; and the parrot told the master, "Jim kissed Ann." Ann did not like Polly, and would call it ugly names: and it would say, "Pretty Polly, poor Polly, Polly has not done wrong. Oh, do not beat poor Polly, nasty thing!"

On one occasion, one of the maids had made some cakes, which she did not wish her mistress to see. So, finding she was coming into the kitchen, she put them under the cushion of a chair. The mistress sat down on that very chair, and the parrot said, "Burn you, ma'am! Burn you! Hot!" The mistress remarked, "I am not too near the fire, Polly!" and did not find out what the parrot meant. When the cakes were removed and found out to be crushed it said, "Ha ha! I am glad too! Naughty Polly!"

The Dover Express, 14 August 1896.

Readers will probably have noticed how vigorously interactive this bird is, compared to the at times almost tape-recording parrot of Mr Aveline. Also interesting here is the way the bird's pranks are woven through the mesh of Victorian class hierarchies. On the one hand we learn something about the small secret luxuries servants might seek to gain behind their Mistress's back. On the other, we realise that these little fragments from a servant's life have been preserved only thanks to an exotic and perhaps rather spoiled pet. A rich person's parrot, indeed, might have more voice than a lowly maid, circa 1896.

100. Feathered Porters.

'A correspondent writes: "I observe your article regarding calling out the names of stations on railways, and beg to recommend a practice followed by the Edinburgh and Glasgow Company's officials on the

point. At almost every station the station-master has a starling or parrot, so trained that, whenever a train draws up at the platform, it commences calling out the name of the station most distinctly, and continues to scream it out until the train starts. This is found an economical mode of informing the passengers where they are; and, as this is the season for securing young starlings (which only can be taught), I would recommend you to make the matter public through the columns of your paper." – We willingly do so, but suggest nevertheless, that, until the starlings are trained, railway porters be compelled to speak distinctly.'
Liverpool Daily Post, 21 May 1861.

In 1893, a reader of the *Portsmouth Evening News* wondered how long it was since this practice had stopped, adding: 'these must have been very primitive times in Scotland [unless] somebody has been hoaxing … I rather suspect so.'
Portsmouth Evening News, 2 June 1893.

Nowadays, it is hard not to read of this ingenious system without comparing it to the robotic dreariness of so many recorded announcements in British trains and stations. Somehow sounding neither quite human nor purely computerised, many of these seem to epitomise the routine misery of Britain's abysmal privatised rail network, where we pay some of the highest fares in the world for some of the very worst services. By contrast, there has always stuck in my head a peculiarly memorable female voice which I heard over twenty years ago on the District and Circle Lines in London. It had an oddly plangent, lyrical, faintly mournful and even philosophical quality to it – as if it some understood all too well the sad inevitability of delays at Earl's Court, the weary necessity of changing at Notting Hill, and the improbability of getting a seat at Bayswater. It is possible that this was the result of a faulty tape, of course – but a happy accident if so.

Next time you hear someone misusing the phrase 'parrot fashion' you might want to point out how humanly responsive a railway bird can sound by comparison with our modern robots.

101. Another Winged Witness.

'At Lambeth Police Court on Saturday, Thomas Joseph Gibbons was summoned for detaining a parrot alleged to be the property of George Simmons. Mr Mayo appeared for the defendant. The complainant [Simmons] stated that he had lost a parrot, and that a friend told him that the bird was in the possession of the defendant. A parrot was found at the defendant's premises, but the defendant denied that it was the property of the complainant, and refused to deliver it up, asserting that he had bought the bird. Mr Mayo said he should call a witness who would prove that [Gibbons] had bought the bird from India, and that it had been twice to India and back with him. He would also produce the bird, which would prove as good a witness as anyone with regard to who was the owner. [Simmons] and a witness declared the bird was the property of the former.

The parrot in a cage was then placed in front of the Magistrate, when Harry Smith, formerly a carpenter on board Her Majesty's ship Crocodile, came forward, and much to the amusement of the Court, proceeded to put the bird to the test. The bird uttered clearly the expression, "Pretty Polly; give us a kiss." The parrot likewise at the request of the witness gave "the call for the dog" and imitated the cry of a cat. It also uttered, "get up missus; want my tea". Mr Mayo said the bird could also say "Hip hip, hurrah for the Queen", but this the parrot failed to do. Mr Mayo continued by saying that the bird had been trained to talk by Smith while on the voyages to and from India. The witness said that he [Smith] had got into some little difficulties, and had sold the bird to the defandant for 25s.

A witness for the complainant tried to put the bird through its paces, but was not nearly so successful as the defendant's witness. Mr Saunders said, looking at the evidence before him, he could come to no other conclusion than that the bird was the property of the defendant, and therefore dismissed the summons. If the complainant was not satisfied with the decision, he had a perfect right to go to the County Court, but he believed the complainant was mistaken.'
Dundee Evening Telegraph, 28 September 1886.

Much more recently, Bud, an African grey parrot, has been considered as a possible witness in a US murder trial. In May 2015 Martin Duram was found shot dead in his Michigan home, with his wife Glenna beside him. She had also been shot, but survived. Police began to suspect a murder-suicide gone wrong, and Duram's family pointed out that, for weeks after the shooting, Bud could be heard shouting 'Don't f***ing shoot!' – evidently repeating what he had heard on that fatal day.

102. I'd Like to Teach the Birds to Sing…
'A well known New Yorker, whose pen and pencil have alike brought him money and reputation, has had an

adventure which discounts by about 10,999 the average conventional parrot story. He was fond of knocking about in out of the way quarters of the world, and left ship on the Central American coast with a party of comrades to explore the wilderness. During a cruise of several months the entire ship's company ... had devoted their odd hours to singing to a parrot. The sailors also had lost no opportunities, and taught the bird all the seafaring lingo, and a few more or less elegant expletives besides.

When the artist and his exploring comrades had bidden the bird and the sailors goodbye they plunged into the heart of the tropical forest. After 28 miles of mortal effort they reached their camping place for the night. Just as the sun was going down they were startled to hear, in the primeval silence, a familiar voice calling down from the top of a tall palm:

"Avast there, yo, heave ho!"

It was the ship's parrot. But before they could recover their startled senses, the faithful bird, having flown ahead to prepare this unexpected treat for its chums of the voyage, fluttered down to the top of a dead stump near by, and, with a shrill call, summoned thousands of the little green paroquets of the country. It is said eleven thousand of them were counted, as they circled around the great grey African oracle on the stump, and finally took their places on the ground, in rank upon rank and row after row. The explorers looked on in dumb amazement. When the feathered assemblage became quiet, the ship's parrot burst into the words of "Nancy

Lee", and to the inextinguishable laughter of the travellers, the consternation of the rest of the tropical world, and the delight of the festive precentor, the whole 11,000 paroquets, with one mighty burst of song, broke into "Nancy Lee".
Dundee Evening Telegraph, 29 June 1888.

Now, if you don't want this story to be true, there is something very wrong with you. There again… did they really manage to count *11,000* paroquets? And did this feathered multitude really learn their new song in a matter of seconds? If anyone wishes to conduct an experiment to find out, I would certainly love to be in the audience. 'Nancy Lee', as its opening lines show, was a popular sailor's song of the period:

Of all the wives as e'er you know,
Yeo ho! lads, ho! yeo ho! yeo ho!
There's none like Nancy Lee, I trow,
Yeo ho! lads, ho! yeo ho!
See, there she stands an' waves her hands upon the quay,
An' ev'ry day when I'm away she'll watch for me,
An' whisper low, when tempests blow, for Jack at sea,
Yeo ho! lads, ho! yeo ho!

Chorus.
The sailor's wife the sailor's star shall be,
Yeo ho! we go across the sea;
The sailor's wife the sailor's star shall be,
The sailor's wife his star shall be.

103. The Deacon as Doctor.
'One of the late Cunard steamers which arrived in Liverpool brought a great living curiosity. It was an odd looking parrot, whose conversation made the cabins lively during the voyage, and whose wisdom filled the forecastle with awe. Externally he is unimpressive: instead of the usual green and yellow plumage he has a grey suit that is not at all handsome. His form is rather striking, however, as he is as big as an owl, and his head is remarkably wide and flattened, making him look like a profound scholar. Among the party of gentlemen who greeted the parrot's owner on his arrival was a member of a well-known wholesale drug house of Liverpool, who sympathetically inquired of the parrot, "What do you want, Polly?" The parrot startled him by the reply, delivered in a gruff tone and with slow emphasis, quite unlike the rapid, rasping ejaculations of most talking parrots, "I – want – to – go – home."

"Home" is now some 14,000 miles away, for the parrot was brought from Australia. He was bought when young from a Sydney bird fancier by Mr Alfred Hay, one of the great sheep breeders of New South Wales. Mr Hay's estate, known as Boonanoomana, is on the Murray river. It contains about 300,000 acres, and pastures a quarter of a million sheep ... The piano in Mr Hay's house had to be hauled by wagon about 100 miles from the railway station. In a family so isolated from society, and so dependent on its own resources for entertainment, the odd-looking grey parrot had a good school. He soon developed an astounding aptitude for speech, and the whole family took a lively interest in his education.

Talking parrots are generally swearing parrots. Mr Hay gave strict orders that the parrot should not be allowed to use oaths. If the parrot picked up a naughty word from the servant he was promptly cuffed, and so decorous became his speech that he was called the "Deacon". Eventually the servants were afraid to swear or do anything wrong in his presence, as the Deacon would be apt to solemnly report the fact to the family. The present owner of Deacon made the parrot's acquaintance last autumn ... which in Australia is the sheep-shearing season ... At Boonanoomana 200 men were kept busily engaged at shearing sheep ... About three sweeps of the long shears will cut off the fleece on one side. Snip, snip, snip. The fleece on the other side is off; the shorn sheep is released, and wildly plunges down the fenced passage leading to another paddock.

It was during such a scene as this that Deacon's present owner first saw the grey parrot. Deacon always enjoyed excitement, and someone of Mr Hay's family had hung its cage where he could see the shearers at work. Deacon was in a great flutter, and he had much to say. If he heard an oath, "hush, you wicked beggar" he would scream at the offender. The thing that most interested him was the occasional snipping of the sheep's hide. In such rapid work the shears would not infrequently slice off a piece of skin and draw blood. The practice was to give the sore place a rub with St Jacob's Oil, which is in high favour in the Colony. Deacon heard so much about St Jacob's Oil that he got his phrases about it very pat. If a sheep had a sore or was nicked by shears, he would shake his feathers, jump from perch to perch excitedly and shout, "St Jacob's Oil", "Use St

Jacob's Oil", "Rub on the oil", "St Jacob's Oil conquers pain".

The gentleman visiting the range took a great fancy to Deacon, and finally Mr Hay presented the bird to him ... Deacon's owner left Australia last autumn, taking the Pacific mail steamer to San Francisco ... Deacon went with his owner across the American continent, and recently crossed the Atlantic to this country, so that he has pretty nearly circumnavigated the globe. He was christened the Doctor by the sailors during the voyage to England, from his habit of recommending his favourite remedy. If he saw anyone get a knock, or bruise, or limp, as if from pain, "rub it with St Jacob's Oil" would be his solemn advice ... the owner of Deacon is connected with the Charles A. Vogeler company, 45, Farringdon Road, London, who are the proprietors of that great remedy, St Jacob's Oil, in which the parrot takes such a lively interest.

As our readers will doubtless readily assume, Deacon's future is provided for; he occupies palatial quarters in the Office of the Company ... he has many visitors, some of whom he treats in the most civil and dignified manner, while others, we regret to announce, he treats most uncivil. For instance, he will scream out to the carriers who bring orders to the office in muddy weather, "Wipe your feet, you lubber – can't you see the rug?" – but on the whole, however, Deacon is a model bird.'

The Leeds Mercury, 22 December 1888.

By the sound of it, Deacon was certainly a helpful creature. And the details of this story also make it clear that he was both intelligent and observant. He had worked out what St Jacob's Oil was for, and would shout about it in appropriate situations. As with other parrots, and perhaps especially African greys, Deacon also had his own emotional life: hence his poignant, apparently heartfelt first words on the dock at Liverpool. We can only hope that Deacon was well-fed by the Vogeler company, which seems to have done very well by him. In February 1889 his picture appeared in the *County Gentleman*, beside a reprint of the above story, and several columns of advertising for St Jacob's Oil.

As Joe Nickell explains, 'August Vogeler (1819–1908) came to the United States from Germany in his early twenties and by 1845 had become a drug manufacturer, operating as A. Vogeler & Co., Baltimore'. St Jacob's Oil, patented in 1878, was the subject of hyperbolic claims in numerous adverts, some of which featured a red-cloaked image of St Jacob himself, looking conveniently like a kind of medical wizard. Rather less miraculously, the chloroform found in the mixture may have had much to do with its long-running success.

104. A Feathered Heckler.

'Children's Day was celebrated in the Methodist Church at Rexford Flats [Saratoga, NY] yesterday, and the church was handsomely decorated with flowers, while numerous canaries in cages suspended about the edifice added their sweet music to the singing of the children. One lady, not having a canary, brought an accomplished but not genteel parrot to church. The parrot behaved well for a time, but finally when a little boy of his acquaintance stood on the platform and began a recitation, the bird commenced to mock him ... greatly annoying the boy. Finally the parrot screeched out, "Hey! You little devil!" which had the effect of completely breaking up the youthful declaimer, and demoralising the congregation. The bird was led out of the church in disgrace.' *Dundee Courier*, 28 July 1885.

In the Saddle

Leaving my office in Durham one evening a few years ago, I noticed as I headed toward Elvet Bridge a strange dog a hundred or so yards away, being led along on a rope. As it grew closer I realised that this was not a remarkably large dog, but a very small pony: a stout creamy coloured beast whose mane would just about reach to the average person's hip. Elvet Bridge, as you may know, is purely pedestrian – and there now ensued a near riot of feminine delight and photography as the animal's handler, remarkably indifferent to all the shrieking and giggling, clopped the beastie uphill, attempting as he did so to hold a conversation on a mobile phone. This creature seemed to belong to The Court Inn, a popular Durham pub, and could occasionally be seen as mascot with the pub's advertising board right outside one of our main lecture theatres. He was a pit pony, and the man with him outside the theatre may have been an ex-miner, or sometime pony handler from the pits (this being, as all right-thinking music-lovers will know, the job once held by the father of Bryan Ferry.) Now, if ever an animal was calm under fire, it was this cute and sturdy pony. If stroked and adored by so many young ladies in such a short space of time, after all, many strong men would probably have a heart attack. I never found out how clever the animal was. But we will meet some striking examples of intelligence and emotion in our brief canter through the world of nineteenth century horses, donkeys and ponies.

105. The Horse that saw the Elephant.

'A very remarkable case of the effects of fright upon a horse, occurred in Franklin, United States, a short time since. A horse, belonging to Mr Joseph Palmer, was grazing in the yard near the fence, when the elephants belonging to the Menagerie recently in this city were passing along. The horse did not observe them until they were quite close to him, when, looking up and seeing the huge animals, he started back in a fright, ran to the opposite side of the yard, stood for a moment quivering, then dropped dead. He was literally frightened to death.'

Westmorland Gazette, 2 August 1851.

Can you really die of fear? The answer, for humans and animals, is a resounding Yes. Loyal readers of *A Century of Supernatural Stories* will be well aware of how many people died of fear of ghosts in the nineteenth century. The same also happened among those who believed in witches or vampires. In such cases, people essentially died through the strength of their beliefs, via a process known as 'voodoo death' – a kind of physiological shutdown which usually takes around one to three days. This might, at a glance, seem to raise questions about the role of animal intelligence in the Franklin instance (did it have beliefs about elephants?) But there is also another type of terror death, whose speed of operation fits the horse's fate more closely. 'Vagal inhibition' takes its name from the vagus nerve, running from the brain down to the abdomen. A surprising number of things can cause this nerve to react violently, slowing or stopping the heart, thus bringing about death in minutes or even seconds. Vagal inhibition was recorded, for example, as the cause of death in Birmingham in early 1973, when a girl of five died of fright after becoming lost in tall weeds a mile from her home.

Another close match for the horse's death involves the pig which was frightened to death by a vampire. Strange, but true… Stranger still, this was no Transylvanian porker of the Dark Ages, but a Huntingdonshire pig, living in the supposedly enlightened 1950s. We know the story is true, because the pig's owner, Mrs Louisa Ann Clark, successfully sued for damages. It was not the vampire, however, but the vampire's owner that paid up the £65 for the sow. Just on the verge of giving birth to piglets in June 1954, Ginny leaped up in the air when a Vampire jet plane swooped over at tree-top level, and was later found to have died from a burst blood vessel. The Ministry of Defence eventually settled out of court.

Ironically, there is evidence that elephants themselves can die of fear. Masson and McCarthy, the authors of *When Elephants Weep*, cite reports that 'captive elephants are subject to "sudden-death syndrome" or "broken-heart syndrome" which happens (most often with young elephants) when they are separated from their social group or put in a new enclosure by themselves'. This situation indeed sounds remarkably like that of that lost girl in 1973.

106. A Pony in a Pram.

'It would be difficult to conceive of a higher piece of animal training than that which was exhibited at a private view on Friday afternoon at the Aquarium. This is the horse Alpha, which has been taught to play "God Save the Queen" on an everyday harmonium fitted with an organ pedal board; to select any letter of the alphabet asked for by the audience; to write his name with a piece of chalk on an ordinary slate; to add, subtract, and multiply lengthy rows of figures, and to execute a number of other clever feats. One act is exquisitely funny. Alpha is "dressed up" in a huge coal scuttle

bonnet, shawl, black shirt and white apron, and in this guise wheels up and down the stage in a perambulator its little stable companion, Beta, a pony so small that it can walk underneath Alpha.'
The Star, 15 October 1895.

107. A Coltish Veteran.
'There is at this moment, in the possession of Mr Martin Colnaghi, of Cockspur Street, one of the most extraordinary ponies that ever was heard of. He is now over six and thirty years of age, was bought by Mr Colnaghi when he was eleven years of age; and during the 25 years he has been in that gentleman's possession, has travelled in harness and saddle upwards of 200,000 miles, or more than 8 times the circumference of the globe. He has repeatedly performed 75 miles in a day, and frequently did the distance between London and Worthing, with a gig behind him, in seven hours. His original colour was grey – it is now nearly white. His shape exhibits the true Arab character and form; small head, intelligent countenance, eyes as bright as a colt's, legs clean and faultless, and a mane and tail as springy and fresh as those of a five year old. This remarkable horse was bred by Lord Heathfield, his sire being Young Arabian. He was never a great feeder, and his manger was never without salt. After hard work [he] has invariably been fed with a mash, for which tepid water was used, and great attention has always been paid to his feet. He requires continual petting, without which he will not take his "grub".

He will face any crowd, and even fireworks. His attachment to hunting is so great that, not longer ago

than March last, while the Queen's hounds were out in Hertfordshire, he leaped the fences of his paddock, and, following the dogs, took the lead of the huntsman and was first in at the death. While in training as a racing pony he was known as Little Treadaway, but in 1815 he was renamed Delpini. On Sunday last he was careering in harness through the parks, to the utter astonishment of many who recollect him a quarter of a century ago; and, from the soundness of his teeth, wind, and limbs, and his invincible "bottom", there is no knowing when he will cease to be what he is. Large sums have been offered for this pony, which have invariably been refused, the family having determined that he shall die "comfortably" in their service.'
John Bull, 13 July 1840.

This account becomes the more startling when we learn that a horse of 30 is considered to be in 'extreme old age', and that age 36 approximates to just over 100 human years. Which rather prompts the question: when did Delpini stop?

108. A Mother's Alarm.
'A favourite pony mare, the property of Mr Field Evans, of Hentaes, near Pool, Montgomeryshire, some time ago had a colt, and both grazed in a field adjoining the Severn. One day the pony, to the surprise of Mr Evans and his family, made her appearance in front of the house, and by clattering with her feet, and other noises and motions, shewed she wished to attract the attention of persons in the house. On observing this, a person went out, and she immediately galloped off. Mr Evans, suspecting from the extraordinary conduct of the

animal, all was not right, desired that she should be followed; and, what was still more extraordinary, all the gates (there were several) from the house to the field, were forced open. How the animal did open them, no person can conceive. On reaching the field, the pony was found looking into the river over the spot where her colt was found drowned, which had no doubt gone too near the river, and slipped in; and its dam finding she could render it no assistance applied, in this interesting and affectionate manner, to her master for help.'
Bell's Life in London, 10 February 1828.

109. The Donkey's Funeral.
'Mr Hector Crighton, of Aldershot, has forwarded to us the following account of a funeral which took place in that town last week. A certain merchant of the peripatetic school … was up to Tuesday last possessed of a donkey which was generally considered to be the embodiment of assinine perfection. Long association, kindred pursuits, and constant fraternity had bound a strong attachment between them, so it is not to be wondered at that when nature claimed her due of the animal last Tuesday, the master, feeling how worthy a servant he had lost, should determine to bestow on his remains the last tribute of respect – a donkey's funeral.

… The funeral entered the town about 12 o'clock, evidently to the great satisfaction of the juvenile portion of the population, and was headed by the bereaved master, who bore in his hand a black wand covered with crape, and advanced with slow and measured steps amidst the encouraging admonitions from the youngsters to "Jee up, Neddy". Next followed four

bearers carrying the remains of the deceased upon a door, his head uncovered and the body enveloped in a white sheet. After them followed four mourners, whose habiliments and appearance might best be described as belonging to the *artful dodger* type, all abreast, and all smoking long clay pipes; and the *pompa mortis* was wound up by a bare-headed fiddler, who capered in the rear and produced an air from his instrument which was pronounced by the bystanders to be, "O Jerusalem! the costermonger's donkey."'
Cheshire Observer, 6 April 1867.

110. Shoed Away.
'A well authenticated and extraordinary case of the sagacity of the Shetland pony has just come under our notice. A year or two ago Mr Sinclair, pupil teacher, Holm, imported one of these little animals from Shetland on which to ride to and from school, his residence being a considerable distance from the school buildings. Up to that time the animal had been unshod, but some time afterwards Mr Sinclair had it shod by Mr Pratt, the parish blacksmith.

The other day Mr Pratt, whose smithy is a long distance from Mr Sinclair's house, saw the pony, without halter or anything upon it, walking up to where he was working. Thinking the animal had strayed from home, he drove it off, throwing stones after the beast to make it run homewards. This had the desired effect for a short time; but Mr Pratt had only got fairly at work once more in the smithy when the pony's head again made its appearance at the door. On proceeding a second time outside to drive the pony away, Mr Pratt,

with a blacksmith's instinct, took a look at the pony's feet, when he observed that one of its shoes had been lost. Having made a shoe, he put it on, and then waited to see what the animal would do. For a moment it looked at the blacksmith as if asking whether he was done, then pawed once or twice to see if the newly-shod foot was comfortable, then finally gave a pleased neigh, erected his head, and started homewards at a brisk trot. The owner was also exceedingly surprised to find the animal at home completely shod the same evening, and it was only on calling at the smithy some days afterwards that he learned the full extent of his pony's sagacity.'
Manchester Courier, 18 June 1881, citing *Orkney Herald*.

Given the number of dogs which managed to take themselves into hospitals and chemists for treatment, we can assume that this was not the only Shetland pony which shrewdly called on the blacksmith on its own initiative.

111. Homesick Horses.
'A French paper states as a fact the following ... "In the night of the 22nd November there was a great fall of snow at Commercy (Meuse) for the first time this winter, and of such violence, that the ground was covered to a depth of eight or ten inches. When the Russian dragoons stationed there, were taking their horses to water in the morning, these animals, surprised and delighted at a sight which doubtless reminded them of their country, began to prance, neigh, and roll themselves in the snow. A number escaped from the

hands of their conductors, who had great difficulty in catching them again."'
The Times, 4 December 1815.

What we have seen so far in the way of animal emotions does indeed suggest that these horses were delighted with sights and sensations which – at least temporarily – cured their homesickness.

112. Bless This Horse.
'Twice each summer, in July and August, the horse-race, or "Palio", and medieval procession take place in the piazza at Siena. The Palio (so called from the banner given as prize) ... has been run annually since 1650 ... Each horse entered for the race must first receive a benediction at the parish church of its Contrada [district] a few hours before it runs. The church doors are thrown open that all who wish to see the ceremony may enter ... The priest stands waiting at the altar - all eyes are turned to the door for the entrance of the horse. Possibly he deems it "an honour to which he was not born", for it is only after much clattering of hoofs and plunging that he can be coaxed to enter and is led up to the High Altar; thus he stands surrounded by the company of the Contrada, the jockey, helmet on head, the Captain in full armour, standard bearer, drummer, and pages ... There is a moment's hush, then the priest steps forward and sprinkles the horse with holy water, reads a few words of blessing in Latin, and sprinkles him again; the spectators give a lusty shout, and the horse is led triumphantly out.'
The Graphic, 19 August 1893.

Field and Farmyard

According to some modern authorities, such as the remarkable nature writer Robert Macfarlane, the basic knowledge of the average child about British fauna is decreasing by the year. My own childhood was somewhat chequered in this respect. Down in the local woods armed with catapults that remind one of the days when private toy shops not only flourished, but doubled as small-arms dealers, we doggedly pursued grey squirrels, in the unshakable belief that they were known pests, and the police would reward us with £2 for each pelt we triumphantly produced at the local station. I am happy to say that we never so much as grazed one. There again, although hardly counting as ardent conservationists, we were at least out of doors on our own, for long spells of time. Nowadays the few British children who do get out in this way are all too likely to be talking into a phone much of the time, relaying their co-ordinates to their parents.

Meanwhile, back in many cities and towns in the nineteenth century, you certainly did not have to get out into the country to see farm animals. Many were routinely being transported or herded through the streets, to say nothing of all the horses working them day by day. (Some readers will still remember, as my mother does, the way that neighbours would compete to snatch horse dung from passing animals, for use as garden manure.) Notoriously, cows at this time were kept in dark London cellars, to supply the capital with milk. And, just now and then, you could find yourself up close and personal with something even heavier, and much less friendly…

113. A Fugitive Bull in Bed.
'A few days ago a bull was being driven from the cattle dock in Railway Street, Newcastle, when it suddenly rushed into the room of a Mrs Watson, an invalid, who was in bed. The bull jumped onto the large four-poster and beat its head against the opposite wall, but, finding no escape in that direction, it turned round in the bed with its head to the foot, when the four-poster, with a crash, gave way under the extra weight, Mrs Watson sinking to the floor in a fainting condition, while the bull stood on the upright portion at the other end. The drover, who followed the beast in, immediately lifted Mrs Watson from the broken bed and placed her in the care of some friends in a place of safety. He then succeeded in getting the animal into the street without much further damage. Mrs Watson, who has been under the care of Dr Ellis, is still suffering from the shock and bruises which she sustained, but happily is not dangerously ill.'
The North-Eastern Daily Gazette, 3 October 1881.

114. Puss and Piglet.
'There are now at Mr Munnerly's, [at the] Legs of Man Inn, in Preston, a kitten and a young pig, which from the time they saw the light, entertained for each other an affectionate and playful attachment, that has at once astonished and amused all who have witnessed its exhibition. They were born about the same time, and the pig being an odd one of a litter, and deficient of a teat, was brought into the kitchen by the cook, and fed with milk, etc, along with the kitten. They soon began to

form and to maintain … "the most amicable relations", and became, indeed, inseparable companions, which they have since continued, although the pig has been transferred to a stable, and has far outgrown his infantine friend.'
Bell's Life in London, 19 August 1838.

115. Co-Drivers.
'Mr Huddy, the postmaster of Lismore [Ireland], lately travelled, for a wager, from that town to Fermoy, in a Dungarvon oyster tub, drawn by a pig, a badger, two cats, a goose, and a hedgehog. The eccentric sportsman wore a large red nightcap, and … used a large sow-gelder's horn, and a pig-driver's whip. Mr Huddy is in his 97th year. This exploit assembled a numerous concourse of spectators, and is the theme of conversation in that part of Ireland where the feat was accomplished.'
Liverpool Mercury, 12 January 1821.

116. Weasel Frenzy.
'A few weeks ago a labourer in the parish of Glencairn was suddenly attacked by six weasels, which rushed upon him from an old dyke in a field where he was at work. The man, alarmed at such a furious onset from an unprovoked enemy, instantly betook himself to flight, in which, however, he was closely pursued; and although he had a large horsewhip, with which he endeavoured by several backhanded strokes to stop them, yet so eager was their pursuit, that he was on the point of being seized by the throat, when he luckily noticed the fallen branch of a tree, and hastily

snatching it up, commenced in his turn the attack with so much success that he killed three, and put the rest to flight. Some idea may be formed of the man's danger, when it is known that two weasels are a match for a dog.'
The Cheltenham Chronicle, 5 February 1818.

Apart from the sheer savagery of this furry ambush, another interesting feature is the implicit teamwork of the animals. This notably sociable co-operation is still more striking in other cases of team weaselling. Writing in 1926 of his Bedfordshire home near the Chiltern hills, the veteran naturalist Oliver Pike spoke of local 'farm labourers who will tell you that fairy dogs still hunt the meadows at night'. Pike went on to assert that, 'remarkable as it may seem our meadows are hunted by night by packs of small but desperate robbers'. What awe-struck viewers had not realised, however, was that 'these miniature hounds' were actually weasels – creatures which, at certain times of year, will hunt in packs of up to forty.

117. Room at the Top.
'A few days since as a man in the employ of Mr. Boorne, of Erpinghan, was pruning trees, he discovered that a rabbit had deposited her young on the top of an ancient elm pollard, ten or eleven feet from the ground. The trunk being decayed, the little animal is supposed to have climbed the hollow.'
Leicester Chronicle, 1 February 1834.

118. The Dog and Ducks.
'Mr F. having a water dog, about a year old, which his father conceived had the effect of drawing too much of his attention from business, advised that the dog should

be disposed of. This was promptly complied with, and Neptune, such was the dog's name, was given to his father's head millwright, a Mr Scott, who resided at a place about three quarters of a mile distant. Although Neptune appreciated the favours of his new owners with evident manifestations of the warmest gratitude, he did not forget his old master, to whom he was in the habit of paying an occasional visit. Some time after our hero had taken up his abode in the house of the overseer it came into the head of his mistress to send a present of a few fine young ducks to Mrs F. They were accordingly forwarded, and duly acknowledged.

On the following morning, however, it was discovered by Mrs Scott, to her great surprise, that all the ducks were back again, safe and sound, at her own door. This created some inquiry and amazement; for, as ducks are bad travellers, and their wings not grown, they could not fly, it could not be surmised how they got back. Off the ducks were packed a second time; but lo! next morning they were back again home at Mrs Scott's door. The girl was strictly examined, who deposed that she delivered them all to the cook. The cook was examined, whose testimony agreed with the girl's. The ducks, however, were once more restored to Mrs F, who ordered two to be killed for dinner, to break the charm. This left seven, there being at first nine. All was now right, but fairies or witches are just not so easily mastered. On the following morning the seven ducks had once again taken up their station at Mrs Scott's door. Back they went a fourth time, and now effectually to prevent their return, the heads were cut off the entire [lot]. This was a settler to all witchery. The mystery, however, of how nine young ducks could make their way through three close-barred gates, and travel nearly a mile in the short space of a summer's night, continued for several months.

It was at last explained. One day a gentleman passing Mr Scott's door observed the dog, Neptune, and recognized him to be one he had met on the road several months before, ere sunrise, driving ducks, and carrying a lame one in his mouth, which was unable to travel. This at once unravelled the mystery, and cleared the "good people" or fairies of the crime of transporting them.' *The Odd Fellow*, 16 October 1841.

119. A Bull Takes Flight.
'Monsieur Poitevin, on Sunday, made an ascent from the Champ de Mars, Paris, in his immense balloon. Attached was a bullock, bearing on its back Madame Poitevin, crowned with roses and clad in a white dress, over which was thrown a purple velvet cloak embroidered with gold! ... the foolish couple effected their descent at a short distance from the fort of Ambervilliers. The bull "was placed in a stable, where it commenced eating with good appetite."'
Westmorland Gazette, 16 November 1850.

Told you. (The idea in this instance was for Madame Poitevin to depict the myth of Europa, the Cretan woman who was abducted by Zeus, in the form of a white bull.)

120. Foster Mother.
'A singular case of adoption by an animal has just occurred at Castleford, Yorkshire. Mr G. Hepworth of

the Crown Hotel, Hightown, has a sow which gave birth a day or two ago to 20 pigs. Three died shortly afterwards, leaving 17 for the mother to suckle. As there were too many for her to properly attend to, and as Mr Hepworth was anxious to save as many as possible of this numerous progeny, he took five of the newly born pigs and placed them with a setter which had only recently had pups. Strange to say, this animal not only displayed no resentment, but actually took the five little aliens under her protection, and is now suckling them, exhibiting the utmost affection towards the little piggies. Mr Peck, veterinary surgeon of Castleford, speaks of this case of adoption as the most extraordinary that ever came under his observation.' *Gloucester Citizen*, 1 September 1892.

121. A Fox in a Tree.

'The East Kent hounds were "drawing" in Knowlton Park, on Friday week, when not having found [the fox], the field was departing. A hound had endeavoured to climb a tree, but had been whipped off as upon a false scent. A gentleman who had observed this, rode under the tree, a large cedar, and examined it narrowly. To his surprise he saw a fox, almost 15 feet from the ground, quietly gazing after the retiring horsemen and dogs. The animal liked his quarters so well that it was not until lashed by a long whip that he would quit them. He descended by a large drooping arm of the tree, which nearly touched the ground. On examining the tree, it was found that he had two kennels in it, which bore every appearance of having been used for some time. The sly gentleman was hunted; but we are glad to say

that he got away from the hounds, and was the same day seen near his tree.'
Westmorland Gazette, 9 March 1850.

Intriguingly, over sixteen years later the East Kent hounds again chased a fox out of a low-branched ivy covered tree, 20 yards from the front door of Sir Brooke Bridges, MP, in Goodnestone Park, after a litter of cubs had been seen up there. It is just possible that it was the same tree; but it was clearly not the same fox. Were they related, or was there was something about the Kent fox which led it to prefer life in the tree-tops? They seem, at any rate, to have been cunning, as this one also escaped (*Dover Express*, 21 December 1866). A recent article by Alice Klein tells of how foxes in Australia have been seen climbing trees at night – possibly to prey on koalas…

122. Motherless Fox Cubs.
'It is well known that, whereas many benighted heathens worship many a comparatively sweet-scented animal, the Christian Englishman, especially if he be a country gentleman, venerates the fox. And, as the Vulpalia … will soon be in full swing, it may be interesting to call to mind a singular occurrence … The occurrence alluded to is akin to a reversal of the process by which Romulus and Remus were, according to the myth, suckled and preserved to found old Rome. Only in this case there is no myth. It is a fact, "known to the late Sir John Honeywood" and possibly "verified by Sir Brook Bridges … Captain H. Cotton … and by most of the gentlemen of the East Kent Hunt", says our authority, that in the year 1829 an enthusiastic British matron, inspired by her more enthusiastic British husband, a well known *earth-stopper, with a due

regard for the sacred sport of fox-hunting … did suckle and rear three fox cubs "until they were able to forage for themselves, when they were turned out, marked, and in after days afforded excellent runs to the much-loved sport … "Old Will", as the earth-stopper was called, was informed "that some malicious vulpecide had shot a vixen" … he went to the spot indicated, and … "his fears were realised – she was dead!" … [Observing that] from the vixen's condition she must have cubs about somewhere … he went to work [in her earth] and in less than an hour he was rewarded with a prize; "three fine cubs" said he, "as ever my eyes did see".

He took them home to his wife, Nan, and said to her pathetically, "Here, if thee must gie suck, gie it to these little poor cubs, that have had their mother killed by some damn poacher or other." Nan at first showed some repugnance, and replied, "Na na, not that; you had better wrop them up in these here old worsted stockings, and put them in the stock-hole in the chimney-corner, and that'll keep em warm." Old Will obeyed with a heavy heart, and went out, but hardly had he gone when "the kind-hearted Nan, hearing the plaintive cries of the distressed captives, took them into her lap" and treated them as if they had been her own babies. Old Will "returned sooner than she expected, and caught her in the fact, and the old man was in raptures." And so great a hold did the matter take upon the minds of sporting gentlemen that the scene was put upon canvas by a favourite sporting artist who painted "a portrait of Old Will's wife in the extraordinary act of suckling a fox cub…". The portrait is, no doubt, still in existence.'   *Morning Post*, 26 Sept 1874.

Well – it might have been then; but, without a precise title or the artist's name, it is not the easiest thing to track down these days. Does it still exist? If not, was it destroyed by chance, or by someone whose tastes in art had changed since the Victorian era? The Brook Bridges in question was evidently the same one who had previously had fox cubs nesting in one of his trees, as he lived from 1801-1875. It says a lot about the social hierarchy of the day that poor Nan was obliged to pose for this portrait by the gentlemen in question.

*An earth-stopper was the person who, the night before a hunt, blocked up any holes into which the fox might escape.

123. Extraordinary Escape of a Boy from the Fury of a Bull.

'On Sunday morning, as the ten o'clock fast train on the North Kent line was nearing Erith station on the way to Stroud, the engine-driver saw a boy, of about 12 or 13, being pursued by a bull from the adjoining marshes. The boy got on the line, calculating that the animal would not venture on the metals. He judged wrongly, however, for the animal dashed over the fence, and had just reached the down metals, when the noise of the whistle caused it to hesitate for a moment and incline its head towards the engine, and, at that instant, it was struck on the right shoulder by the near buffer, and the guard-iron in front having entered the body, tore it up in [such] a manner that death must have
been instantaneous. The engine passed on uninjured, and the boy had been fortunately delivered from his danger.'

Hereford Journal, 25 October 1862.

On Safari

Apes

'An ape', wrote the poet and contemporary of Shakespeare, John Donne, 'is a ridiculous and an unprofitable beast, whose flesh is not good for meat, nor its back for burden'. This sadly utilitarian attitude, so unable to view an animal on its own unique terms, had changed at least slightly by the time of that great Restoration diarist, Samuel Pepys, when confronted by a baboon in August 1661:

> by and by we are called to Sir W. Batten's to see the strange creature that Captain Holmes hath brought with him from Guinea [ie, sub-Saharan coastal Africa]; it is a great baboon, but so much like a man in most things, that though they say there is a species of them, yet I cannot believe but that it is a monster got of a man and she-baboon. I do believe that it already understands much English, and I am of the mind it might be taught to speak or make signs…

Although Caroline Grigson thinks that this animal may in fact have been a chimp or even a gorilla, Pepys's reaction is typical of that of many others in and after this period. (Given my own title, I should add that I do know the difference between a monkey and a gorilla – I just find 'primates' a rather too dry term.) Various types of higher ape were seen to be curiously inbetween creatures. Hence the reference to a chimp exhibited at Moncrieff's London Coffee House, in 1698, as 'the monster' (*Menagerie*, 53) – this being a term then used to indicate not so much hideous strangeness as hybridity.

Again, the artist who portrayed a female chimp, arrived in London in 1738, seems to have humanised it to a surprising degree, with the Angolans of its native home themselves allegedly referring to it as the 'chimpanzee or mock-man'. Among the hundreds flocking to view it at a shilling a time, one observed that she was 'a very pretty company at the tea-table, behaved with modesty and good manners ... gave great satisfaction to the ladies ... [and] would drink tea' (*Menagerie*, 54-55). Little wonder, perhaps, that the word 'chimpanzee' itself means, in the Tshiluba language, 'mock human'.

Grigson and others have stressed that the curiously inbetween quality of higher apes was, for this pre-Darwinian age, more a matter of the Great Chain of Being than any kind of proto-evolutionary argument. Yet when the author Philip Thicknesse wrote to Lord Monboddo, in 1789, stating of a London baboon, 'he understood everything said to him by his keeper, and had more sense than half the brutes erect we meet in the streets' (*Menagerie*, 92-93) he had chosen his listener wisely. For James Burnet, aka Lord Monboddo (1714-1799) was one of the first notable figures to propose a version of Darwin's theory of evolution – an effort for which he was ridiculed by the public heavyweights of his time.

One hundred years later, the biologist and friend of Darwin, George Romanes, was taking some trouble to downgrade the intelligence of Sally, London Zoo's popular celebrity chimp (of whom much more below). Her speech, he asserted, was limited to three types of grunt expressing assent, dissent, or thanks; she was apparently colour-blind; and she, like all other animals, lacked a sense of humour (*Dover Express*, 14 June 1889). Whilst Sally in particular may have been colour-blind, chimps in general are not, having the same three-colour vision as humans. As for sense of humour? Many certainly seem to have a sense of fun, and their smiles and laughter were persistently reported by the American Richard Lynch Garner, a man who emphatically counted many monkeys and chimps as his personal friends. A few years after Garner's work of the 1890s, the Russian scientist, Nadezhda Ladygina-Kohts, would compare the raising of an infant chimp, Joni, to that of her own son.

Viewing these intimate relationships against the longer history of humans and apes, we begin to see a curious paradox. The closer you get, the more you learn, and the closer the apes become. That is, the more you *treat* them like humans, the more human they become – which, thinking about it, is partly similar to the raising of any child. But if your prejudices keep them at a distance, then apes will seem and be more distant. Even Romanes, indeed, briefly admits that 'there is no knowing what might be done with Sally by prolonged education'. In terms of intimacy and close observation, the Victorians had one big advantage over their predecessors. This was the zoo. Visitors could judge for themselves up close. Most of all, if you really wanted to know about a particular ape, the person you should talk to was their keeper. As we will see, these relatively anonymous individuals were friends, teachers, or even parents to various chimps and orangutans.

Garner himself is now known for his pioneering research on the speech of monkeys. Let us close this survey, however, by reminding ourselves how powerfully two individuals can sometimes communicate without speech (a medium which, as we all know, is too often used to conceal our true feelings). In about 1891 Garner befriended Nellie, a Capuchin monkey owned by a Washington animal dealer. Presently Nellie was visited by 'a little girl who was deaf, dumb and blind … accompanied by her teacher, who acted as her interpreter. One of the greatest desires of this little girl's life was to see a live monkey – that is, to see it with her fingers'. Knowing how unfriendly Nellie was to anyone but himself, Garner 'stroked the child's hair and cheeks with my own hand first, and then with Nellie's' – upon which the monkey looked up at me in an inquiring manner, and uttered one of those soft, flute-like sounds a few times, and then began to pull at the cheeks and ears of the child. Within a few moments they were like old friends and playmates, and for nearly an hour they afforded each other great pleasure, at the end of which time they separated with reluctance. The little Simian acted as if she was conscious of the sad affliction of the child, but seemed at perfect ease with her … She would look at the child's eyes, which were not disfigured, but lacked expression, and then look up at me as if to indicate that she was aware that the child was blind, and the little girl appeared not to be aware that monkeys could bite at all.

We can only guess how much this girl actually knew about monkeys. But one moral of this story may well be: the less you know, the closer you get.

124. A Child Stolen by a Monkey.
'A local paper reports a somewhat remarkable case of purloining a child, which occurred in the small village of Manxbridge, in Somersetshire, on Monday last. It appears that Mr. Judcote, a gentleman of independent means, has for a long time past kept a large monkey, who has been accustomed to range over his master's garden and grounds, as the creature was esteemed harmless, and to use a sporting phrase, "…was esteemed to be free from vice".

On Monday last, Mrs Hemmingway, near neighbour of Mr Judcote, while walking in her garden, was surprised and horrified at beholding "Hulch", Mr Judcote's monkey, suddenly snatch her baby from the arms of her youngest sister Clara, who, as a special favour, had been permitted to take charge of the infant.

The monkey, gibbering and chattering, rushed off with its prize, and gained the roof of an outhouse with very little difficulty. Mrs Hemmingway was driven to the utmost extremity of despair, and she vainly strove to repossess herself of her last born. She beheld, to her infinite horror, the monkey pass over the roof of the outhouse, until he and his burden were both lost to sight. The anxious mother at once hastened to the house of her neighbour Mr Judcote, who appeared to be as much troubled as herself at the unlooked for disaster.

His man servants were despatched in every direction in search of "Hulch" who was, however, too wary to allow his hiding place to be discovered. In the meantime the parents of the child were kept in a constant state of anxiety and trepidation. It was impossible to say what had befallen the child.

The day passed without any news of either Hulch or the infant, and it was by the merest chance that both the fugitives were discovered by some farm labourers in an adjacent wood towards eight o'clock in the evening. At this time Hulch seemed to be tired of his companion, whom he purposely resigned to the farm servants. The delight of the parents upon regaining their child may be more readily imagined than described.'
Illustrated Police News, 9 July 1870.

We can only wonder what might have prompted the monkey to steal

Clara, and what went through its head as it bore her up to the roof and away into the woods. Was the animal male or female? If the latter, did it (like those various adoptive parents seen above) have some strange maternal instinct toward the girl? Or was it after a playmate, and found presently that young Clara was rather too dull for this purpose? Both Kohts and Garner found that chimpanzees could grow extremely fond of human company, and get highly distressed when realising they were to be left alone. We can safely assume that in later life Clara dined out many an evening on this tale.

125. A Gorilla by the Fire.

'For a fortnight past the district round about Madely Wood, Salop, has been in a state of intense excitement, [from] the alleged depredations committed by a gorilla, which is said to have escaped from a wild beast menagerie travelling to Bridgenorth. The animal was stated to have first made his appearance in the neighbourhood of that town, where in the darkness of the night it was severally seen by a clergyman and a policeman, both of whom fled. It is also said to have appeared in several places in the immediate neighbourhood.

A few evenings since the occupier of a house at Madely Wood went to bed at a reasonable hour, with the greater portion of his family, leaving his good wife up, who took the opportunity to visit a neighbour, leaving the door open and the candle burning. Returning in a short time, she was horrified at seeing a bent form, with a goodly array of grey hair round its face, crouching over the expiring embers of the fire, apparently warming itself, the light having gone out.

Too frightened to shriek, she ran to her

neighbours, who quickly armed themselves with pokers, iron bars, guns, and pitchforks ... and marched in a body to capture the gorilla. The form was seen sitting at the fire, but, evidently aroused by the approaching body, rose to its full height and revealed the figure of an eccentric character, well known in the neighbourhood as "Old Johnny". Seeing the door open, [he] had quietly walked in to light his pipe, accidentally puffed the candle out, and was very near being captured, if not exterminated, in mistake for an escaped gorilla. The animal has not been heard of since.'
The Cornishman, 12 December 1878.

Ironically, the gorilla had in fact been recaptured over a week before (*Sheffield & Rotherham Independent*, 4 December 1878).

126. The Monkey Theatre in Munich.

'After this we went to the wäffeln-booths, where we ate hot-baked wäffeln ... and then, resisting a wonderful elephant show, we hastened to the monkey theatre, the poor elephant's rival exhibition; the "Grand Monkey Theatre from Paris," in which forty-two apes and poodles, the property of Monsieur Le Cerf, would exhibit the most wonderful and artistic feats. At length we were seated in the little theatre; and, after a fearful charivari from the orchestra, the curtain drew up, and we beheld, seated at a long table, a company of monkeys! It was a *table d'hôte*. A dandified young fellow - perhaps Monsieur Le Cerf himself - in the most elegant of cravats, the most elegant white wristbands, the most elegant ring, and the most elegant moustache, performed the part of host; the waiter and waitress were monkeys. The waiter - a most drunken, good-for-nothing waiter he seemed - a fat, big ape - drank behind the backs of the guests the very wine he was serving them; he seemed so very tipsy, that he could hardly walk; he staggered backwards and forwards, and leaned against the wall for support, as he emptied the bottle he was bringing for the company.

But the little waitress! She was a little darling, the tiniest of little monkeys, and she came skipping on the stage in a little broad-brimmed straw hat, and a bright-coloured little dress, with the daintiest of little white muslin aprons on; she looked just like a little fairy. Everybody was enchanted with her. Even Monsieur Le Cerf himself caressed her, and gave her not only, every now and then, a nut, but a kiss. She behaved beautifully. But as to the guests! They quarrelled, and even fought—Monsieur Le Cerf said it was about paying the bill.

I can't pretend to tell you half the clever things the monkeys did in the way of swinging, dancing, firing off muskets, riding on a pony, etc. Wonderful things, too, were performed by the dogs, splendid spaniels and setters ... A beautiful white spaniel came walking in most grandly on her hind legs, as Madame de Pompadour, in a long-trained dress which was borne by a tiny monkey in livery, bearing a little lanthorn in his hand.

The finale was the besieging of a fortress; and to see some twenty milk-white spaniels rushing up and down the stairs of the burning fortress, illumined by brilliant rose-coloured, green, and blue lights, was very curious indeed. If I could have forgotten the terrible

training through which these poor creatures must have gone, I should have enjoyed it much more.'
Belfast Newsletter, 5 March 1851, quoting *An Art Student in Munich.*

Anna Mary Howitt, author of this first-person account, was a British painter and writer. She was in Munich to study painting because, at this time, women were not allowed to study at the schools of the Royal Academy. Over time, the enterprising Monsieur le Cerf seems to have become rather more obscure than his monkeys and dogs.

127. "The Missing Link!"

'An attempt is being made at Boston, US, to teach an ourang-outang to speak. Already its education in this unwonted direction has progressed favourably, for although only two years old, the animal distinctly utters the words "Mama" and "come back". "Mama" is the name by which he knows the wife of his keeper. He wears clothes, and is able to dress himself like a child, even putting on shoes and stockings. He has learned to eat exactly the same food as the trainer's family.'
Portsmouth Evening News, 22 August 1899.

'As an appropriate climax to a series of experiments in educating a monkey, Mr. J. L. Buck, now in Boston, will try to make the monkey talk. The animal is one of the greatest curiosities in the simian line ever seen. The point to which his education has been carried is wonderful. He rejoices in the name of Sambo, and is a Bornean of the orang-outang species. Sambo eats at table with as much complacency as a Christian, and behaves better at his meals than some Christians. In describing his method of teaching Sambo how to use a spoon, Mr. Buck explained that he placed the food in a very deep cup. Sambo's natural intelligence at once showed him the use of a spoon, but he at first made the mistake of bringing his provender from the depth of the cup by means of the spoon and then laying it down on the table to be grabbed in his fingers. Mr. Buck cured Sambo of this habit by placing a hungry monkey at the table beside him. When Sambo would lay the food down the hungry one would snatch it away. After a while Sambo saw the point, and foiled the thief by carrying the food directly from the cup to his mouth by means of the spoon. The accomplishment once acquired there was no more trouble.

Sambo was taught the value of clothing by being left for a time in a cold place and afterward taken in and warmly clothed. In this way the advantage of wearing clothes soon became apparent to his monkey mind. What caused Mr. Buck most perplexity was how to get Sambo to wear a cap, for he seeemed to have a rooted antipathy to any kind of headgear. The trainer was almost on the point of giving it up, when one warm day he noticed that the flies were annoying the monkey very much. When they were particularly persistent around his head Sambo would pull up his coat to protect his poll. Inspiration came to Mr. Buck. Daubing a little molasses on Sambo's head, he left him to be tormented by the flies for a time, and then placed a cap over his head to show him the use of the covering. Sambo realised the utility of a cap at once and has worn it without protest ever since. By these methods, and without the use of the whip that is considered so indispensable by most trainers of animals, Sambo's education was carried on.

He can dress himself without assistance, putting on his shoes and stockings as carefully as an orderly boy, at meal times carrying his chair to the table and sitting up like a regularly recognized member of the family, eating his meals decorously and daintily, with his napkin tucked under his chin, and behaving, in short, with the best of table manners. At night Sambo will sedately remove his clothing and climb into the little white enameled bedstead provided for him, cover himself with the bedclothes and dream blissfully of his happy emancipation from the ignorance of his ancestors. Sambo breakfasts, lunches and dines on the food that Mr. Buck and his family eat. He relishes vegetables cooked in any manner, and all kinds of bread, pie, cake, cheese, and, strangest of all, he has learned to eat meat and grown very fond of it. Naturalists assert that the orang-outang is a vegetarian, but Sambo has never had a day's illness since he has partaken of a meat diet. All food given to him is prepared in the same manner as that intended for the family.

The most interesting experiment is the attempt that Mr. Buck is making is to develop Sambo's vocal organs. After a careful examination, Mr. Buck concluded that these were perfect and capable of the power of speech. The method employed to teach the monkey to speak he is not desirous of giving in detail. He says, however, it consists of parts of each of the methods used to teach birds, feeble-minded children and the blind, deaf and dumb. Although Sambo is hardly of an age to grasp the advantage of speech, his trainer considers that even a year of unavailing effort will not be time wasted, as he is confident that as Sambo grows older he will learn the language. At his present age, 2 years, Sambo is very nearly as far advanced as most babies, as he uses the words "mamma" and "come back." Mrs. Buck has petted Sambo to such an extent that if she leaves the room he will cry continually, "Mamma," and on her reappearance will say distinctly, "Come back."

Mr. Buck admits it will require time, labour and patience to get anything like a vocabulary of words, to say nothing of teaching Sambo to put them together intelligently. While his trainer does not hope to make an accomplished orator of Sambo, he feels very sure that within a reasonable time he will be able to show to the scientific world a simian who speaks in the English tongue. Such sounds as Sambo is learning to use are absolutely foreign to the natural guttural sounds of the ourang-outang. Mr. Buck has made arrangements with an East Indian trading house to bring over a wild simian at least once a year, so that Sambo may not forget his mother tongue. Should the efforts to educate the monkey to speak prove successful, the time may come when Sambo will act as interpreter between man and the missing link. Sambo is what is known as a cage bred animal. His parents were captured when young and tamed in a cage by the Rajah of Somabayo. So Sambo has never known a wild existence, which may account for his genial and tractable disposition.'
The Anderson Intelligencer, 11 August 1899.

When I first read this story, I had my doubts. But I started to take it more seriously when I came across recent reports on the speech-like behaviour of Tilda – an orangutan in Cologne Zoo, who had been studied by Dr Adriano Reis e Lameira and others. Tellingly, when the *Daily Mail* covered this in January 2015, an only half-joking headline about the Planet of the Apes recalled the edge of nervousness evident in 1899 ("The Missing Link!"). Subtext? Interesting, but a bit too close for comfort…

Dr Lameira's team video-taped Tilda, and analysed these recordings. They found that she was making extremely rapid speech-like clicks (around seven times faster than, for example, ordinary chewing) and doing so in the same way that humans move their mouths to form consonants. Among other things, these results suggested to the team a model for the early evolution of human speech.

Having sent the story of Sambo to Adriano, I was pleased to find that he had never come across it, and was keen to include it in his research (his opening words, indeed, were 'what a precious piece of journalism!'). He also added that he had been 'contacted recently about a chimp in the US that was able to say "more" to request peanuts from a vending machine in front of his enclosure but to which only visitors (of course!) had access'. Now, three words are not much to go on: but notice that two of them begin with 'm', and that variants of 'mamma' are one of the first words spoken by most infants – prompting us to wonder if the 'm' consonant is easier (for babies and primates) to vocalise than others.

Looking at the century-long gap between Buck's achievements and Adriano's work, it is hard not to be struck by the question: 'Why so long…?' It is said that the Ancient Egyptians had designed a form of steam-power, but did nothing with it other than opening temple doors in a pleasingly magical way. Perhaps in a hundred years people will be wondering why on earth it took so long to exploit all the technologies derived from the study of animal homing instincts…

As Adriano pointed out, a colourful American character, Richard Lynch Garner (1848-1920), had claimed in the early 1890s to have identified and understood the speech which chimps used to communicate with each other. Proving that it was not merely advances in 21st century technology which allowed recent studies on primate speech, Garner took a phonograph to the Washington Zoo, and recorded some utterances of a female chimp. He then moved the phonograph over to the male chimp's cage and played back the recording. Bewildered by the production of monkey speech in the absence of the monkey, the chimp thrust its arm into the horn of the machine and peered into it repeatedly (*Pall Mall Gazette*, 2 June 1891). Garner would go on to claim that he could speak primate languages, and could also teach human speech to apes. For this (notes his biographer, Jeremy Rich) he was often mocked by the scientific community of the time (*Missing Links: The African and American Worlds of R. L. Garner, Primate Collector*, 2012). As Garner's intriguing activities deserve a little space, I hope to return to them in my second volume.

What did Sambo and Tilda have in common? Perhaps most importantly, contact with humans. In many ways Buck evidently treated Sambo like a human child, whilst Tilda's behaviour (which also included whistling and arm waving) prompted Adriano and co to suspect that the animal had at some point been trained for the purposes of entertainment. Readers may have noticed that the ever-observant Pepys was well ahead of the game here, almost 250 years earlier.

128. Wrestling an Orangutan.

'A remarkable struggle took place yesterday at the Royal Aquarium between a young negro named Dock Perry, a keeper of the wild animals in that establishment, and the ourang-outang, familiarly known as "the Wild Man of the Woods". It appears that the animal in question, which has been on exhibition at the Aquarium for a period of nearly twelve months, has been purchased by the proprietor of a menagerie in Paris, and that yesterday it became necessary to take the animal from its cage in order to send it to its place of destination.

At the hour named the negro Perry entered the cage (which has three compartments) with a cane in his hand, and having opened one of the slides, which usually admits the keeper, attempted to drive the ourang-outang out into the cage. The ourang-outang, however, showed fight, and closed with the man, clasping his great arms, which are twice the length of those of a man, around the negro. The keeper, who is a stalwart fellow, grappled with his opponent around the neck, and, in the sight of a number of spectators, a most exciting wrestling struggle took place. After about five minutes the ourang-outang was overpowered and driven into the cage intended for him, and about six o'clock he was despatched from the Aquarium to his destination. The negro was bitten in the left hand during the struggle.'

Nottingham Evening Post, 23 September 1881.

129. A Monkey Celebrity.

"'Sally' has spent more than five years in Regent's Park, having been acquired by the [Zoological] Society in October 1883, and is probably better known than any other inhabitant of the Gardens ... She is very intelligent and well educated ... [and] uses a spoon with such dexterity that even this action seems natural to her, and ... she will, when she has done drinking, wipe her mouth as carefully as any person whatever.

Her education has, however, not been confined to table manners; in fact, they are among the least of her accomplishments, the greatest of which is that she is able to count up to five, picking up and handing to her keeper, without mistake, the number of straws that he may ask for. Her method of proceeding is curious, as she puts all the straws in her mouth, with the exception of the last one. For example, if she is asked for five, she puts four in her mouth, picks up the fifth, and hands the whole number to her keeper ... She also has an idea of colour, or at least can distinguish between a light straw and a dark one; for, being asked for a black straw, she will hunt in her litter until she finds a really dark one ... [these] accomplishments are apparently not so appreciated by the public as such comparatively simple tricks as leaving her food untouched until told to take it, finding fruit in her keeper's pocket, or kissing or shaking hands with him through the bars of her cage.

Sally would appear to be sufficiently advanced to have some crude ideas of sale and barter; for on one occasion a lady who was watching her had in her arms a suricate [meercat], and Sally, who is fond of rats,

evidently mistook it for one, and desired to possess it, and to this end produced all her valuables, consisting of a piece of wood, a penny, and the tin from which she had just drunk her beef tea, and offered them one by one, evidently in exchange for the little beast, and her fury and indignation on finding her offers refused were most amusing.'
Birmingham Daily Post, 19 February 1889.

What we saw earlier of our chimp and her pet kitten suggests that Sally may have wanted the meer-cat for similar reasons. Any flint-hearted readers who doubt so fluffy a theory might want to consider the incident at Basle Zoo cited by Masson and McCarthy: 'When a young sparrow crash-landed in the chimpanzee cage … one of the apes instantly snatched it in her hand. Expecting to see the bird gobbled up, the keeper was astonished to see the chimpanzee cradle the terrified fledgling tenderly in a cupped palm, gazing at it with what seemed like delight. The other chimpanzees gathered and the bird was delicately passed from hand to hand. The last to receive the bird took it to the bars and handed it to the astounded keeper' (*When Elephants Weep*, 142). Time for more on Sally…

'A "Missing Link" at the Zoo.'
'I have always laughed at the "Missing Link" theory, but I was shaken in my faith at the Zoo one day last week. I was introduced to a lady: her name was Sally. She did not live in an alley, but in a cage, and from that domicile as I passed a paw was suddenly thrust into my face with a wisp of straw clutched in its hairy grasp. A keeper called out, "For shame, Sally! That's very bad behaviour." Whereupon, to my utter astonishment, Sally, who is no other than the chimpanzee, went into a

corner and blubbered piteously. Her feminine pride had been wounded by the reproof, and she took it to heart sadly. The keeper then said, "Well, Sally, you shall give me a bouquet for my button-hole, and the chimpanzee gathered up some straws, broke them off neatly to equal lengths, and in the neatest manner, drew them through two button-holes of the keeper's coat.

Later on the man gave Sally some beef-tea, and she handled the spoon with the grace of a Court lady. There was a look of keen intelligence in her face, which I remarked to the keeper, who said, "Yes, if some of these animals could talk, I expect they would be as sensible as most of us." Sally came to the gardens when only two years old. She has now reached the mature age of eight.'
The Penny Illustrated Paper, 17 August 1889.

'"Sally", the chimpanzee, is rather inclined to sulk just now. Nevertheless her keeper is able to cause her to take a straw and at word of command, without guiding her hand in any way, poke it first through a keyhole, and then through a little hole in a board. He then offers her two pieces of pear, a large and a small piece, telling her to take the small piece, which she obediently does. Then he puts two more unequally sized pieces in his pocket, and tells her to take out the small piece, and again she obeys. Then she places a flower in the keeper's button-hole with a grace – using both hands – a duchess might envy. After which she is told to pick up three straws, which she does, and hands them to the keeper.'
Pall Mall Gazette, 18 October 1889.

'The Zoological Gardens have sustained a serious bereavement in the death of "Sally", the black-faced chimpanzee from the west coast of the Gaboon, who for eight years has entertained many thousands of folk of all ages and of both sexes in the popular gardens in Regent's Park. The intelligence of "Sally" has been the subject of comment among men of science, of sages and philosophers, and possibly theologians. Perhaps the most remarkable of her feats was that of counting. "Sally", in the presence of a crowded room, when called upon, say, for bits of straw in her cage, would give you the exact number you named, up to ten, and the keeper has found her when alone counting in this way up to twenty. If one of the public asked for five, six, or nine straws, or whatever quantity up to ten, she would pick each deliberately up without any mistake, put them one by one into her mouth until all were got together, and then give them into your hand. If asked for a "button-hole" she would take a straw, break off part of the stalk, and put the ear into the button-hole of the keeper's coat. She knew right from left; would use a spoon, and sip with it till the cup was empty. She was four years old when first brought to this country, and was therefore twelve years of age. Though seeming to understand almost all that was going on round her, she could never frame any articulate speech. Her memoir deserves to be written by someone who is qualified by intimate acquaintance. Unlike most other biographers he will have nothing to conceal. Poor "Sally's" death has been previously reported, but it actually took place on Friday last.'

Daily News, Monday 31 August 1891.

By an odd coincidence, the headline 'Death of a Chimpanzee' which appeared 1 August 1891 in the children's paper *Chatterbox* referred not to Sally but to a chimp which had come over with her to the zoo over seven years ago. Sally was said to have nursed this ape (which caught a northern chill) until it died, sitting by it and wrapping it in a blanket. This story seems consistent with Sally's affection for her keepers, and her general sociability. Many of the feats of skill or intelligence she performed seem, after all, to have been inspired by a desire to please her keepers, or the visiting public. The counting of straws does not seem to have been rewarded with food; whilst taking the smaller piece of pear is something one can imagine many toddlers refusing to do. As the following story shows, Sally's celebrity by this time was such that the public could not do without a replacement.

130. Monkey Music.

'A correspondent of *The Spectator* who has been making experiments with various musical instruments on the animals at the Zoological Gardens, writes as follows with regard to one of his latest tests: "Our first visit was paid to Jack, the young red ourang-outang, which, since the death of Sally, the chimpanzee, claims the highest place in animal organisation among the inmates of the zoo. He is a six months' old baby, of extremely grave and deliberate manners, and perhaps the most irresistibly comical creature which has ever been seen in London. He is extremely well behaved, not in the least shy, and as friendly with strangers as with his keepers. His arms are as strong as those of a man, whilst his legs and feet seem to be used less for walking than as a subsidiary pair of arms and hands. He is thus able, when much interested, to hold his face between two hands, and to rest his chin on a third, which gives him an air of pondering reflection beyond any power of human imitation.

'He knows there's something up', remarked his keeper, as we entered the house, and the ape came to the bars and sat down to inspect his visitors. As the sounds of the violin began, he suspended himself against the bars, and then, with one hand above his head, dropped the other to his side, and listened with grave attention. As the sound increased in volume, he dropped to the ground, and all the hair on his body stood up with fear. He then crept away on all fours, looking back over his shoulder like a frightened baby; and taking up his piece of carpet, which does duty for a shawl, shook it out, and threw it completely over his head and body, and drew it tight round him. After a short time, as the music continued, he gained courage and put out his head, and at last threw away his cloak and came forward again. By this time his hair was lying flat, and his fear had given place to pleasure. The piccolo at first frightened the monkey, but he soon held out his hand for the instrument, which he was allowed to examine. The flute did not interest him, but the bagpipes – reproduced on the violin – achieved a triumph. He just flattened his nose against the bars and then, scrambling to the centre of the cage, turned head over heels, and lastly, sitting down, chucked handfuls of straw in the air and over his head, 'smiling', as the keeper said, with delight and approval."'
Sheffield Daily Telegraph, 31 August 1892.

'The sunlight drifted through the browning leaves of the trees by the Marsupial House, and there was an occasional drip from the branches due to the last shower that passed. The house itself was desolated ... Even the two black monkeys .... for once in a way behaved sedately, and cuddled up to each other on their barkless tree stump, instead of racing up and down it. No one watches them now. They used to win a reflected glory for their near presence to Jack the Ourang-Outang, but his death has sunk all his neighbours to a level of indistinction. Jack had become a public favourite since that day, almost two years ago, when he came to this country a hairless baby, wrapped in a rug.

The keeper mourned for him. Sighing, he said, in a monologue in a minor key: "It was with Jack as it is with interesting children; they die young. But it was a pity. You see I was just beginning to educate him, and he was learning well. He could count. Why? this way. I used to take an apple and cut it into pieces, and tell him to take three. He would eat the three pieces, but he would not touch the fourth till I gave him it. I began him with straws just as Sally learned to count. He was real human too; he could put a buttonhole bouquet in my coat quite natural. You should have seen the way he would eat ... He supped with a spoon, and held the bowl ... He was a great favourite, so good-tempered. There was nothing he liked better than, when I let him out of his cage ... to sit alongside of somebody who had given him a banana ... on the rail in front of his cage ... He was a good 'un. Yes, it was the same old complaint – consumption – that carried him off; none of them seem able to stand against it."' *Graphic*, 21 Oct 1893.

Despite his sad early death, Jack clearly managed to become famous in a matter of months. As to his responses to music… many animal experts would probably write them off as evolutionary reactions to some perceived threat. But this theory surely would not explain his apparently genuine delight in the bagpipes. Once again, animal pleasure rears its furry head in an unexpected way. Much more recently, a gorilla called Michael has become so fond of Luciano Pavarotti that 'he has been known to refuse an opportunity to go outdoors when a Pavarotti performance was on television' (*When Elephants Weep*, 192).

More recently, we have the Thai Elephant Orchestra formed by conservationist Richard Lair and American composer Dave Soldier. Reporting on this in November 2000, Sarah Strickland of *The Independent* felt that six year old Tadpole, 'banging the drum in perfect time with his trunk' certainly seemed to be 'enjoying himself' (*The Independent*, 8 Nov 2000). Having now listened to the CD several times, I can recommend it as strange, lovely, and remarkably soothing.

One of the earliest experiments on the musical tastes of elephants was arranged by the surgeon Everard Home (d.1832) at Exeter Change in 1822. Having become interested in the hearing of elephants after he received the pickled head of a Sumatran elephant, Home persuaded Broadwood to bring one of his pianos to the Exchange, where a tuner tried out various chords for the elephant's delectation: "the higher notes hardly attracted notice, but the low ones called up the elephant's attention. He brought his broad ears forward … and made sounds expressive of satisfaction than otherwise. The full sound of the French horn produced the same effect" (*Menagerie*, 207-8).

131. A Monkey's Baptism.

'A few days ago an infant ourang-outang was presented to the Zoological Society of Kansas City, and a question at once arose as to what name might be most appropriately bestowed upon the newest recruit of the collection. "Ham Junior" was decided upon by a majority of the council, at the close of a long and animated discussion, and it was further resolved to give the baby ape a public christening. As no duly ordained minister of any religious denomination could be induced to perform the ceremony, that important duty devolved upon the executive [officers] of the Zoo, and was solemnly gambled for by the principal lion-tamer, the chief bear-ward, and the unique elephant-trainer, Captain Matthew Johnson. Euchre was the game, and the last-named official won ... whereupon the date on which the christening rites were to be publicly celebrated was conspicuously advertised in all the local papers. On the appointed day, in the presence of an enormous and hilarious gathering, Captain Johnson did the needful for the simian catechumen, laying on hands, sprinkling water, and reciting the words of the Christian baptismal service with superlative gravity. He was much applauded.

A day later, the episcopal ministers of Kansas City, in high conclave assembled, passed the following resolution: "We, the bishop and clergy of the episcopal church, do hereby put on record our solemn denunciation of the blasphemous travesty of the Christian Sacrament of Holy Baptism recently perpetrated at the Zoo in this city." Captain Johnson's only comment on this withering rescript was: "Well, the baby had to have his christening anyhow. No offence was meant to the ministers, you know!" He will probably be excommunicated; but in Kansas City it is considered likely that he will suffer the extreme displeasure of the Church with considerable fortitude and exemplary equanimity.'   *Dover Express*, 19 May 1899.

132. London's First Gorilla.
'A distinguished – though very unprepossessing and extremely unsociable – guest has just been received at the Gardens of the Royal Zoological Society in Regent's Park, in the shape of a young male gorilla. He comes at the wrong time of year for the public as well as for himself, for the leaves are falling, and the cold winds blowing in the "Zoo" ... His own opinion of the English climate – if it may be gathered from his present demeanour – is one of the profoundest disgust ... "Mumbo", as he is sometimes called ... was captured in the Gaboon, as an infant, and kept for some time by his negro masters, before being shipped to Liverpool to join the well-known menagerie of Mr Cross'.

All too typically, Mumbo seems to have caught severe cold before or during his railway trip from Liverpool to London.

'Mumbo lives in the same house with Sally, the amiable and highly accomplished chimpanzee, but, of course, in a separate compartment ... He is indeed evidently not at all well, for as he crouches in his dark corner at full length he twitches his hairy legs ... [He] is about as large as a human child of twelve or thirteen years, covered with a dark grey fur, reddish upon the head, which is ugly even beyond the appalling plainness of his neighbour Sally ... Deep sunk eyes glitter now and then from under the cavernous brows ... Thinking to cheer him up a little, the authorities of the Gardens have introduced a small Indian monkey, a macacus, into the gorilla's den. No friendly approaches seem to have ensued. The macaque skips and climbs about, almost utterly regardless of its hideous relative, except when it fancies a little taste of the gorilla's food ... It is a bad sign at present that he will not eat much, for in their native wilds the appetite of his race is something tremendous and insatiable. They will devour fruit and vegetables till their huge stomachs swell like balloons, and they can crack cocoa-nuts with their prodigious teeth, and tear to pieces, it is said, the leopard and the lion ... Possibly it may rouse and comfort young Mumbo, by and by, when he hears every night ... the roaring of the great carnivores in the new house near at hand ... But certainly, at present, what he seems to say as he sprawls in a fluffy mass amid his straw is "I don't like London!"'

Daily Telegraph, 14 October 1887.

Other reports of the time were urging Londoners to see Mumbo while they could – and their gloom about his imminent end was sadly accurate, for he was dead some time before 7 January 1888 (*Penny Illustrated Paper*). Given the great efforts of the Zoo to keep him warm, with his cage heated to 72 degrees fahrenheit, we have to wonder: did Mumbo die of homesickness?

For the thirty years preceding poor Mumbo's short stay in England, gorillas had in many senses been creatures of myth. Whilst various types of ape or monkey were found not only in zoos but romping about country and city in the Victorian age, the only gorillas seen here initially were stuffed ones. An adult specimen of over five foot was on display in the Crystal Palace from late 1858, and another, '"little Bill," the baby gorilla' could be seen at a charity bazaar in Regent Street in summer 1861. The Mr Fisher who captured it had sought to bring this animal back alive, but it seems to have died of shock after falling into a river. Interestingly, although the French explorer Paul du Chaillu had seen a live gorilla in Africa in the late 1850s, and brought dead specimens to Britain in 1861, Fisher had come to doubt their existence until his own encounter in that same year. If true, the story of how Fisher caught his ape may help explain some of the myths about gorillas, credited at this time by Africans and Europeans.

They were frequently misrepresented as immensely fierce and violent, with Du Chaillu referring to them as 'monsters' and reporting his great terror on seeing them beat their chests. Du Chaillu's misapprehension may have been created by his habit of pointing a rifle at every gorilla he met. At any rate, it prevailed for some time, and the specimen which the British Museum bought from him to display at the top of the great staircase was described by one reporter as having its 'head inclined forward as if about to spring, the mouth, wide open … the right arm extended above the head … while the left, drawn across the chest, appears ready to deliver one of those blows which M. du Chaillu so vividly describes' (*Bell's Life in London*, 28 July 1861). Three years before, an account of the one in the Crystal Palace had explained: 'the negroes of Africa live in constant terror of these animals, and it is stated by the natives that they frequently descend in considerable force, sack the villages, carry away the young children, and devour them, and further that they have a very ugly custom of attacking men, and wrenching off the heads of those whom they attack … it is very certain, from the formation of the teeth, and the great strength of the animal, that the gorilla is not a vegetarian' (*Stirling Observer*, 25 November 1858).

Tellingly enough, the Crystal Palace gorilla had thirteen wounds, and two bullets in its body – and in the circumstances one can see how these animals may have got into the habit of pulling off a human's head first and asking questions later. But in fact Fisher's story casts doubt on even this reasonable precaution. He had got hold of Little Bill when he spied a frightened African boy, Gorumba, who got into Fisher's boat, shortly followed by Bill. Gorumba explained that 'a large gorilla stole his mother and himself; and she dying in a few days, he became the playmate and friend of the ugly beast'. Whilst this account leaves it slightly unclear if the death was of Gorumba's mother or the adult gorilla, it seems clear that the boy was not harmed – and indeed possibly treated rather like one of the family (*Belfast Morning News*, 24 June 1861).

With Darwin's *Origin of Species* published in November 1859, following years saw numerous articles with headings such as 'The Gorilla War' or 'Gorilla Controversy', driving the desire to see this purported relative of *homo sapiens* in the flesh. When in autumn 1862 a live gorilla was said to have arrived by boat in Liverpool, 'a scientific gentleman from the Zoological Society started by express train, with his pocket full of gold, to acquire the valuable specimen for the gardens in Regent's Park' – only to find that this simian rarity was nothing more than a common chimpanzee (*Cork Examiner*, 28 November 1862). A real gorilla, named Jenny, turned up alive in Liverpool in autumn 1885, but had died before September was out (*Daily Telegraph*, 24 September 1885). Thus the stage was set for the sadly brief fame of Mumbo, scrutinised by curious Liverpudlians and Londoners until his death a few weeks after October 1888.

Like myself, readers are probably struck not just by Victorian delusions about the habitual ferocity of gorillas, but by repeated references to their supposed ugliness – especially if they have seen the remarkable 1970s footage of a young David Attenborough rolling about in the midst of a gorilla family. These early nineteenth century reactions seem to have been coloured by more than just the shock of the new – the unwanted kinship argued for by Darwin must surely have been unsettling many of these observers and reporters.

133. A Monkey Postman.

'The Madrid journals contain an account of the arrest of a street organ-player of that city on a singular charge. This man, whose name is Juanito, had a monkey which he dressed in the uniform of a sailor, and sent up to the windows of the houses before which he played his organ, to receive the money that was given. In this the police saw no offence; but, it appears that Juanito was in the habit of putting under the jacket of his monkey love letters and assignations with which he was entrusted, and for delivering which he was well paid. This was regarded as an offence against public morals and the honour of the married senors of Madrid. The mode in which the letters were delivered was as follows: when the monkey ran up to the windows Juanito kept pulling his cord, and caused him to shift from place to place until he arrived near the lady to whom the letter was addressed. He then ceased to pull the cord, and the monkey, knowing what he had to do, drew out and presented the letter.'

Leicestershire Mercury, 25 September 1852.

134. Special Ape Service.

'There was a splendid fête in the Surrey Zoological Gardens on Monday, in honour of the birthday of the Princess Victoria. The weather was favourable, and the real attractions of the grounds ... - the excellent exhibition of living specimens of Natural History – and other amusements, including several bands of music ... led to the assemblage of an immense multitude of well-dressed persons, who remained in the Gardens till dusk. Among other objects of curiosity was the ascension of Mr Green in his balloon, from a platform on the lake, in the most magnificent style. Mr Green took with him a monkey belonging to the establishment, called Jacopo, who exhibited no small surprise at the novelty of his situation, a surprise which was, however, succeeded by indignation on finding himself bundled out of the car without ceremony, in a parachute, which soon expanding, enabled him to reach *terra firma* in safety.

He fell in a garden belonging to a policeman in East Lane, Walworth. A label, affixed to the parachute, promised a reward of £2, and a free admission to the Zoological Gardens for the present season, to anyone who might find "my nabs" and convey him back to his numerous family. He chattered most vociferously on being taken up, and, it was supposed, protested strongly against the repetition of such freedom with his amiable person. The fortunate finder, not having an interpreter at hand, was at first at a loss to discover from what star he had descended; but the label catching his eye, Signor Jacopo was, without loss of time, conveyed to the Gardens, where he was received with loud acclamations and congratulated heartily on his safe descent. We have the authority of Mr Tyler, the Secretary of the Society, to state that the aerial traveller suffered no injury internally or externally, as might be inferred from "his acceptance and munching of the

hundreds of cakes and oranges that were presented to him by the delighted multitude". ... Mr Green descended with equal safety in Dagenham, Essex.'
Bell's Life in London, 31 May 1835.

Charles Green (1785-1870) was the leading balloonist of his day, making over 500 flights and suffering many close shaves in the process. Whatever Jacopo thought of this strange business in May 1835, just over two years later he must have been about ready for the monkey SAS. On 15 May 1837 *The Morning Post* promised its readers that 'the celebrated monkey, Signor Jacopo, having engaged the only vacant seat at an enormous expense of 20 guineas, will ascend positively for the last time with Mrs Graham today and tomorrow, and perform the daring feat only attempted by himself of descending in a parachute, in or as near the gardens as may be practicable.' Two days later we hear that Jacopo, described as 'the monkey who has seen the world', had descended safely onto Kennington Common from Mrs Graham's balloon.

 Meanwhile, on Monday 4 September a grand gala was held in Surrey Zoological Gardens to celebrate Queen Victoria's becoming its patroness. As well as wild beasts, bands of music, the eruption of Mount Vesuvius, Bedouin Arabs and fireworks from a platform on the lake, the crowds were regaled with the ascent of Mr and Mrs Graham in their balloon, just as two other balloons were passing over from Vauxhall. Perhaps trying to think of England (or of cakes and oranges) Jacopo in his parachute was suspended under the car. When released by Mr Graham 'the little gentleman contained in it came slowly to the earth without experiencing either dread or danger'.

 Mrs Graham was an impressive character of the day, now unjustly near-forgotten. She made her first ascent around 1820 at about age 16, with her future husband, aeronaut George Graham.

She survived several accidents across the period from 1836 to the 1850s, dying a natural death in her old age. Given that most of her ascents seem to have been made with George, it was a particularly memorable day when, on 9 August 1837, she ascended from the Mermaid Tea Gardens in Hackney with two other female aeronauts, Mrs W.H. Adams and Miss Dean.

Not to be outdone, the balloon-loving Parisians were regularly parachuting a monkey named Jocko out of a balloon in the 1850s. The monkeys might have been consoled to know that, owing to uncertainty about the effects of altitude on the human body, the world's first ever aeronauts, sent up in a French balloon in 1783, were a sheep, a cockerel and a duck.

135. King Kong's Rehearsal.

'On Sunday morning a large-sized baboon, which had been sent as a present from a gentleman at the Cape to a friend, and which had been brought from on board ship but a few hours before, managed to slip his chain, and sallying from the house, No.12 Duke Street, London, soon made his way to the roof of the houses in New Martin Street. On gaining this eminence Master Jacko commenced amusing himself by stripping the tiles off and flinging them at the crowd in the street. His pursuers got from the garrets of the houses onto the roof, but the instant they made their appearance the cunning animal shifted his quarters, and recommenced taking off the tiles, and flinging them into the street, to the amusement of some and the terror of others.

Jacko thus moved from house to house, until he at length reached the roof of the Anchor and Hope, opposite to the London dock, in East Smithfield. Here he descended to a low building over the long-room, over the

roof of which there was a skylight. Having minutely surveyed the place, and seeing no one below, Jacko took a fancy to get in, and having smashed several squares of glass with a piece of tiling, let himself drop from the opening thus effected onto one of the tables. After much difficulty, and a desperate resistance on the part of Master Jacko, he was secured, and brought back to the house from which he had escaped.'
The Bath Chronicle, 13 June 1844.

136. A Baboon Hits the Bottle.

'A remarkable story of the antics of a drunken baboon comes from Omaha, via New York. The baboon, it seems, was a member of a trained animal show that was doing a turn at the Creighton Theatre, and the animal by some means got loose and invaded the stage one afternoon. Being muzzled, it was harmless, but also being very large and ugly, it frightened those upon whom it chanced to burst. The stage hands tried to catch the animal, but this only served to make the creature angry, and it rushed at its pursuers, seizing them with its great hands, and throwing them about as though they were children. Finally it dashed through the door of the theatre and into the café adjoining. The bartender fled for his life, and the baboon leaped behind the bar, where it drank portions of a bottle of whisky, beer, brandy, and other liquors, then hurled the bottles at the mirrors, and at length rushed back into the theatre with bottles under both arms and grasped in each hand. These missiles the ape hurled in every direction, smashing three long mirrors in the principal dressing rooms, and destroying a number of costumes

by tearing them to bits. For half an hour the animal raged thus without hindrance, at the end of which time its keeper arrived and succeeded in chaining it up.'
Yorkshire Telegraph and Star, 17 January 1899.

137. A Monkey Secretary.

'A Governor of Jamaica, who had his peculiarities, but was nevertheless considered a good Governor, was in the habit of noting down on the back of a letter, or any other slip of paper near him, such matter as he deemed it necessary to notice in his dispatches, and when these were to be transmitted, the notes were all arranged to be officially communicated to the Colonial Secretary. It happened, on the eve of the sailing of a packet, that one of these scraps was missing, containing some memoranda of importance, which the Governor could not call to mind. The Secretary and his clerks were all set to work to hunt for the lost scrap, and whilst they were busily ransacking the cabinet, a servant entered with the stray fragment. The Governor, pleased to recover his lost memoranda, and being tired with the search, summoned his suite to repair to the breakfast room, to partake of a lunch before he completed the dispatches, which they had still time enough to finish; but, in quitting the cabinet, they locked up in it a huge African monkey, who had been the curious spectator of all their proceedings.

When they had nearly finished their lunch the whole house echoed with an hideous yell; the monkey dashed into the room, jumped over the table, and bounced out at the window. On repairing to the cabinet, the cause of the outcry was explained. The monkey had

imitated all he had seen; he had searched out and torn to atoms all the papers he could lay his paws on, and amongst others the recovered memoranda, and finally he raised the wax to the lighted taper to seal his labours, but unluckily, catching at the heated wax, he burnt his fingers, which occasioned the yells which alarmed the Executive, and which further caused the postponement of the packet; an event creating, as usual, sundry conjectures and manifold murmurs amongst the Kingston politicians.'
The Morning Post, 26 September 1833.

138. A Pet Chimp.

'I was once the owner of a highly-educated chimpanzee. He knew all the friends of the house, all our acquaintances, and distinguished them readily from strangers … He never felt more comfortable than when he was admitted to the family circle and allowed to move freely around, and open and shut the doors, while his joy was boundless when he was assigned a place at the common table and the guests admired his natural wit and practical jokes. He expressed his satisfaction and thanks to them by drumming furiously on the table. In his numerous moments of leisure his favourite occupation consisted in investigating carefully every object within his reach. He lowered the door of the stove for the purpose of watching the fire, opened drawers, rummaged boxes and trunks and played with their contents, provided the latter did not look suspicious to him. How easily suspicion might be aroused in his mind might be illustrated by the fact that, as long as he lived, he shrank with terror from every common rubber ball …

He knew perfectly his time for retiring, and was happy when some one of us carried him to his bedroom like a baby. As soon as the light was put out he would jump into the bed and cover himself, because he was afraid of the darkness. His favourite meal was supper with tea, which he was very fond of. He sipped it from a cup, and ate the dipped bread slice with a spoon, having been taught not to use the fingers in eating.'
Manchester Courier, 14 January 1893.

139. A Monkey's Pet.

'A highly educated chimpanzee has recently been added to the Paris *Jardin d'Acclimatation*, who is worthy to rank with the orang-outang "Jacko" we recently described in the *Jardins des Plantes*. The new arrival is called "Timbuctoo", is very tame, of most amiable temperament, and while residing with his former master at Sierra Leone supplied the place of a servant in the house; he opened the door to visitors, greeted them, and on their departure showed them out with the utmost courtesy, handing them their hats, etc.

Timbuctoo's very domesticity, however, nearly caused a fatal accident on the voyage to France. One day his mistress missed her baby, a child of eight months, and after a long search descried to her horror Timbuctoo perched at the top of the mast, rocking the unfortunate infant to and fro. Nobody dared move lest the chimpanzee should be startled and let the baby fall, so Timbuctoo hopped about the rigging with his plaything, finishing his performances by swinging from the mast by the edge of his tail.

Suddenly the vessel gave a lurch, down went

monkey and baby, but Timbuctoo saved himself by catching at a rope, and climbing down to the deck, where he was speedily relieved of his precious burden, and carefully watched for the rest of the voyage.

Monkeys in Acheen, however, are made useful members of society. They are bred and taught to pluck cocoa nuts, and their owners let them out for this purpose in the Straits. The apes have a line attached to them and scale the trees, where, like human beings, they obey command, and choose the fruit which is pointed out to them. They then twist it round and round till it falls, celebrating their success with a jump and a chuckle of satisfaction.'
Edinburgh Evening News, 11 August 1875.

This drama of course reminds us of Clara's escapade with the wayward Hulch in Somerset. Here we can see that the adoptive monkey parent is definitely a male. Despite that, it seems to have been as careful as any monkey mother with its borrowed baby – not least given the sudden fall…

140. A Local Hero.
'The municipal council of Grenoble, France, has voted a large sum for the purpose of erecting a bronze statue of the famous chimpanzee Charlemagne, who has just died there. He was brought to Grenoble by an African explorer, and for nine years had enjoyed the freedom of the town, being allowed to enter practically every home and to help himself to anything in the vegetable and fruit shops. Charlemagne, who was perfectly tame, dressed like a labourer, though he preferred to travel on all fours. He used to sit with the card players in the

cafés or by the fishermen at the riverbank by the hour, looking to be the wisest and most sedate individual among them.

   Five years ago he rescued a child from a well by going down and climbing back by the help of the rope and the projections of the wall. Nobody was present but the drenched child, who told the story. Charlemagne was also a great favourite at the children's hospital. There he spent hours playing in the different wards with infinite kindness. His funeral was attended by a very great number of persons.'
Leamington Spa Courier, 18 January 1901.

Given what we have seen of monkeys snatching children, this tale offers a bit of karmic balance. It is especially striking that Charlemagne made the rescue on his own initiative, without any human prompting. Sadly, the statue seems at some point to have succumbed to the ravages of war.

141. The Flying Pieman and Jacko.
'On Monday last, an itinerant showman, who for some time past exhibited two dancing monkeys about the town, pitched his stage, on his way to St Bartholomew Fair, in Covent Garden Market. When his poles and cords were fixed, and the monkeys in their full dress were about to commence, the celebrated flying pieman came by with his basket, and, having furnished himself with a bottle of gin, he leaped upon the stage, and treated the showman and one of the monkeys with a glass each; but the other monkey declined taking any, and was leaping about to avoid it; but the pieman served out the second glass, and the other monkey took

his with apparent gladness. The pieman again seized the monkey who declined it before, and he still scorned to take any. The bystanders called out to the pieman to throw it at him. The pieman instantly flung it in his face. Instantly, the monkey who drank the gin, and who was half-drunk by this time, sprung upon the pieman, seized him by the arm, and would have torn that piece of the flesh entirely out, only for its master, who with much difficulty made him relinquish his hold. The pieman was dangerously wounded, and was carried to a doctor's shop to get his arm dressed; he was then carried home to his lodging at the seven dials.'
Bell's Life in London, 8 September 1822.

The flying piemen of London were so called because they moved around selling pies – probably often containing more or less life-threatening ingredients, from what historians of food have claimed. Several of these characters have survived at least fragmentarily in newspaper accounts from the period. Our culprit here was probably not William Francis King (who emigrated to Australia in 1829), given that this individual was born only in 1808. A more likely bet is one John Crayford, referred to as 'the flying pieman' in the report of an assault hearing from July 1822. Upon being asked by 'a respectable pawnbroker' to shop shouting 'Hot pies' outside the man's house, Crayford had whacked him in the mouth with a slice of this dubious comestible, and was brought up before a Lambeth magistrate for his pains. If this is indeed the correct match, then our pawnbroker may have felt that there was a touch of karma at work when Crayford was so savagely repaid for his monkey business that September.

    A polite biography of Crayford might have described him as 'a bit of a character' – which would also fit the unnamed flying pieman who, back in July 1809, stood on one of the towers of Lambeth Bridge, calling, 'Hot Pudding, All Hot!' This was just one of innumerable inventive and reckless wagers of the eighteenth and nineteenth century – part of a culture in which the wealthy were said to have lost thousands betting on which drop of rain would be the first to reach the bottom of a windowpane. (If you don't believe me, do watch the excellent documentary *The Real Casino Royale*.) In the present case, one Mr W. had bet a Mr F. that our pieman could be heard bellowing about puddings as far away as Battersea Bridge – a distance which is now over three miles by road... Sadly, the result of this escapade has since vapoured away on an old Thames breeze.

142. More Monkey Talk.
'Miss Esther Williams, a bright Chicago belle, has devoted a good deal of time and talent to the study of the monkey language. While other Chicago society girls were studying French and German, Miss Williams was devoting her spare hours to the language of the chimpanzees and the gorillas. Miss W has come from Chicago to New York with a phonograph to pursue her studies in the monkey languages in Central Park ... Miss Williams's idea was to come to New York so she could enjoy the advantage of talking with Chico and Johanna, the pair of chimpanzees in Central Park. She believes that she can say words to Chico which he will be able to understand, and that she can engage him in conversation. She may thus draw from him an expression of his views on New York, Hoboken, and other interesting subjects. It is the opinion of his keepers that he is not able to understand any sound which a human being makes, except that he is able to

distinguish the voice of kindness and to comprehend a command.'
Tamworth Herald, 21 April 1894.

143. A Monkey Detective.
'The following wonderful story is told by a Bombay paper. A Madrassie going on a journey took with him some money and jewels, and a monkey, of which he was very fond. The poor man, however, was waylaid, robbed and murdered by a party of ruffians, who went their way after throwing the corpse into a dry well, and covering the latter up with twigs and dry leaves. But they had overlooked the monkey, who saw the whole proceedings from the top of a tree. As soon as the road was clear, the intelligent beast set off for the Tehlsidar's, or police officer's house, and having drawn his attention by cries and moans, lured him on by dumb signs to the tell-tale spot. In due time the body was discovered, and then with the monkey's help the Tehlsidar found the stolen property where the thieves had buried it.

He then followed the monkey to the bazaar. There the monkey picked out one of the murderers, ran after him, and with his teeth held him fast by the leg until the man was secured. This feat he seems to have repeated until all the murderers were caught. It is added that they have since confessed their crime, and been committed for trial before the Tellicherry Court. An Agra contemporary suggests that such a monkey ought to be made an inspector of police. Would that not be rather a descent for the monkey?'
Royal Cornwall Gazette, 17 February 1872.

144. A Monkey in a Sweetshop.

'A capture of a most unusual character was effected by the Warrington police on Sunday morning about two o'clock, a burglar being caught not only on the premises but laden with spoil. About the time named, the occupants of a provision shop in Church Street were considerably alarmed by hearing a crash in their shop, followed by noises that clearly indicated that someone was on the premises with felonious intent. Thoroughly aroused by the successive crashing of glass, an alarm was given; and when the police arrived the husband and wife were found standing at the door leading into the shop, the one armed with a pair of fire tongs, and the other with a sweeping brush, ready to repel any attempt at escape on the part of the ruffian, who was heard smacking his lips and crunching the spoil.

A light was procured, and all were considerably astonished to see a monkey sitting amidst a ruin of broken glass jars, sweets, cakes, etc, stuffing himself with all that was within reach. He was promptly taken into custody, and had so gorged himself as to be unable to make the least resistance. Further evidence of guilt was found in the fact that each paw was full of sweets, and the distention of paunch ... showed clearly that he had made the most of what must have been a very golden opportunity. The culprit had gained access to the premises by means of a broken window at the back, and not satisfied with a full indulgence in the good things with which he was surrounded, did considerable damage to the breakable articles which were scattered in all directions. As he could give no account of himself,

and no one knew where he hailed from, he was taken to the bridewell, where he soon made himself comfortable.'
York Herald, 29 December 1880.

145. A Monkey College.
'The Cinncinati Inquirer is responsible for the following news: "The latest thing in educational news is the college of monkeys in London. Half a dozen evolutionists and naturalists of the very advanced school are attempting to teach monkeys to talk or express their wants. The method is at first by letter blocks. A block alphabet, in which the letters are all distinctly coloured, is arranged before the monkey student, which is first taught to select some simple word, as pie, and when he picks out the letters and forms the word he is given a piece of pie, so there is a constant incentive to learn … "And what are the results?" asked the visitor? "They have not been divulged yet" was the reply, but one of the authors of the scheme states that there is to be a public exhibition, when the monkeys can be heard for themselves. If a pig can be taught so many wonderful things, I see no reason why a monkey should not.'
Dundee Evening Telegraph, 9 Sept 1884.

Sadly, I have not been able to find out more about this venture – something which would doubtless have appealed to both Garner and Williams.

146. A Monkey Maestro.
'A well-known American *savant* has educated a favourite monkey to become a good pianist; all monkeys, this gentleman maintains, have more or less a musical

faculty. If men had not invented the piano, the learned American seriously maintains, monkeys would infallibly have done so. After only 48 lessons the monkey Tabitha, who is a real ornament to her sex, could play scales with surprising dexterity. The suppleness of their fingers, their agility, their strength, all tend to show, at least according to Tabitha's master, that all monkeys are born pianists. Patience is the only thing required to bring out this hidden faculty. There is another fact which strikes one. Monkeys have this great advantage over human pianists; they have four hands, while men are unfortunately not endowed with more than two. A monkey ... can thus ... play a duet without the assistance of a companion.'
Dundee Evening Telegraph, 28 May 1886.

147. A Curious Monkey.

'In the Zoo connected with the National Museum at Washington, there is a fine male grivet monkey, who shares a large cage with four opossums. To human beings he shows himself anything but amiable, but he takes kindly to his strange companions, and they have been the best friends from the first. The attention of the attendant was lately drawn to the cage by the excitement of a crowd in front of it, and on going to ascertain the cause he was surprised to see the monkey seated in the middle of the cage, with one of the opossums lying quietly on her back on his lap, and her head under his arm. The monkey had just discovered the marsupial pouch of the opossum, and was diligently investigating it. Had he not been a close observer it certainly would have remained unseen, for it was so

tightly closed as to be perfectly invisible in its normal condition. The monkey carefully lifted the outer wall of the pouch, and peered into the cavity. Then he reached in with his hand, felt about for a moment, and to the astonishment of everybody took out a tiny young opossum, about 2 inches long, hairless, blind, and very helpless, but alive and kicking. Jock held it up to the light, where he could get a good view of it, scrutinized it with the air of a savant, and presently returned it to the pouch, very carefully. After replacing it he looked into the pouch again, and presently drew out another for examination, which he looked at with solemn interest, smelt it, and then carefully put it back. It was thus it became known to the attendants that the old female opossum had the young ones, which had previously been looked for in vain.'
Sheffield Evening Telegraph, 23 July 1888.

148. A Monkey Guardian.

'An instance of the instinct and fidelity of a young monkey comes from Batignolles, a suburb of Paris. A little boy, the son of an inhabitant of that part of the city, was playing in one of the rooms of his father's house with the monkey, which is a most intelligent and domesticated member of its species. The boy, in a fit of juvenile caprice, tied the cord of a window blind around his neck and pretended to hang himself, to the immense amusement of his simian playmate, which grinned and chattered on a chair. Suddenly the boy became livid and began to cry, for the cord had got into a real noose round the neck.

In a very short space of time the monkey took in

the situation and tried to undo the noose with its paws, but had to give up the attempt. It then hopped away to another room where the boy's grandmother was sitting, and began to pull her gown, to chatter, grimace, and look wistfully towards the door. At first, thinking that the animal wanted to bite her, the old lady was frightened, but, seeing that it was endeavouring with might and main to drag her towards the door, she rose from her seat and went, piloted by the monkey, to the room where her grandson was moaning. The boy was instantly extracted from his perilous position, though it was some time before he recovered from his pain and fright. Jacko, the deliverer ... received a nice little tablet of chocolate cream for his splendid action, and he deserved it.'
Dundee Evening Telegraph, 27 October 1888.

149. More Monkey Music.
'Here is the "latest" from Paris. A monkey is creating sensation and earning fame by giving brilliant performances *a quatre mains* on the pianoforte, making graceful and becoming use of his long tail in turning over the leaves of the sheet music from which he draws his inspiration.'
Dundee Evening Telegraph, 5 December 1888.

'The *Philadelphia Inquirer* proclaims the existence of a monkey violinist. The animal belongs to Mr John O. Warren, a young musician of Philadelphia who bought him of an organ-grinder. He now executes several waltzes.'
Yorkshire Evening Post, 19 January 1898.

Disappointingly, there is no record of a duet between this talented pair.

150. A Monkey in a Highland Church.
'On Sunday forenoon a most unusual event happened in the Bellie Parish Church, Fochabers. A monkey belonging to Mr Milne, draper, had broken loose in the morning, and after disporting itself through the town, entered the church along with the congregation. During the singing of the first psalm it made its appearance in a very prominent part of the gallery, making itself quite at home, walking across the seat-rails and grinning most knowingly and composedly in the faces of the congregation, who could barely suppress their mirth at such an unlooked for addition to their number. The minister himself – the Reverend J.P. Watt – evidently felt the ludicrous nature of the situation. As such a state of matters could not possibly be tolerated within the precincts of the sacred edifice during divine service, one of the elders tried to eject the intruder, driving him downstairs before him. Our Darwinian ancestor, however, eluded him ere he opened the door, and again turned upstairs, grinning complacently at his futile attempts to entice him outside. Two of the congregation, however, joining issue, he was ejected, but only to appear in the opposite gallery; whence, however, he was re-ejected ere he could try any more pranks. Later on Mr Milne and others secured him roaming about, and he was returned to captivity.'
Dundee Evening Telegraph, 18 March 1890.

151. The Wild Man Of The Prairies.

'An old hunter, writing from Grayson, California, to the *Antioch Ledger*, on the subject of a report that a gorilla had recently been seen in the state, says that he caught sight of one of the wild men of California last year, while hunting in the mountains 20 miles south of Grayson. Finding on returning to his camp one evening that the charred sticks from his fireplace had been scattered about, he kept watch next day in the bush, and, after about two hours waiting, saw standing by the fire a creature in the image of a man full five feet high, and disproportionately broad and square at the shoulders, with arms of great length; the legs were very short, and the body long. The head was small, compared with the rest of the creature, and appeared to be set upon his shoulders without a neck. The whole was covered with dark brown and cinnamon-coloured hair, quite long on some parts, that on the head standing in a shock and growing close down to the eyes, like a Digger Indian's.

The creature stooped and grasped a stick from the fire; this he swung round and round, until the fire on the end had gone out, when he repeated the manoeuvre. The hunter sat and watched him as he whistled and scattered the fire about. Having amused himself apparently as long he desired, he started to go, and having gone a short distance returned and was joined by another - a female, unmistakably - when they both turned, passed within twenty yards of the hunter, and disappeared in the bush. The whistling was such as boys produce with two fingers under their tongue. The writer adds that several persons have come across the tracks of the immense feet of these creatures, and he

has met with one person who has seen them.'
Tamworth Herald, 24 December 1870. Original letter 16 October.

Just what were these beings? Some parts of the description would indeed fit gorillas, although these creatures are not known for standing upright for very long, nor for walking on two legs, which they seem to be doing in this case. If they were gorillas, then where had they come from? These animals were still rare as captives at this stage, and the loss of two from a menagerie seems fairly unlikely. The hunter's description is certainly eerily precise. We will probably never know exactly what it was that he saw. But if some kind of missing link was going to live on in the wild in the late nineteenth century, then California was probably a pretty good place to hide out.

Claws

Any readers of a nervous disposition should be warned that most of the bears, lions, and tigers to be met in following pages were not safely penned up in zoo cages. Indeed, as far as travelling menagerie animals went, there seems to have been no such thing as a safe cage. As John Simons notes, in 1816 a lion from Ballard's menagerie 'escaped and became a highwayman. It lay in wait by the roadside and attacked the Exeter Mail Coach near Salisbury', killing a horse and a dog. Before the coach's guard could shoot it with his blunderbuss Ballard had intervened, saving an animal which had cost him £500, and which was still being exhibited, in all its happy notoriety, in 1825 (*The Tiger…*, 67).

Whilst you had a surprisingly good chance, in these days, of seeing a lion or tiger or even a Tasmanian devil on the loose, probably the commonest thing with claws, encountered in streets across the country, was the bear. Given the lives suffered by these performing animals (still seen in Britain some way into the twentieth century), it was little wonder that they escaped from their captors at every opportunity. But even those still under control could occasionally prove fatal. In 1876, after fleeing in terror from a performing bear outside his house in Derby, two year old Joseph Dence went into a state of prolonged shock, and finally died on 2 May; and something very similar happened to three year old Elizabeth Thorlby, of Helpringham, Lincolnshire, in May 1879.[8] These were almost certainly not the only cases. We begin, however, with a famous animal escape and rescue from 1857.

152. A Child Snatched by Tiger.

On Monday 26 October 1857, about 1pm, a tiger belonging to the animal dealer Charles Jamrach escaped and, at the corner of Bell's Street, seized a child. Jamrach later wrote up the following first-hand account of his part in this incident.

'It is now a good many years ago, when one morning a van-load of wild beasts, which I had bought the previous day from a captain in the London Docks, who brought them from the East Indies, arrived at my repository in Bett Street, St. George's in-the-East. I myself superintended the unloading of the animals, and had given directions to my men to place a den containing a very ferocious full-grown Bengal tiger, with its iron-barred front close against the wall.

They were proceeding to take down a den with leopards, when all of a sudden I heard a crash, and to my horror found the big tiger had pushed out the back part of his den with his hind-quarters, and was walking down the yard into the street, which was then full of people watching the arrival of this curious merchandise. The tiger, in putting his forepaws against the iron bars in front of the den, had exerted his full strength to push with his back against the boards behind, and had thus succeeded in gaining his liberty. As soon as he got into the street, a boy of about nine years of age put out his hand to stroke the beast's back*, when the tiger seized him by the shoulder and ran down the street with the lad hanging in his jaws. This was done in less time than it takes me to relate; but when I saw the boy being carried off in this manner, and witnessed the panic that had seized hold of the people, without further thought I

266

dashed after the brute, and got hold of him by the loose skin of the back of his neck. I was then of a more vigorous frame than now, and had plenty of pluck and dash in me.

I tried thus to stop his further progress, but he was too strong for me, and dragged me, too, along with him. I then succeeded in putting my leg under his hind legs, tripping him up, so to say, and he fell in consequence on his knees. I now, with all my strength and weight, knelt on him, and releasing the loose skin I had hold of, I pushed my thumbs with all my strength behind his ears, trying to strangulate him thus. All this time the beast held fast to the boy.

My men had been seized with the same panic as the bystanders, but now I discovered one lurking round a corner, so I shouted to him to come with a crowbar; he fetched one, and hit the tiger three tremendous blows over the eyes.

It was only now he released the boy. His jaws opened and his tongue protruded about seven inches. I thought the brute was dead or dying, and let go of him, but no sooner had I done so than he jumped up again. In the same moment I seized the crowbar myself, and gave him, with all the strength I had left, a blow over his head. He seemed to be quite cowed, and, turning tail, went back towards the stables, which fortunately were open. I drove him into the yard, and closed the doors at once. Looking round for my tiger, I found he had sneaked into a large empty den that stood open at the bottom of the yard. Two of my men, who had jumped on to an elephant's box, now descended, and pushed down the iron-barred sliding-door of the den; and so my tiger was safe again under lock and key.

The boy was taken to the hospital, but with the exception of a fright and a scratch, was very little hurt. I lost no time in making inquiry about him, and finding where his father was, I offered him £50 as some compensation for the alarm he had sustained. Nevertheless, the father, a tailor, brought an action against me for damages, and I had to pay £300, of which he had £60, and the lawyers the remaining £240. Of two counsel I employed, only one appeared; the other, however, stuck to his fee right enough. At the trial the judge sympathised very much with me, saying that, instead of being made to pay, I ought to have been rewarded for saving the life of the boy, and perhaps that of a lot of other people. He, however, had to administer the law as he found it, and I was responsible for any dangerous consequences brought about in my business. He suggested, however, as there was not much hurt done to the boy, to put down the damages as low as possible. The jury named £50, the sum I had originally offered to the boy's father of my own good will. The costs were four times that amount. I was fortunate, however, to find a purchaser for my tiger a few days after the accident; for Mr. Edmonds, proprietor of Wombwell's Menagerie, having read the report in the papers, came up to town post haste, and paid me £300 for the tiger. He exhibited him as the tiger that swallowed the child, and by all accounts made a small fortune with him.'

Charles Jamrach, 'My Struggle with a Tiger', *Boy's Own Paper*, 1 February 1879.

*This detail, which does not appear in all contemporary newspaper reports of the incident, should be treated with some scepticism –

implying as it does that the child was partly to blame for the attack.

Well before the days of Harrods' resourceful pet department, Jamrach (born Johann Christian Carl Jamrach in Germany in 1815) was London's dealer of choice for anything from a parrot to an elephant. John Simons tells of how Jamrach's first wife, Mary was one day trapped in their parlour by three escaped lions. As the parlour door was glass, Mary 'had the bracing experience first of seeing three lions prowling in the hall way and then of realising that the lions could see her'. The lions then went upstairs to pay a visit to Charles, and finding him barricaded in a bedroom, wandered up and down the stairs until Jamrach managed to lock them into the second bedroom. Ironically, when their keeper, Clarke, returned it was claimed that the animals had been frightened 'by the sight of Jamrach whom they didn't know' (*The Tiger...* 41-2). Perhaps rather against the odds, Jamrach died a natural death at this same house (Wellington Street, Bow) in 1891.

Readers may have noticed that amidst all the arguing about Jamrach's heroism and the boy's suffering, no one appears to have spared a thought for the tiger, who was royally whacked for making a pretty understandable bid for freedom. Indirectly, Jamrach was almost certainly responsible for many other dramatic animal escapes of the day, given how many beasts he sold to private buyers and menageries.

153. A Child Shoots a Panther.

'A few days ago, while W.H. Higgins, living about two and a half miles from Renovo [Pennsylvania] ... was working in his field making hay, he saw an animal in a distant part of the field making off with a hen. He thought it a fox, and called the attention of his son George, a lad of 14, to it. George is fond of hunting, and getting his gun, he started off for the fox, accompanied by his five year old brother and a hound. They had not been gone long when Mr Higgins heard several continuous yells of the most terrible kind. The animal had been treed by the dog, and its half human shrieks rent the air with terrible distinctness, like the shrill agonised voice of a woman in dire distress. The excited father and his field hands at once made for the spot whence came these foreboding sounds, and ere they reached the spot they met George dragging a huge female panther, measuring five feet one inch in length and two feet high.

The boys had followed the dog to a big tree, up which the panther had gone about 65 feet. When the eldest lad saw the animal, crouched and glaring above, he felt that it was either to be a dead panther or a death struggle between it and himself and little brother. He was a good shot generally, but here was to be the severest test his young eye and nerves had ever been put to, and one that might well have tried an older and stouter hunter. He drew the bead and fired, feeling as he did so, he says, as if had been lifted clear off his feet. But there was the hungry brute yet, crouching on the limb, its eyes fairly fit to burst in their malignant glare. Bang went the gun of our brave young hunter, just as the panther sprang. It seemed, said the lad, as though the animal sprang out from the tree about 25 feet, then came straight down, lighting on the dog about sixteen feet from the boys. The young hunter again thought he had missed. Clubbing his gun he advanced upon the brute to strike it, but it rolled over dead before he could so so. Examination proved that his first shot had struck

about four inches back of the heart; the last one in the heart. It was bravely and well done, and but for the steady nerve and true aim of the lad, he and his little brother would doubtless have fallen victims to the animal's ravenous hunger.'
Aberdeen Weekly Journal, 11 October 1879.

154. Extra Housework.
'The La Grange, Texas paper, gives the following incident, which occurred near Douglas, Nacogdoches County: A panther came into a house in which there was no person but a young lady and her little brother. The young lady, being very busy attending to her little household affairs, did not see the panther until he had entirely got into the house; but so soon as she discovered him she seized hold of him and called to her little brother to bring the axe. After waiting some time for this weapon, still holding onto the panther, the young lady then told her brother to bring her a smoothing iron, with which she soon succeeded in putting the intruder to death. The screams of the heroine during the encounter were heard by some of the neighbours, who went immediately to learn the cause; but when they arrived they found her the conqueror, and viewing with much composure the lifeless body of the frightful intruder.'
Age and Argus, 11 January 1845.

In both the above cases the 'panther' was probably a mountain lion (this being one name among others for the animal). The Pennsylvanian panther was unusually large in length for such an animal, but the description (down to an inch) does sound precise.

As both the above stories suggest, children were tough in these days. Funnily enough, it was in May 1845 that a would-be robber was forced out of a Lancashire farm-house occupied solely by children. The oldest girl was only twelve, but despite this the whole bunch made such a noise, together with the brandishing of axe, spade and bill-hook that the villain slunk away empty handed. The little boy who briskly shut the door on him was four years old.

155. A Berwick Bear Dance.

'Something akin to a panic was caused on Saturday night in High Street, Berwick, by the escape from a stable, in which it had been lodged for the night, of a performing bear. After visiting a public house bar, where it caused a stampede, the bear sallied out onto the crowded thoroughfare and was soon tackled by a dog, with the result that the people scattered in all directions amid exciting scenes. The dog being put out of the lists, the bear made after a man who had ventured near, and he sought the protection of the old stocks near the Town Hall, and round the ancient seat of correction he dodged the animal until he very cleverly caught its chain, which he smartly secured to the stocks. The owner of the bear now arrived on the scene, and led off the captive, much to everyone's relief.'
The Evening Telegraph, 10 September 1894.

156. The Lions at the Ampitheatre.

'The other evening, just before the animals were fed, a most extraordinary scene took place – a scene which few of the number present would have missed for more than their price of admission. Mr Carter having gone through his performances, left the den, as usual, accompanied

by one of the leopards. He had hardly been off the stage a minute, when the lion and tiger commenced a terrific fight. The scene was most extraordinary; the whole of the company assembled on the stage prepared to take flight, and the audience were in a moment in the greatest excitement. Mr Carter hearing something unusual, rushed on the stage, and in an instant was in the cage, and threw himself between the combatants, felling the lion on one side, and hurling the tiger to the other. A wild burst of applause rewarded this daring feat, and was loudly continued when the excited animals were seen to cower into the corners of the den in the most abject state of subserviency. The effect of this was remarkable in the extreme. In a cage, hardly 10 feet square, stood a man unarmed and alone, so perfect a master of the wildest and most savage creatures of the forest, that they forgot their animosity to each other, and actually trembled with fear at his presence. The attitude of the "lion-tamer" and the position of the animals immediately after they were parted, formed one of the finest and most interesting groups ever beheld.'
Cleave's Penny Gazette, 26 December 1840.

John Carter was a celebrated American lion-tamer, who had first been introduced to the public in October 1839. Readers will probably have noticed how the writer's approach to this incident typifies the era's notions of rightful human dominance over the animal world. Indeed, the way in which spectators treat Carter's intervention as one more piece of entertainment makes us wonder if perhaps the Victorians, at such times, had more in common with the Romans and their gladiators than they did with us.

157. The Fat Boy at the Zoo.

'Mr Frank Buckland states, in *Land and Water*, that by the kindness of Mr Bartlett he has been enabled to examine a beautiful little polar bear cub which has just arrived at the Zoological Gardens from the arctic regions. "It was presented to the society by Mr Smith, who has lately returned from a voyage to the high latitudes in his private schooner Sampson. He brought home this little bear with him. The sailors have christened the little beast Sampson, in honour of their vessel. He is a jolly little fellow, about a year old, as far as we can judge. He has a private den next door to the original polar bear which everyone knows so well, and which came to the Gardens in September 1846. I am sorry to say that polar bear No. 1 does not welcome his young relative, polar bear No. 2, with the same cordiality as one might expect at this Christmas time, for I saw him this morning run at and snarl at him like an ill-tempered old beast as he is. Sampson is about the size of a large Newfoundland dog, but more short and stumpy. He has a splendid shaggy coat of long yellow hair, and his general appearance reminds one of an animated doormat. When he stands on his hind legs he looks like a fat boy with an Ulster coat on … The old polar bear is about 6ft in length, and stands about 3 ft 2 inches high. It is therefore not safe yet to let out the cub into his den, as the cub would have no chance if the "old man" pitched into him.'
The Times, 20 December 1871.

Glimpsed briefly above amidst our choirs of trilling mice, Francis Trevelyan Buckland (1826-1880) was a sometime surgeon and ardent naturalist, who in 1865 founded his own nature journal, *Land and Water*. Becoming one of Britain's major experts on fish and fishing in later life, Buckland made key contributions to the collection of the South Kensington Science Museum. When at Christ Church, Oxford, in the 1840s, Buckland kept a monkey, an eagle, a marmot and a bear, 'all of which, it seems, were allowed to roam about the college fairly freely' (M.G. Watkins and Giles Hudson, Dictionary of National Biography). Devoted as he was to the monkey Jocko, Buckland found his patience strained on the day of an important exam, when he realised that the beast had torn his precious revision notes to pieces. Mercifully, Buckland's tutor accepted this excuse – presumably on the grounds that it was so much more original than 'the dog ate my homework'.

In our own age of often relatively sterile scientific description, there is something charmingly creative about Buckland's likening the bear to 'a fat boy with an Ulster coat on'. This and other phrases also suggest a certain sharpness of attention, as if the strangeness of such creatures, seen up close in captivity, has not yet worn off.

For all that, polar bears had been seen in Britain, on and off, since the time of Shakespeare, whose most famous stage-direction (from *The Winter's Tale*) was indeed, 'Exit, pursued by a bear'. Grigson points out that two live polar bear cubs were captured by a British arctic expedition of 1609. Placed in the care of theatrical impresario Philip Henslowe (played by Geoffrey Rush in *Shakespeare in Love*) and Shakespeare's star actor Edward Alleyn, the bewildered beasts presently found themselves transformed into showbusiness celebrities. They first appeared in the anonymous play *Mucedorus*, privately performed before James I on Shrove Tuesday 1610, and not unlike Carlo were considered such an asset that new scenes were written specially for them. We next hear of them in another royal command performance, this time a masque by Ben

Jonson staged on New Year's Day 1611. In these peculiarly elitist entertainments, royals were actors as well as spectators. Here James's son, Prince Henry 'in the title role, rode on to the stage in a chariot drawn by the two white bear cubs'. With *The Winter's Tale* first being performed in May 1611, we are then led to wonder: did Shakespeare's company use a real bear? And if so, was it white, rather than brown?

158. Hunting a Tiger in Paris.

'A frightful mishap, accompanied by the most tragic circumstances, spread terror on Sunday morning last through the district of St Jacques. The Zoological Gardens has for a long time been in the possession of two magnificent Bengal tigers, one of which was to be forwarded to London. To avoid accident the animal was placed in a wagon secured with strong iron bars. The greatest precaution was therefore taken to avoid a catastrophe.

At half past three in the morning the railway servants perceived an enormous animal clearing at a bound the wall which separates the Zoological Garden from the railway station. The tiger had in fact escaped, having bent and broken two of the iron bars of his cage. The first object of his fury was the cart-horse of a night-man, who happened to be passing. The tiger bounded on the unfortunate horse, biting him in the flank, and tearing the straps that attached him to the cart. The driver, who at first sought safety on the horse's back, hid himself under the cart, but not before receiving a wound in the leg from the tiger's paw.

Meantime the horse, mad with terror and pain, galloped furiously towards the market of St Jacques, pursued by the tiger. Here another deplorable event occurred. A gardener who was passing the street attracted the fury of the beast. The tiger sprang at him, tearing his breasts, neck and leg in a fearful manner. Having finished his victim the animal dragged the body some distance; he then abandoned it and rushed into St Anne's Court, where his presence caused indescribable terror. M. Vekeman, the Director of the Zoological Gardens, having been informed of the escape, proceeded with his staff in pursuit, and came up to the animal at the corner of St Jacques Street, near the house Verstrepen. A night watchman and three or four other persons took refuge in a small shop opposite this house. The tiger spied them, and stood for a moment as though he intended to rush at them through the window. He pursued his course, however, through the market.

M. Vekeman with his assistants, after the animal got into St Anne's Court, barricaded the entrance and placed a trap in it with the view of taking him alive. They then got into the houses of the court in order to frighten him into this trap. The tiger lay crouched against the door of the *atelier* of M. de Braekeleer, the sculptor, but perceiving one of the men in pursuit on the roof of a house, he leaped on the roof of a lower house, and assumed a most menacing position. Monsieurs Vekeman, Braekeleer, Werbronk and Verhoven were armed with guns. The tiger having perceived them, slowly descended from the roof, evidently bent on making an attack, and when about four metres off he couched to make his spring. The order to fire was given, and three guns were discharged in succession. The first shot appeared to have missed,

the second struck the animal, the third inflicted a mortal wound. He tottered back to the entrance of the court, where M. de Braekeleer finished him with a fourth shot. These gentlemen behaved with great intrepidity, and but for their coolness and the measures they adopted much greater injury would have been done. The gardener who was attacked never spoke, and died in the hospital at six o'clock the same morning.'
The Derby Mercury, 17 June 1868.

159. A Lion Loose in Surrey.
'Another instance of the contagion of fear and its effect on the imagination has been afforded by the panic in some parts of Surrey, caused by the report that a lion had escaped from a menagerie and was wandering at will, and no doubt very hungry, among the woods near Banstead Downs. Very soon there were authentic stories of one or two people being attacked and devoured, and so alarming were the rumours that the Messrs Sanger, the circus proprietors, from one of whose vans the lion was said to have escaped, found it necessary to write to the papers, denying that any such escape had occurred, or that they had any lions at present travelling in this country. Now an explanation has been offered. The old sign of a country inn, a rampant lion, was either blown down or removed, and some funny person remarked, "Look out! There's a lion got loose." The words were winged and flew through West Surrey. Funny people should really be looked after by their friends.'
The Illustrated Household Journal, 1 November 1880.

The impressive degree of panic which this jape had indeed sparked is shown by a report of 29 September, which told of 'mounted soldiers, with huge dogs', patrolling St Leonard's Forest (*Bristol Mercury*).

160. A Bear Takes the Bus.

'On Saturday last the Brentford Bench of Magistrates were engaged for some time in investigating a charge against the two Frenchmen, Le Trim Salim and Joseph Jerrant, of creating an obstruction with a performing bear and dog, and of also assaulting and wilfully endangering the life of a police officer in the execution of his duty.

Whilst the prisoners were under examination the bear was secured to the stout railings in front of the Town Hall, and carefully watched by four policemen. In the course of a few minutes, however, Master Bruin, after giving one or two tugs at his chain, showed signs of making a fight for liberty, and Jerrant was sent down by the magistrates to quiet him. It appeared from the evidence that the prisoners were found performing with the bear in the streets of Hounslow. A constable interfered, telling them the law did not allow them to obstruct the streets in the way they were doing. They pretended not to understand English, but moved on at a sign from the constable. Shortly afterwards they were again found performing, and, instead of moving on this time they assumed a threatening aspect towards the officer. Jerrant threw down the drum which he had been playing, and drew a large jack-knife, which he flourished over the constable's head. The latter, however, procured assistance, and the prisoners were taken to the station, where a singular scene occurred.

When they found that they were to be detained Jerrant seized the heavy pole with which the bear performs, and knocked one of the constables down. He next gave a sign to the bear, and the animal, rising on its hind legs, struck a second constable to the ground. The officers then resorted to their truncheons, as the prisoner Salim was attempting to unmuzzle the bear. When Jerrant found himself effectually subdued, he gave a sign which caused the bear to make its way up the staircase. Upon its making a determined effort to make its way into the rooms, the female occupants were so terrified that they threw open the front windows and screamed for assistance. The policeman seized the pole used in the bear performance and made an attack on him with little or no effect, but eventually succeeded in compelling one of the prisoners to control the brute, and it was ultimately locked up in the patrol's loose box. During the night it tore down nearly all the fittings in the loose box, and broke the scabbard and sword of one of the patrols. It, however, quietly followed the prisoners to the town hall at Brentford.

The Chairman of the Bench, addressing the prisoners, said they had promised the police-magistrates in London that they would leave the country, but they had not only not done so, but they were now found committing the very offence with respect to which they had been cautioned. They exhibited their bear to the danger of horses and alarm of women, and when they were told to desist acted with violence. They must now be taught that such things were not tolerated in this country, for they would go to the House of Correction for one month's hard labour.

A difficulty arose as to what should be done with the bear during the incarceration of its owners, and on the suggestion of Superintendent Fisher it was resolved to make application for its reception into the Zoological Gardens. Sanction having, in the course of the afternoon, been obtained from the authorities of the gardens, the next difficulty was how to convey the bear thither, for it would follow no one but the prisoners. Ultimately it was decided to pack them off in an omnibus, and after a great deal of trouble the trio were on their journey, followed for some distance by a crowd of urchins. Before they arrived at Kew Bridge, however, the bear smashed the window, and made its way out of the omnibus, to the terror of the spectators. The animal seemed to be more frolicsome than anything else, and was soon captured, and led on foot to the gardens.'
North Devon Journal, 8 April 1869; *Daily News*, 6 April.

161. Delmonico and the Tiger.

'A terrible panic occurred at Wombwell's menagerie yesterday ... at Bolton ... It appears that at about three o'clock, Delmonico, the lion-tamer, who puts the tiger cats and lions through a series of performances, entered the den occupied by the tiger cats, and he had scarcely had time to close the door when one of the tigers slipped between his legs and bounded into the middle of the menagerie, which was thronged at the time with spectators. A scene of the wildest excitement followed. The tiger rushed about the tent foaming with rage, but as it was followed by Delmonico, it slunk into a corner, and attempts were then made by the regular attendants to secure it by covering it with a large empty barrel.

In the meanwhile, the mass of people, young and old ... were filled with horror, as well they might be, and some ran to the steps leading to the menagerie. Many were thrown down on the ground, and not a few were trampled upon. The force of the crush was such that at one corner the hoarding between two caravans was thrown down, and from the aperture thus made, women rushed out, screaming and fainting, while others came pouring out by the main entrance ... During the time the terrible excitement prevailed, one young woman was thrown against a cage, whereupon a tigress in it immediately thrust out its paw, and caught her by the back of the neck, tearing off her bonnet, and lacerating her neck. She was taken to the infirmary.

While all this was going on the tiger cat had been secured by means of the barrel, and it was again placed in its den. The space in the centre had scarcely been cleared when a report spread that the animal had escaped a second time. Once more there was a frightful rush among those inside the menagerie. The second report was, however, groundless, and gradually the excitement subsided; and the hoarding broken in the first push was replaced, and the band having struck up a lively air, tranquility was restored. Women rushed about the town in all directions, and the most painful rumours prevailed.'

Birmingham Daily Post, 3 January 1884.

Born Joseph Ledger in Milton, Delaware in 1841, the lion-tamer known across Europe by his stage-name, Ledger Delmonico, was African-American. By 1884 his fame would have been the greater, following the death (in 1871) of the famous black lion-tamer Martini

Maccomo. Delmonico was badly injured in late November 1891, when one of a pair of recently imported lions sprang on him during a rehearsal at the Grand Theatre, Liverpool. Despite this, he seems (unlike a fair number of other lion-tamers of the day) to have died a natural death, in 1901 at his home in Christchurch, Hampshire. This may in part have been because he decided on a change of career not long after the close shave in Liverpool. In August 1896 a Signor Ledger Delmonico is listed in the cast of the drama *Ups and Downs of Life*, then playing in Gravesend. A year later this same name features in reviews of the controversial new play, *Secrets of the Harem*, at Halifax's Grand Theatre. Considered offensive to British morals by some, and equally so to the Turks by others, this saucy oriental romp fell foul of the censors, but enjoyed continued success when subtly repackaged as '*Secrets* ---- (*The banned play Secrets of the Harem*)'. Given the period's rather loose notions of ethnicity, it seems likely that Ledger would indeed have been considered a suitable choice for a Turkish character.

162. Escape of the Tasmanian Devil.

'This wonderful animal, the chief attraction of Wombwell's menagerie, effected its escape in the latter part of last week, and up to Saturday night had not been discovered. The menagerie was being exhibited at Bideford, North Devon. The animals had just been fed, in the presence of the spectators, and the establishment was about to be closed, when loud shouts rang through the place that the "devil" had escaped. The man who fed it omitted to fasten the door of the cage, and while he was getting a shutter the animal took advantage of his absence by leaping among the crowd and escaping into the town.

The excitement was immense. The animal was

chased along the quay side, and it boldly plunged into the water. Boats were immediately launched, and diligent search made for the devil, but it was quite dark, and he could not be found. This is the third escape of the animal during its captivity – the first occurred at St Day in Cornwall, and the second at St Just, in the same county. It is believed that the animal was drowned. It was of great value to the proprietors of the menagerie. Accompanied by some of the inhabitants of the town, they continued the search till Saturday night.'
The Dundee Courier & Argus, 19 August 1868.

'...on Thursday last, the "devil" was discovered in the farmyard, at Penhill, by men in the employ of Mr John A. Vellacott. It was found that he made havoc among the poultry, and was in the act of devouring the carcass of a hen when he was captured. A reward of £5 had been offered for the recovery of the "devil", which will reward the exertions of the men and compensate their empoyer for his loss. The "Tasmanian Devil" is described as a little animal just about the size of a badger, covered with strong black hair similar to a dog, with a white mark on each side of the flank, very short legs, and strong claws similar to a bear; the head and tail resembling that of a bull terrier.'
The North Devon Journal, 3 September 1868.

One wonders if Jamrach would have taken on a Tasmanian Devil as readily as he did that tiger. Recognised as being almost extinct by the 1860s, this remarkable animal entered Wombwell's collection at Edinburgh in February 1866. 'Without the least cause' (wrote the journalist who recorded its arrival) 'it will fly at the bars of the cage and endeavour, by dint of teeth and claws, to wreak its vengeance on the keeper, while it gives vent to its passionate feelings in short hoarse screams of rage' (*Reading Mercury*, 10 February). Like myself, you have probably guessed very quickly that the Tasmanian Devil had very good cause for all this rage. Simply, it did not like being in a cage. Come July 1875 another specimen had escaped from confinement on board the ship Bella Mary, somewhere off the coast of New Zealand. Having bounded over the head of the chief officer, it escaped its pursuers by jumping overboard. Happily, 'it appeared to be an expert swimmer'. Against all the odds, Wombwell's still had the beast in captivity when it visited Cornwall in May 1877. Beset by facial tumours since the late 1990s, the tasmanian devil was officially listed as Endangered in 2008.

163. A Lion Celebrates its Liberty.

'A panic, caused by the escape of a lion, occurred on Wednesday, on the market-place of Lisieux, where a fair is being held. Owing to the negligence of an attendant at the menagerie exhibiting at the fair in omitting to fasten the door of a cage, one of the animals escaped and stalked into the marketplace. The people disappeared, screaming, into the neighbouring houses, and doors and shops were closed at once. The lion sat down on his haunches near a cart and began to roar, no doubt with the novelty of being at large. With the help of ropes and an unsparing use of loaded whips, the tamer of an opposition menagerie, together with a woman tamer, succeeded in leading the lion back to its cage.'
Portsmouth Evening News, 2 January 1885.

164. Devoured by a Polar Bear.
'At Fleurance, Gers, during a fête to celebrate the completion of the Agen Railway Works, a polar bear escaped from a menagerie. It made its way into a pastry-cook's, and devoured all the cakes and ices.'
Illustrated London News, 17 June 1865.

165. The Lion's Afternoon Tea.
'The Welsh newspapers give the following details of the escape of a lion from Wombwell's Menagerie at Llandrindod Wells. A lion having broken loose from his den, hurried down the principal street, and dashed through the window at the Bridge Hotel into a sitting room, occupied by a Mr Osborne, a visitor from Neath. Mr Osborne, horror stricken, seized a chair as the only means of defending himself in what appeared to him an inevitable and terribly unequal struggle for life.

   At this instant the lion's keeper appeared on the scene. The keeper, grasping the situation at a glance, said quietly to Mr Osborne, "My good sir, don't stir an inch, or your doom is sealed!" The lion paced the room in an evidently angry mood, and the terrified human occupant strictly obeyed the injunction of the keeper to remain still; with as little delay as possible the keeper and his assistants made their way to the room with the necessary appliances for recapturing the animal. With some difficulty they succeeded in throwing a sack over the lion's head, after which he was firmly secured with ropes.'
The Sheffield & Rotherham Independent, 4 July 1889.

166. A Fussy Eater.

'Sarah Bernhardt and her pet tiger cub "Minette" had a royal time a few days ago at the Hotel Richelieu, which was not so pleasant for the other parties concerned. After wrestling with the startling artistic and emotional ecstasies of "Fedora" at the Columbia, Mme Bernhardt gathered her feline pet in her long graceful arms, and was driven to the Hotel Richelieu. Here she had ordered for herself and party a sumptuous dinner, which was served according to her lavish and expensive tastes. "Minette", the pet infant tiger, was not to be overlooked; and Madame, calling the chef of the hotel to her side, ordered a special dish of consommé and poached eggs for the snarling little brute which was attached to her wrist with a golden chain, and was gazing with hungry eyes at the tempting viands upon the daintily spread table. While this dish was in preparation the young tiger could hardly be restrained from mounting the table and devouring the unpronounceable dishes upon which Madame and her party were feasting.

When the consommé appeared in a silver tureen, borne by a trembling and awe-stricken waiter, named Frank Zogelman, the hungry young tiger made a spring and fastened his teeth in the arm of the terrified attendant, which caused him to utter a howl of agony, and hastily deposit his assailant's dinner on the richly carpeted floor. This little episode, artistic in its natural gracefulness and emotional in its painful realisation of suffering, diverted the attention of Madame for a moment; but, finding her pet uninjured, she laughingly resumed her repast. The bitten waiter rushed from the room, and in a short time his wound became so painful that he was put to bed and a physician summoned to attend him.

Hugo Zieman, the head waiter, gallantly offered to take charge of Sarah's amiable pet, and as he reached out his hand to take the chain, a warning "Take care!" in Madame's most dramatic tones was heard, and the terrified Hugo stepped back just in time to escape the sharp teeth of the snarling animal. This was enough menagerie for one afternoon, and no one could be induced to offer any further civilities to the angry Minette. When train-time arrived, Sarah gathered up her voluminous wraps, and, fondly caressing her delightful though somewhat carnivorous pet, left the hotel and was driven to the depot without so much as an inquiry after the welfare of the poor fellow who was groaning with pain in another part of the hotel. It is said that Zogelman's injuries are serious, and blood poisoning is feared.'

Leeds Mercury, 29 June 1887.

All in all, a fairly ordinary meal for perhaps the most flamboyant actress who ever lived. Bernhardt, daughter of a Dutch-Jewish courtesan and an unknown father, was a miracle of self-invention and re-invention. Her belief that 'Life begets life. Energy creates energy. It is by spending oneself that one becomes rich' was pretty convincingly borne out by many phases of her career – but perhaps nowhere more powerfully than the way that she continued her stage roles after the amputation of a leg in 1915, age 71. One suspects that Minette did not get on well with Bernhardt's pet lynx.

167. A Lion Goes to Ground.

'The lion which escaped from Wombwell's menagerie during the Biriminingham Onion Fair was a full grown African, and, after being at liberty since noon on Friday was recaptured early on Sunday morning. The police and show managers arranged a quasi capture two hours after the escape, in order to allay public anxiety.* Steps were, however, taken by the police and Wombwell's people to effect an actual recapture. Shortly after midnight on Saturday the fairground was cleared, and Mr Bostock the manager of the menagerie, with a dozen of his men superintended the work of barring the sewer outlet into the Aston brook with the trap cage.

A move was then made to a manhole at the corner of Aston Brook Street, and two young men, employees at the menagerie, volunteered their services, and armed with a policeman's lantern and a loaded six chambered revolver each, and with instructions from Mr Bostock "not to spare the ammunition" they descended the manhole. The sewer was almost dry, and there was plenty of evidence that the lion had been about. Before very long a growl was heard further up the pipe, and the men climbed to the road again. They then went to the manhole at the corner of Bracebridge Street and Elkington Street, but from there it was found they were still behind the runaway. The next move was to the manhole in Miller Street, but no clue could be obtained from there and the company went to a manhole at the back of St Stephen's Church. One of the men known as "Dick" called out that they headed him, and that he had gone off in the direction of Bracebridge Street.

At this point several sewers converge, and the bottom of the manhole there has a large circumference. Mr Bostock resolved to try the experiment of entrapping him there, and after calling upon the men not to start upon their hazardous journey until they received a signal, ran off to the Bracebridge Street opening. Here he obtained a strong rope, noosed it at the end, and let it into the manhole until the slipknot covered the mouth of the Bracebridge Street sewer. The signal was now given to the two men to start; but before this the lion had made an attemtpt to return, and would have done so had not "Dick" as he came up, fired one of the chambers of his revolver at him, and thus sent him howling down the sewer again. With some difficulty the two men – Dick first and his companion behind – squeezed themselves into the 2ft 6 inch pipe, and amidst the shouts of "good luck to you" from the men above ground, disappeared.

Meanwhile, Mr Bostock sat with his legs down the manhole, and with a tight grip on the rope, waiting for the first movement from below. It was some time before this came. The lion disputed his ground, and time after time turned in the sewer and came towards his pursuers. One barrel after another was fired at him until at last the twelve chambers of the two revolvers had been emptied. The men had then followed him nearly 200 yards, and were nearly at the Bracebridge Street outlet, where they were aware they could obtain a fresh supply of ammunition, supposing the trap which they had laid had not been successful. Dick, who as already stated was leading, asked his companion to pull off his boots, and this having been done, and handed to him, he banged them backwards and forwards against the sides of the piping, and shouting and waving their lamps they crawled a little further. One of the men stated that the lion, before emerging from the pipe, turned round and fought at them with one of his paws, but that he appeared to be afraid of the light. Presently a loud and continuous howl told them that he had been caught in the trap laid for him. And they lay quiet awaiting the signal that all was safe.

It was now the turn of the people above ground. As the lion stepped out of the sewer into the bottom of the manhole Mr Bostock gave his rope a sharp tug, the noose tightening around the animal's loins, and by steady pulling he was soon brought within sight. The excitement amongst the small body of captors became intense. It was decided to place a trap cage over the top of the manhole and run the rope through a hole in the top and pull him into it. Had the cage been large enough, this piece of strategy might have worked very well; but it was not, and the lion could not be got into it. The cage had been pulled from over the manhole, and the lion lay upon the road, his body with the rope still firmly round it, being underneath, and his head outside. The animal whose head was wedged closely between the edge of the box and the road, roared and fought desperately, and it required the most determined exertion of as many as ten men to keep the cage upon him.

By this time a crowd of people had assembled, but as soon as the brute was seen struggling on the road, they fled in all directions; some climbing lamp-posts,

and others begging … householders to admit them. The policemen not actually engaged in the fray stood their ground, but many of them were armed with revolvers, and others had drawn their staves. After a delay of about ten minutes – which most of those who stood near said seemed nearly an hour – and as the cage showed signs of giving way, a large den was brought from the menagerie. This was placed over the top of the cage, and the lion and the cage pulled into it and the door secured. The proceedings from start to finish occupied two hours and a half. The two men who had all this time remained in the sewer were called out, and as they stepped into the road everyone present cheered lustily. Mr Bostock was particularly warm in his congratulations, and presented each man with a sovereign. The den containing the recaptured lion was subsequently dragged onto the fair ground and early on Sunday morning the menagerie left town.'
The Derbyshire Times, 5 October 1889.

*This strategy seems to have been partially successful, but come 30 September, the *Birmingham Daily Post* was wondering if two lions had in fact escaped.

Slither

Which came first? the serpent or the Devil? As readers might recall, once upon a time there was a naughty snake, which tempted our first mother, Eve, to go scrumping forbidden fruit in God's own orchard. And, as we know, it was all downhill from there... Do snakes have such a bad reputation because of Eden? Or: was it the bad reputation of snakes which caused that ancient storyteller to drop this one down at Eve's feet, as she was innocently raking and hoeing?

Anyone who really hates snake can be reassured that in fact alligators and crocodiles manage to crowd them out in following pages. This consolation, of course, hardly promises an abundance of fluffiness, and there is no denying that this is one of the least cuddly chapters of my book. A little glimmer of crocodile cuteness, however, does show its teeth in a few moments, down in the Brighton Aquarium. I am told that you should never smile at a crocodile – but perhaps just this once, from the safety of your armchair...

168. 'Voracity of a Boa Constrictor.'

'A singular instance of the voracity and power of appetite of this reptile occurred a few days since in the Zoological Gardens in the Regent's Park. Two fine tiger boa constrictors were brought over by Captain Redman,

from Calcutta, and presented by him to the menagerie on the 4th of September last. They were respectively eleven feet and nine feet in length, and had lived in harmony together in their cage until last week, when the smaller one being sickly would not eat at the usual time of feeding. The larger one had just eaten a rabbit and three guinea pigs, when it appears he made a gorge of his more weakly companion, which was proved by the sudden disappearance of the latter, and the more bulky size of the former, who exceeded three feet in diameter in the greatest proportion of his body. So singular a case of the carnivorous power of this reptile is not previously on record.'
The Leicester Chronicle Saturday, 10 April 1841.

On 23 October 1894 there was a report of this happening again at the zoo, with a 9 foot boa constrictor swallowing its mate of 8 foot – allegedly by accident, when trying to take the pigeon which the mate was itself consuming.

169. Post Office Scales.
'A few days ago publicity was given to the proposal that a shoal of crocodiles ought to be imported by the London municipal authorities for cleansing the Thames and the sewers, these unlovable monsters being insatiable consumers of impurities – which may account for the thickness of their hides. It is presumed that some philanthropic gentleman on the banks of the Nile has seen the suggestion, and is desirous of its practical realisation. At all events, the officials at the Post Office are at this moment much puzzled what to do with four young alligators which have reached London by parcel

post from Egypt. Their temporary home was a wooden box, out of which proceeded mysterious sounds that raised in the minds of the Post Office people visions of infernal machines and dynamite. When the parcel was opened the alligators were discovered, wriggling and frisky, as if impatient to commence eating either Thames mud or a commissioner of sewers. At present the reptiles are detained in the Dead Letter Office until their fate is decided. The City is empty just now, and they therefore cannot be sold for turtle soup; the Thames water is too cold for experiments; they could not be expected to derive any pleasure from recognizing Cleopatra's needle covered with snow. Still, the philanthropic but misguided intentions of the sender should not be completely overlooked.'
Gloucester Citizen, 19 April 1892.

170. Killed by its Own Dinner.
'A story so strange that it seems almost incredible comes from the Zoological Garden [in Cincinnati] ... Yesterday afternoon a little squirrel killed a rattlesnake about to devour it, and the aggressor became the victim. It is customary to place live animals, such as the rabbit, the rodent, or the squirrel in the dens of the reptiles. The snakes, when they are hungry, with fearful deliberation approach their terrified prey, and relentlessly devour it. The squirrel crouched trembling in a corner of the snake's abode, and seemed to understand that it would soon be food for the disgusting creature. Slowly but surely the rattlesnake crawled towards the squirrel, but the bunnie quickly jumped on a perch above the deadly reptile's head. The long flat

head was raised upon the perch, and the forked tongue spat forth its venom. But the squirrel, with a sudden spring, alighted on the back of the snake and bit off one of his rattles. The wounded reptile wheeled quickly round, and struck the little hero a fearful blow, breaking the right hind leg. Brave little fellow, once more he leaps beyond the reach of his maddened foe. Another spring and the squirrel was triumphant. He caught the snake behind the head, and with one firm thrust of his sharp white teeth decapitated the slimy monster and fell exhausted by the wriggling mass. But the battle had been won and the snake was dead.'
Portsmouth Evening News, 17 January 1882, citing *Cincinnati Enquirer*.

171. Be Careful What You Fish For.

'A singular circumstance, which may not occur again for centuries, took place yesterday. A man in the employ of Mr Arthur Willock, of the Custom House, while steering his barge past Galley quay, observed a black motionless object in the water, which, on attempting to draw it out, moved, and his hand was immediately severely lacerated; he, however, succeeded in getting it into the barge, when it proved to be a young alligator. It was purchased for, and removed to, the Zoological Gardens.'
The Times, 13 October 1836.

172. Clammy Embrace.

'During the week the inhabitants of Oxford have been much concerned at the statement that a young lady living in the High Street had been severely bitten and crushed by a boa constrictor, kept in the house by an undergraduate of Brasenose College, who lodged there … It appears that the owner of the boa constrictor is the Hon. Mr Fitzpatrick, of Brasenose College, who lodges at Mrs Seager's, at 116, High Street. Before entering upon the lodgings Mr Fitzpatrick mentioned to Mrs Seager that he had a snake in his possession, which he should wish to keep in his rooms, but that it was only a small thing and harmless, and that it was well secured. Mrs Seager naturally objected to so loathesome a reptile, but nothing further was said on the matter until its arrival at the house as a box of "Books". The box being ventilated … excited some suspicion, and on the owner being questioned … he assured Mrs Seager that it was "all right"; that the serpent was well secured, and that if it was objectionable he would send it away. He did not do so, however, but kept it for a companion in his sitting room, amusing himself occasionally with feeding it, after having whetted its appetite with a fast of some duration.

Yesterday week the boa constrictor was fed with three rabbits during the morning, its usual meal being five, and by some carelessness on the part of the eccentric owner, the lid of the box in which it was kept was left unfastened. Miss Seager entered the room for some purpose, and noticed that the lid of the box was opened. On going to it to shut down the lid, the serpent sprang at her from another part of the room, seized her right arm with its jaws, and quickly coiled itself around her arms and body. Miss Seager screamed for help, and did her utmost to free herself from her perilous position, until her mother and sister came to her aid, in company with Mr Fanning, of Trinity, who also lodges in the house. Miss Seager's sister, with extraordinary courage, seized the jaws of the snake, and forced the reptile to relax its hold, Mrs Seager and Mr Fanning at the same time doing their utmost to free Miss Seager from its folds.

After great exertions they succeeded in releasing her, and throwing the snake to the floor, when it began licking up the blood which had flowed from Miss Seager's hand. Miss Seager was then found to be seriously injured; her hand was dreadfully bitten, her arms were crushed, and her nervous system was fearfully shaken. It seems that after the snake had coiled itself round Miss Seager it began to cover her arms with a coating of saliva, after the manner of boa constrictors, and there can be no doubt what her fate would have been if timely assistance had not been at hand. Meanwhile Mr Fitzpatrick had arrived, and he securely lodged the snake in its box. Mr Briscoe, surgeon, was called, and through his great skill and unremitting attention Miss Seager is going on favourably, although she is still in a lamentable condition. The boa constrictor is some seven feet long, and 4 or 5 inches in thickness, and we are glad to find that its owner, who ought never to have had such a thing in his rooms, has sent it away from Oxford.'
Jackson's Oxford Journal, 2 April 1870.

It is a shame that no one ever managed to take a census of all the interesting pets in residence at Oxford or Cambridge University around this time. Given what we know of Byron (who, finding that Christ Church in Cambridge forbade dogs, kept a tame bear in his rooms instead) and the mini-menagerie of Buckland, the above tale suggests that now and then these ancient seats of learning boasted a quantity and range of creatures rivalling London Zoo. Thinking about it, this is not so surprising. After London, these two cities contained a high concentration of wealthy young men, with time on their hands and a desire to impress or outrage their peers and neighbours.

173. A Valuable Animal.

'A correspondent, writing from Chandbally to an Indian paper, gives some particulars of a man-eating alligator: "The rivers of Orissa are infested with alligators, and every now and then one of these acquires a reputation as a man-eater, and is then hunted down. Early last week information was brought to Mr Chapman, inspector of police at Chandbally, that a man had been carried off. It appears the poor fellow was lying in his boat with his feet hanging over the side, when the alligator made a snap at his feet, pulled him into the water and made off. On receiving this report Mr Chapman manned his boat and set off to the Damrah River, some miles from Chandbally, in pursuit. After several hours search the alligator was seen crossing the river, and was allowed to gain the opposite bank. After crawling up the bank, it proceeded to make a meal off its victim, and whilst so engaged was, by a lucky shot, killed on the spot. The inspector had it cut open and there were found in its stomach 26 pairs of brass anklets and bangles, weighing no less than fourteen seers*. There were also two sets of gold ear-rings, and a number of toe-rings. It is supposed this alligator must have devoured four women, five children, and an unknown number of persons who wore no jewellery. Mr

Chapman deserves credit for his promptness."'
The Cornishman, 12 December 1878.

*A seer, one fortieth of a maund, was around two pounds in weight.

174. 'To be Seen Alive!'

'At the house of Eli Hoyle, Rawson's Arms, Tenter Street, a wonderful sea monster, weighing 3 and half stones (London weight) which was taken Saturday 10th June. The head of this water wonder closely resembles that of a mastiff; and the hair or down is as smooth and fine as that of a mouse. Music, which has "strange charms to sooth the savage breast", affects it in a most peculiar manner, and the concord of several instruments excites it in a most extravagant degree … the animal will be exhibited in Mr Hoyle's famous Club Room, which is capable of containing 150 spectators, without the slightest inconvenience to any who may do him the honour of calling to see this phenomenon of the deep'.
Sheffield Independent, 27 June 1835.

Now this, surely was worth three pence of anyone's money – even if it was, as I rather suspect, a baby seal.

175. A Scaly Mouthful.

'Considerable commotion has just been caused at the Brighton Aquarium by a singular escapade of a young alligator, which had been placed with three or four older specimens in a pond in the new tropical room. A day or two since, the little pachyderm, which is about two years old and about 18 inches in length, was missed from its favourite corner. The attention of the curator, Mr Lawler, was directed to the matter, and noticing

something unusual about the jaws of one of the larger alligators, he had the animal's mouth gently prised open, upon which the missing little one was found to be inside. The "baby" was at once withdrawn tail foremost, and appeared to be none the worse for its adventure, saving a somewhat severe abrasion just above the left hind leg. The two alligators both came from South America, and have shared the pond in peace for about six weeks, and from the generally pacific disposition of the larger reptile (which measures over 5 feet) it is conjectured that the little one had of its own accord unsuspectingly crawled into its open jaws. The authorities, considering the confidence to be rather misplaced, have prevented a repetition of the feat by giving the innocent infant separate accommodation in another part of the building.'
Edinburgh Evening News, 25 January 1877.

176. A Slippery Passenger.
'On Saturday last a boa constrictor, 17 feet in length, forming part of a collection of wild beasts which were being conveyed by the train from Havre to Paris for the purpose of being exhibited at the Hippodrome, escaped from the box in which it was confined and wound its way up to the top of the train, where it promenaded for some time without being discovered. It afterwards announced its presence by suddenly thrusting its head up close to the engine driver, to the great terror, as may be supposed, of that individual. The train was immediately stopped, and M. Hebert, who was placed in charge of these animals, with the assistance of two Africans by whom he was accompanied, with some

difficulty re-captured the animal, which had coiled itself around the machinery of the locomotive, and ultimately secured it in a strongbox.'
Illustrated London News, 29 May 1852.

177. Strange Bedfellow.

'A correspondent at Ajmere sends the *Times of India* particulars of a curious adventure with an alligator. At the sacred city of Pokur, near Ajmere, one of the numerous alligators which abound in the lake there, and which are looked upon with the greatest reverence by the Brahmins, managed to crawl from the water up a flight of high stone steps into the courtyard of a house used by the European officials … as a dak bungalow. It is supposed that the reptile was frightened by some noise. Turning, it missed the steps which would have led it back in safety to the water, and entered the room in which the servants were sleeping. The astonishment of the men at finding themselves lashed by the tail of the monster in the dark may be imagined. Their master, in coming with a light, found the alligator, which was ten feet long, hard up against the wall on one of the servant's beds. The Brahmins are highly incensed at this gentleman for shooting the alligator, even under these circumstances, and have preferred a complaint to the Commisioner of the district. It is doubtless very necessary to respect the feelings, especially the religious feelings, of our fellow men; but it does seem rather hard to object to one's shooting an alligator when he gets into your servant's bed in the middle of the night.'
Edinburgh Evening News, 1 Dec 1876.

A Mixed Menagerie

At Sheffield Fair in May 1869 the Horse Fair and Cheese Fair were disappointing, but Wombwell's Royal Menagerie, with its lions, tigers, leopards, its ocelot, Tibetan sun bear and polar bear, wolves, elephants and birds, was as successful as ever. Just as well for the owners, as even an unsuccessful show still had to feed its animals. A lion or a tiger, for example, required about twelve pounds of solid flesh per day, a leopard five pounds, and the bears and monkeys a great deal of bread, sop and fruits. The flesh-eating animals alone consumed about 225 pounds of meat every day.

 Another way of looking at this is to say that the menageries of this age were relatively big business. One particularly memorable proof of this is given by Simons, when he describes 'two angry and frightened elephants rampaging down the Oxford road from Reading to Henley' in May 1833. Behind them animals were roaring and stamping in their cages, a caravan was on fire, and a pitched battle was raging, with whips, crowbars and tent poles, between the staffs of Wombwell's and Hilton's menageries. Why? Because they had been racing more or less neck and neck to get the best pitch at the Henley Fair (*The Tiger*, 57-8).

 At a different level, a great deal of money also went into private menageries. By the time that Lord Derby's collection, at Knowsley Hall near Liverpool, went under auction in October 1851, this acquisitive peer had accumulated antelopes, gazelles, zebus, yaks, llamas, zebras, alpacas, kanagroos, porcupines, lemurs, an arctic fox, Egyptian and Arabian vultures, eagles, toucans, parrots, macaws, cockatoos, an ostrich, emu amd cassiowary, as well as storks, ibis and pelicans – to say nothing of his tamer or more homely animals.

We can only begin to imagine the varied miles which these creatures had covered by track, road, rail and ocean, from diverse corners of the Empire, to arrive in the improbably green and chilly pastures of Knowsley (which nowadays, curiously enough, is home to a safari park). But we can certainly see the usefulness of an estate so close to England's major port, where the sight and sound of exotic cargos was a more or less routine one for Liverpool dock workers and sailors. 'On Monday' 14 October 1867, for example, 'a strange cargo arrived at Liverpool from Hamburg. It consisted of the largest elephant in Europe, weighing ten tons; two fine dromedaries, a gorilla, a cub lion, and other zoological specimens. The whole lot was valued at £7000. The corporation of Liverpool are likely to become the purchasers for the zoological sections of the new Sefton Park.' (Long before this, incidentally, an elephant travelling by ship could cost £4000 in insurance costs alone.) In a much more unofficial way, exotic pets entered the country through such routes: I recently met someone whose grandfather's small suburban house in Liverpool was enlivened by the presence of a monkey, acquired from a sailor at the docks.

Even these few details give us some idea of the colourful and many-voiced web of creatures traded and displayed by the overlapping worlds of travelling menageries, permanent zoos and private collectors (with Lord Derby himself being sometime President of the Zoological Society). My own private menagerie, still more convenient than Hilton's or Wombwell's, comes direct into your hands, and is impressively varied – even though, in the interests of good housekeeping, its apes, elephants and clawed things are largely displayed elsewhere. The management accepts no responsibility for anyone who gets too close to the exhibits – see the Brighton octopus for details…

178. Riding a Rhinoceros.

The famous actor, 'Mr. Kemble, had been dining with a noble duke of high convivial habits, and on this particular occasion the libations to Bacchus were so frequent and of so long a continuance, the party did not wend homewards until four o'clock in the morning. At a quarter past four, Mr. Kemble (who insisted on walking) found himself alone in the Strand, opposite Exeter 'Change, in the upper apartments of which was exhibited the menagerie of the celebrated Polito. The matins roar of a lion called forth Mr. Kemble's attention; he paused — and, with the fumes of wine floating on his brain, he was seized with a peculiar whim, and uttered to himself, "To be or not to be, that's the question."

"It shall be! — no man ever attempted it. In any book of natural history — nay, in all the voyages and travels I ever perused, no man ever did it. I — I will do it! — the world shall say, alone I did it. I will have a ride on a rhinoceros !" He here took a pinch of snuff, and exclaimed, "What ho! Exeter 'Change ! Nobody stirring ?" He then made a staggering effort to pull the bell. After he had rung the bell several times with tipsy vehemence, one of the keepers of the wild beasts, who slept in their apartment as a sort of groom of the chamber, made his appearance in an ancient beefeater's dress, and a Welsh wig.

Kemble — "Sir, are you Mr. Polito?"
Keeper — "No, sir; master's abed, and asleep."
Kemble — "You must wake him, good fellow."
Keeper — " I daren't, sir, unless it's werry particlar."
Kemble — "Next time say 'very particular.' Hark you, it

is very particular. You have upstairs, if I remember rightly, an animal denominated a rhinoceros?"

Keeper — "We've got a rhinoceros, and a fine feller she is."

Kemble — "Introduce me to him. You object. Go call Mr. Polito, your very noble and approved good master."

On the arrival of Mr. Polito, Kemble addressed him — "Mr. Polito, I presume?" Polito bowed.

Kemble — "You know me, I suppose?"

Polito — "Very well, sir. You are Mr. Kemble, of Drury Lane Theatre."

Kemble — "Right, good Polito! Sir, I am seized with an unaccountable and uncontrollable fancy. You have a rhinoceros?"

Polito— "Yes, sir."

Kemble — "My desire is to have a ride upon his back."

Polito — "Mr. Kemble, you astonish me!"

Kemble (elated) — "I mean to astonish the world. I intend to ride your rhinoceros up Southampton Street to Covent Garden market."

Polito—"It is next to an impossibility."

Kemble — "Were it an impossibility I would do it."

Polito — "Suppose any accident should happen — the beast is valuable. I would not permit him to be led down in the street under the sum of ten guineas."

Kemble — "Here are ten guineas, Mr. Polito — a bargain. Lead forth my charger — speed! speed!"

Polito finding that he could not get rid of the extraordinary application, pocketed the ten guineas, and told the keeper (who was on intimate terms with the rhinoceros) to bring the animal out, with the provision that it was to go no further than Covent Garden. When

306

in the street, ridiculous as it may appear, the grave John Kemble actually mounted on the back of the beast, who hardly knew what to make of it, but led in the strap of its feeder, went quietly enough, until his rider, highly elated by the achievement of his whim, thought it necessary to spur with his heels.

Keeper — "Gently, sir. Let vel alone. This is raytlier a crusty buffer; if you makes him unruly he'll pitch you off, and rip you up."

Kemble — "Rip me up! Ha! ha! ha! What would they do at Drury?"

It was daylight; and, of course, a mob was collected from Covent Garden market. At this moment [fellow actor] Emery, who was also returning from a late party, saw the extraordinary cavalcade. Emery, somewhat startled at the situation of Mr. Kemble, immediately went up to him, and walked by his side to the top of Southampton Street, when Kemble deliberately dismounted, gave a crown to the keeper, patted the rhinoceros, saying, "Farewell, poor beast!" and, holding Emery's arm, uttered, "Mr. Emery, I have doubtless committed a very silly action; but after imbibing a certain quantity of wine, no man's deeds are under control; but, nevertheless, I have done that which no living being can say he ever accomplished ... Mr. Emery, will you have the goodness to see me home?"'
Northern Star and Leeds General Advertiser, 11 April 1840.

Notwithstanding a bit of embroidery and creative licence in the above version, it seems clear that this did actually happen – albeit a good while before 1840. Aside from the fact that John Philip Kemble died in 1823, we also know that Stephen Polito ran the Exeter Change menagerie from 1810 until his sudden death in April 1814. Grigson notes that Polito had acquired his Indian rhinoceros in July 1810. The animal was on tour and therefore out of London at times; though Grigson's guess that the famous ride took place after it returned in December 1811 cannot be correct, as daylight would hardly break before 5am in winter. By 1810 Kemble was an immensely famous Shakespearean actor, drawing crowds at Covent Garden – imagine Laurence Olivier or John Gielgud cantering through Bloomsbury in such a fashion by way of a twentieth century comparison… As we will see in a moment, this was arguably not the stupidest thing an actor ever did with a wild animal.

179. A Tight Race.
'Extraordinary as it may appear, there has been a genuine kangaroo hunt this week in the vicinity of Dorking. One of these animals some four months ago escaped from the pen in which it had been confined at Wotton, the seat of Mr W.J. Evelyn, MP, and has been running wild in the neighbouring woods ever since, bidding defiance to several attempts to effect its capture. On Monday last, however, by Mr Evelyn's direction, a regular hunting party was formed to accomplish this object.

The clever pack of beagles kept at Wotton, with huntsman, whipper-in, and a train of followers, started at noon for Abinger Common, where the kangaroo had been seen on the previous day. Not finding him "at home" there, however, the party proceeded to the Duke of Norfolk's copses in the immediate neighbourhood. Almost immediately the extraordinary animal broke cover, evidently determined to show sport. The beagles were speedily on the scent, and off they dashed to Mr Evelyn's wood, then making a circle of it by returning to the copses. They then made for Abinger Rectory, where a check of a few minutes threatened to spoil sport, but "Found!", "Tally ho!" was soon the cry, and off they went again, the kangaroo once more trying the Duke's copses. Forced to abandon this his favourite spot, however, the chase got warm; and dogs and men in close pursuit, he reached the foot of Leith hill.

Here the animal's peculiar mode of progression was exhibited in a style which astonished the field – a singular succession of leaps carrying it over the ground at a rate perfectly startling. Those who were well mounted alone were enabled to go the pace, and they speedily found themselves at the top of Leith hill, where the kangaroo took to the road, and for about a mile and a half they all dashed along, "the field" rapidly augmenting in numbers as they proceeded in their novel chase. At last, hard pressed, the animal took refuge in a pond on High Ash Farm, Abinger, where a groom succeeded in capturing him, though not without receiving a fraternal embrace, from which his shoulder suffered for some days.'
The Times, 5 October 1850.

An adult kangaroo can maintain a speed of 43 miles per hour for short distances. The nature of the Surrey hunt can be gauged when we realise that the world record for a racehorse is 43.97 mph (Winning Brew, Penn National Race Course, Grantville, Pennsylvania, United States, 14 May 2008). Why no one has ever thought of mixed kangaroo and horse races remains a mystery.

180. 'The Worst Excuse I Have Ever Heard...'

'The following curious occurrence is said to have taken place at Brighton. The performance of "Man and Wife" at the Theatre Royal was delayed some little time in consequence of it having been discovered that Mr Charles Collette, who was playing the part of Sir Patrick Lundie, was not in the theatre. Before, however, an apology was made, Mr Collette arrived, wet to the skin and in a state of great exhaustion. He dressed hurriedly, and appeared on the stage exhibiting no traces of the ordeal he had gone through.

It appears that Mr Collette had learned the art of snake charming in India, and was explaining the process to Mr George Reeves Smith, the courteous general manager of the Brighton Aquarium. Notwithstanding the entreaties of Mr Smith, Mr Collette insisted on exercising his science upon the octopus, and succeeded in luring the monster from its hiding place, and caused it to follow him round the tank. On [Collette's] bending down to the surface of the water, however, the creature seemed to shake off all control, and, turning his snaky feelers round Mr Collette's neck, drew him by main force into the tank. A desperate struggle ensued beneath the water, whence Sir Patrick Lundie was with difficulty extricated by Mr Smith and several bystanders. Mr Collette has since confined his powers of charming to the patrons of the theatre, and with greater success. We believe that Mr Smith, of the Brighton Aquarium, will vouch for the truth of this.'
Edinburgh Evening News, 2 July 1873.

The Brighton octopus was not the only one on record to take offence at human foolery. Masson and McCarthy recount the twentieth-century case of Charles, an octopus on whom experiments were performed. If Charles could pull a lever which turned on a light, he was rewarded with a small piece of fish. After some initial success the creature clearly tired of this. Having yanked the lever so hard that he broke it, Charles dragged the light itself into the tank, and then 'took to floating at the top of the tank, with his eyes above the surface, accurately squirting water at the experimenters' (*When Elephants Weep*, 145-6).

181. A Sturdy Baby.

'The infant hippopotamus held his first levée yesterday, and holds his first public reception today. The Fellows of the Royal Geographical Society and their friends are allowed the privilege of visiting the Gardens in the Regent's Park on Sundays; and the general public is admitted on the first working day of the week - quite as often a holiday with the industrial orders - at the low charge of sixpence a head. To judge from the extraordinary influx, it seems probable that there will be an immense attendance today; and it can only be hoped that the delicate nerves of mother and child will not be disturbed by the rush of kind inquirers. Guy, as the little stranger is called – he weighs only 160 pounds – from the interesting accident of his coming into the world on the 5th November, is barely three weeks old; but he has all the appearance of being a full-grown, well developed specimen of a miniature variety ... There is a marvellous intelligence about this sturdy infant. He looks about him with eyes of mature judgement, evidently preferring Mr Bartlett and the attendants, to all persons of untried, and therefore doubtful, character.

While he has unpleasant suspicions of Mr Frank Buckland, he regards Mr Edwin Ward, the taxidermist, with downright distrust.

… Almost as soon as Guy was born he began to take his proper nourishment. When about four hours old, it being then a little earlier than midday on the 5th November, he accompanied his mother into the bath, and remained in the water for nearly two hours, keeping below the surface for fifteen minutes or so at a time. As he had only sucked for six or seven minutes after his birth, and before his immersion, it has been conjectured by Mr Bartlett that he repeated this operation while under water … When fatigued with swimming and diving the young animal got on its mother's back, and lay there lengthwise, his head in the same direction as hers, with a quaintness resembling that of some grotesque Eastern carving.'
Daily Telegraph, Monday 25 Nov 1872.

182. "Four and Twenty Fiddlers" in a Whale's Belly.
'An entertainment has been given by Mr Kessels, the naturalist, of Gand, for the purpose of exhibiting an enormous whale, which M. Cuvier and others think must have reached the age of nine or ten centuries. The orchestra was arranged in the interior of the stupendous animal, and there were 24 performers.'
Salisbury and Winchester Journal, 16 June 1828.

Later research has revealed the lifespan of the blue whale to be a more modest 80-110 years.

183. The Devil in Your Doorway.

'At the Cork Quarter Sessions, on Monday last, an action was brought by the plaintiff, Jeremiah Desmond, a labourer, against the defendant, Mr Thomas Batty, circus proprietor, to recover £15 damages alleged to be sustained ... through a camel belonging to Mr Batty entering his house and crushing him ... "The plaintiff claims £15 damages for loss, injury and damage sustained ... through the carelessness, negligence and mismanagement of the defendant, he having confined in his circus ... a certain animal called a camel ... which animal he did in the month of December, 1871, negligently and carelessly permit and suffer to escape and break loose from said circus, and wander through the streets, and up to the Lower Glasheen Road, where said camel did force its way into the plaintiff's house, and there injure and knock down and bruise said plaintiff, by which injuries he has been damaged, put to expense, and loss of time."

The plaintiff was examined, and deposed that on the Friday before Christmas he was sitting at the door of his own house minding some pig's food; about half past six o'clock in the evening "a queer thing" came up to the door; he did not know what it was; he thought it was the devil (laughter) – it had a long neck, big legs, and a hump "ever so big" on its back; he screamed but could not stir, he was so frightened; it put its long neck and two forepaws in and crushed him against the side of the door with its shoulder; it got in a couple of feet inside the threshold, and left the print of its paws there.

Mr Hayes: And why didn't it come in further?

God Almighty sir, the hump (loud laughter). The hump was so big, he could not get in the door. I got such a fright that I was not able to eat as much in three days after as I would in one day before.

Mr Hayes: How did it get out?

He backed out again, sir, the way he came. I could do nothing to him.

Cross-examined by Mr O'Connell: What did you think you had when you saw it?

The devil.

I believe you had been talking about him.

Maybe I wor.

But were you?

I wor (laughter).

... But what sort of a thing was it?

My God, sir, his neck was as far as from this over to that (pointing to the jurybox, which was about fifteen feet distant). (Roars of laughter).

Had he anything on his neck?

Oh, faith, he had a hump up on his back ever so big, and he had long legs, and a mouth.

Do you see anything in court that you could compare him to?

Faith then, I don't, I am sure. When he came in the door, I would have given all the world to get him out of my sight.

Did you get up off the chair?

No, I did not. A better man than me could not do it.

Did you attempt to shove him out?

I did not try to shove him out. I did nothing at all to him, for I was afraid of my life of him. I was not able to work for four days, for I got a pain in my heart.

Mrs Desmond, the plaintiff's wife ... added: "All at once I heard him giving a bitter screech out of him. I looked down and I saw the animal "blow" with his neck stretched in as far as he could. 'Pray to the Almighty God', says I, 'for it's nothing good. Pray to the Lord to resave our sowls', and then I fell in a faint." (loud laughter).

Did you ever see the like before?

Oh, wisha, I didn't, sir. The boys about the place took the thing away afterwards.

Cross-examined by Mr O'Connell: What is that you were talking about when the camel came to the door?

My husband was blaming me for being out too long, and he was talking about ghosts and the devil. When I looked out and saw the animal, said I, "It is the devil that is there now, surely." (Loud laughter).

Mr Hayes: That is the defence at the other side, sir – that it was the devil who was there.

Mr Gregg: Did your husband say to you, "the devil take you"?

He did, sir.

Mr O'Connell: Is he in the habit of talking about him?

Well, he is sir; he is too often in his mouth, as I told him before this. (Laughter).

Don't you think it was a just judgement on him, that the devil should make his appearance to see after him under those circumstances?

Wisha, I suppose so, sir; it was after calling on him too often; and it was serving him right.

has he been talking about the devil since?

Indeed, no sir. (Loud laughter).

Mr Julian: Mr Batty has a claim for the reformation of

her husband (laughter).

His Worship considered that the plaintiff was injured on the occasion, and gave a decree for £3.'

North Wales Chronicle, 3 February 1872.

It is difficult to be sure just how much Desmond was playing up in hope of maximum damages (£15 being, of course, a hell of a lot of money at the time). But as we will see presently, there is evidence to show that the alleged trauma of this encounter was not unique. By this I mean psychological shock, rather than physical injury. Simons has convincingly argued that Victorians across Britain had a surprisingly good chance of seeing an exotic animal at least once, despite the fact that many country-dwellers in particular stayed very close to home most or all of their lives. This was in part due to all the travelling menageries which brought the zoo to you; and in part due to the animals which escaped from various places across the period.

Desmond's mingled terror and bewilderment prompted me to consider something I had never thought of before. Whilst Simons is broadly right about the familiarity of exotic animals, there was always a first time for such an encounter – and, if that was unscheduled, rather than booked in via a trip to menagerie or circus, then the result could be a kind of basic existential shock. Just *what* were you looking at? We might roughly compare this kind of experience with a modern encounter between humans and extra-terrestrials. But… by now, after so many films, and so much iconic alien merchandising, even that would arguably lack the strangeness of Desmond's experience – a meeting with something he had never seen, and so terrifying that Hell seemed its most likely place of origin.

184. London's New Penguin.
'The penguin recently added to the collection in these gardens is, we believe, the first time that a living specimen of this strange bird has found its way to England. The present visitor, which will doubtless prove a "welcome guest" to many curious observers, has been presented to the [Zoological] Society by Captain Fenwick, and is a native of the Falkland Islands. Waddling along in the manner shown in our engraving, its great flappers dangling by its side, it presents a most comical appearance, and looks very much like a lump of a boy with an overcoat too big for him. It carries its head, for the most part, sunken between its shoulders; and only occasionally, when alarmed or at feeding-time, thrusts its neck out and displays its natural length. The colouring of the plumage is bright and harmonious. The upper part of the head is black, round which runs a broad band of orange, narrowing as it approaches the middle of the throat. Its back is of a bluish grey, the upper part of the chest yellow, verging rapidly into white as the feathers descend, with black feet. It feeds principally on fish. This bird, which is naturally gregarious, seems to feel its solitary condition, and frets when left to itself. The keeper remains with it the greater part of the day, and seems to have excited in his charge a strong attachment, for it waddles after him like a child.'
Illustrated Times, 8 April 1865.

I am sure most right-thinking readers will agree that a penguin deserves some space simply for being a penguin, rather than doing anything extraordinary. One other reason for including this fragment, however, is the way it supports the hunch presented along with Desmond's story. The penguin at this stage remains strange enough to need that quite careful and wondering description – as though readers still need to be told, and the reporter himself, faintly captivated, is still getting to grips with the curious spectacle.

185. Rescuing a Rhino.
'Mr Frank Buckland tells the following: "I went up early on Wednesday morning to the Zoological Gardens, to study the footsteps of wild animals in the snow. I was unfortunately just too late to witness a curious and most unexpected accident to the rhinoceros. The animal had been turned out that morning as usual in the paddock behind the elephant house, while the dens were being cleaned. The snow had fallen thickly during the night, so that the pond was not to be distinguished from the ground. The rhinoceros, not seeing the pond, put her fore feet on the ice, which immediately gave way, and in she went, head over heels, with a crash. The keepers ran for Mr Bartlett, the resident superintendent. When he came … he found the poor rhinoceros in great danger of drowning, as she was floundering about under great sheets of ice, under which she had probably been kept down till her great strength enabled her to break up the whole mass.

Here, then, was a most awkward accident … putting Mr Bartlett's readiness of action to the test. My friend, however, with his usual courage, quickness, and readiness of resource, was quite equal to the occasion. He immediately let the water off the pond by knocking away a large plug which he has thoughtfully fixed, instead of a tap … In the meantime the poor rhinoceros was in great danger of drowning, as the pond is nine feet deep; so, while the water was running off, Mr Bartlett, losing no time, sent for all the available keepers and a long and strong rope. Barrow-loads of gravel were at the same time strewed on the sloping sides of the pond, to give the exhausted animal a foothold. The rope was then tossed round the haunches of the rhinoceros, like the kicking strap of a horse in harness, and twenty six men, one half at one end of the rope and one at the other, pulled hard on the rhinoceros, so that in her struggles to get up the bank she would not only be supported but pulled forcibly forward. After much hauling on the part of the men, and much plunging on the slippery bank of the pond, the rhinoceros was at last landed on *terra firma.*

The salvers of this valuable living property had then to look out for themselves. Mr Bartlett had anticipated this, for he had left the sliding gate of the enclosure open just wide enough to let one man out at a time, but not a rhinoceros. An absurd scene then took place: everybody rushed to the gate, but the first of the fugitives from the rhinoceros, naturally stout, and possibly stouter at Christmas time than usual, jammed fast in the open gate, so that the other twenty five men were in the paddock with the rhinoceros. The poor frightened and half-frozen beast luckily behaved very well; she did not rush after the men but stood still, pricked her ears, and snorted, giving the keepers time to get out as fast as they could and how they would, through the ingenious 'man-hole' or guard in the railing, made in case of emergencies. Neither the rhinoceros nor the men received the slightest injury. Shortly after the accident I saw the rhinoceros munching her breakfast as if nothing had happened. The rhinoceros was the big female; she is about 10ft 6 inches long and about five foot high at the shoulder, and she weighs at a guess between three and four tons. The ice I found was four inches thick."'

Birmingham Daily Post, 3 January 1871.

186. Playmates.

'In a quarter of the town of Hingham [USA], known as Rockynook, there is a pond, where a little girl, not six years old, who resides near the bank, has tamed the fishes to a most remarkable degree. She began by throwing crumbs in the water. Gradually the fishes learned to distinguish her footsteps, and darted to the edge whenever she approached; and now they will actually feed out of her hand and allow her to touch their scaly sides. A venerable turtle is among her regular pensioners. The control of Van Amburgh over his wild beasts is not more surprising than that which this little girl has attained over her finny playmates. Visitors have been attracted from a distance of several miles to the spectacle she exhibits. The fishes will have nothing to do with any one but their friend. They will trust no one else, let them come with provender ever so tempting. Even fishes are not so cold-blooded but they will recognise the law of kindness, and yield to its all-embracing power.'

The Bradford & Wakefield Observer, 18 November 1847.

New York born Isaac Van Amburgh (1811-65) was the most famous lion-tamer of his day, known among other feats for putting his head into a lion's mouth.

187. The Kangaroo's Day Out.
'An amusing adventure ... occurred at Burton-on-Trent the other day, when either by accident or design a kangaroo was allowed to roam from Ginnett's Menagerie, which is on a visit to the town. The animal, which is said to be an exceptionally docile one, was chased by members of the staff down some of the main streets, and eventually onto the Shobnall Road. Here the interesting specimen of mammalia caught a glimpse of open country, and evidently distinguishing some resemblance between the undulating landscape in the vicinity of Sianin Park and its Antipodean home, it bounded lightly over the railway crossings and made for the picturesque suburb at a double. As the prodigal passed through Bass and Co's Maltings the men turned out in great numbers and formed a cordon, but the kangaroo gave a tremendous spring and got clear in the direction of the canal ... It was eventually captured in a garden by the waterside. Wild rumours gained currency throughout the town, which lost nothing by frequent recital, until many people were of opinion that the whole menagerie had broken loose and worried half the juvenile population of the borough.'
Evening Telegraph and Star and Sheffield Daily Times, 14 March 1893.

188. A Faithful Pet.
'The wombat is a little animal belonging to the family of marsupials found in Tasmania and adjacent places. It

resembles in appearance a small bear with short legs, broad flat back, and very short tail. It eats only grass and other vegetable matters. It is a harmless, helpless little animal, shy and gentle in its habits, though it can bite if very much provoked ...

On one occasion an English settler in Tasmania found one of these harmless little creatures and took it home to his children, telling them that here was a little bear which they might keep as a plaything. The delighted little ones made a bed for the wombat in an old box, giving it at the same time a piece of blanket as bedclothes.

It soon showed great docility and affection, played with the children and followed them about as a dog would do, and when put into its box at night, would get under the blanket and settle itself in a very comfortable manner. Indeed, it loved heat so much that it would make its way into any other bed from which a scrap of blanket hung down to serve as a climbing ladder.

However, as the little creature became troublesome in some respects, the farmer determined, much to the grief of his children, to part with their clumsy plaything. He carried it away into the forest, and left it there, returning home with the story of his success; but, just at bedtime, a well-known scratching sound was heard at the door, and the delighted children, who rushed to open it, carried in the weary creature who had found his way without help to his adopted home. A second time, however, the farmer conveyed it away, and to a greater distance, but still it came back; but the third time, in order to make sure that the unwelcome little animal would not return, the farmer conveyed it across the river in his boat and left it on the opposite bank. The river was broad and deep, and the wombat has not feet adapted to swimming; therefore the farmer felt sure he had got rid of the troublesome and persistent pet.

But, no! by the time the boat had reached the home shore the little creature had found a huge fallen tree which lay half across the stream, and had crawled to the extreme end of it, where it sat, wistfully gazing at its departing friend. But the farmer was kinder-hearted than he knew himself to be; he could not bear the wistful gaze with which the discarded pet was watching him; he therefore paddled back again, took his fat little passenger on board, and carried it home, where it was received with open arms by the children, who told it that it would never, never be sent away again!'
Chatterbox, 1896.

It is, I admit, just possible that this one was a pure invention. But I for one do not want to be the person who casts the lovely wombat out of this book, just after it has had so many lucky returns...

189. Curious Creatures.

'One of the kangaroos which have been exhibiting with the large male elephant, some time at the Grand Menagerie over Exeter Exchange, brought forth a young one on the 10th of September last, which it kept concealed in a cavity or pouch that nature has provided it with, in the centre of its breast, far more curious than anything ever yet observed by human eye, until Tuesday 14th when it came out for the first time, to feed; and ever since it comes out and feeds, and returns back into the

bag, and it is seen with its head and shoulders out, eating hay and other food. The delicacy of this young animal is beyond expression. They are all three exhibited at the above place. This is absolutely one of the most extraordinary subjects that nature has presented us with, and is truly deserving the attention of the curious.'
The Times, 24 October 1800.

See what I mean about first encounters…

190. An Animal Auction.
'The sale of Manders's Royal Menagerie … took place at the Agricultural Hall, Islington, yesterday, August 4th. Caravans containing the cages of the animals were arranged on four sides of a square; Mr Brinsley, the auctioneer, taking up his position in front of the principal van … a large number of people were present … I now give some of the prices realised:

> Orange coloured cockatoo, a good talker, £7;
> Wombat £1 10s;
> Mongoose, £1 2s.

The "variegated mandrill, or red and blue faced gorilla monkey, from Abyssinia, the only specimen in England". This blue nosed mandrill was the first lot that caused any excitement. For a long time there was no bidding at all. The first offer was £100; he was ultimately knocked down for £105. My friend Bob (Mr Jamrach's head keeper) informed me that this was £25 more than Jerry, for that is this huge monkey's name, realised four or five years ago. Jerry is supposed to be fourteen to fifteen years old. His neighbour, a black Canadian bear, only fetched £1 6s. A big Russian bear – the size of a small cab horse – only fetched £1, worth much more than that to a barber to fatten up for bear's grease. His skin is worth 10s at least. The market price of a good bear is £5. This bear was old and not a good show animal; he was probably bought for his skeleton. A very nice zebra fetched £30 ... the gnu, or "horned horse" fetched 50 guineas only; the market price of a good gnu is £100 at least.

The five camels were then paraded and marched past the auctioneer in single file. The large male came first, a splendid looking animal. The first bid was two shillings, and it was a long time before he got over four-and-sixpence. He was very nearly knocked down for fifteen shillings. After a great deal of chaff he realised £7 10s only. Bob let me into the secret of this. "If them as has bought him don't know how to manage him he'll eat up the lot on em, clothes and all." This shows what bad temper will do in depreciating an otherwise splendid animal. Camels have, as your readers are aware, very long sharp teeth, very like dogs' teeth ... A camel's bite is a very serious thing. I hear that this animal has already bitten one man ... A female "llama that goes in harness" was purchased for £16 10s. Lot 37, the spotted hyena, which had bitten off the bear's nose, fetched £5 only.

The excitement culminated when the sale of the lions commenced. A lioness five years old fetched £30. Two lion cubs eighteen months old, born in the Agricultural Hall, fetched £150; the lioness, in cub, £115. The auctioneer prophesied that the purchaser would ultimately obtain more than one lion for his money. Bob, however, shook his head at the auctioneer. "They'll never get any cubs from her; she's the worst mother out. She'll eat her lot of cubs before they can be took from her. She eat the last lot of cubs when I was travelling along with her in the provinces." The leopardess fetched £5 only; if she had a tail she would have fetched more. Some other animal had bitten her tail off at some time or other, and converted her into a lynx. Two very handsome South American jaguars fetched respectively £30 and £32 … Two small monkeys, with a tame cat thown in, only fetched £3; the cat lives with the monkeys. The two "Tasmanian devils, male and female" only fetched £3 the pair … The Tasmanian devil is a bear-like, savage animal; he lives in a burrow, and is a great poultry-eater …

At one time there was a little commotion when lot 48, the young black mule "Topsy" began to lash out with her heels amongst a crowd that had pressed too near her. The lioness happened to roar just at the same time, as if in sorrow that the menagerie had broken up, and she and her lion relations would have to go to fresh masters … The principal buyers were Mr Charles Jamrach, the well-known London dealer, and agents or proprietors from Wombwell's and Edmonds's menagerie … the Bristol gardens, Hamburg, etc. The prices ought to have been much higher, but animals are not fetching good prices at this time. Winter is not far off. Shows cannot travel about without difficulty in the winter, and if they do travel the animals are very apt to die in cold weather.'
Daily News, 5 August 1875.

One poignant detail concerning the under-valued Russian bear is omitted from Buckland's account. Thanks to Simons, we know that at some point Bob was also keeper to this animal – either because it began its life in that great static menagerie belonging to Jamrach, or because Bob had occasional employment on the road with Manders. At any rate, Simons adds that 'Bob almost wept when [Johnny] was knocked down for only a pound', asking Frank if he would buy him and make a present of him'. Buckland would not, owing to the fact that 'the bear's teeth were gone and he had a moth-eaten coat'. Bob, we further learn, 'used to dance with Johnny and told Frank that "he has nursed me in my lap more often than my mother"' (*The Tiger*, 62).

Elephants

If you asked people to name their favourite wild animal, the elephant would probably be first choice for many. A strange combination of sheer bulk and gentleness, along with their intelligence and their fondness for humans, might go some way to explaining their popularity. Even in an age when they were all too likely to find themselves involved in human wars, elephants were recognised as remarkable by the Roman encyclopaedist Pliny the Elder (23-79AD). Despite being struck down fairly young by the eruption of Vesuvius, Pliny found the time to say something about almost everything – and in the many cases when it wasn't true, it was usually entertaining. Witness, for example, the origin of the phrase 'lick you into shape'. Funnily enough, whilst this now usually connotes some degree of roughness (as in army training and the like) it actually derives from ancient ideas about the maternal love of bears. Baby bears, Pliny tells us, are born as round furry lumps, and then licked into the shape of actual bears by their mothers. This and many other charmingly wayward ideas held sway well into Shakespeare's time, when Pliny was translated into English in 1601. (Greatly excited when I first opened an original copy of this in the British Library by the inscription 'William Shakspere his booke', I later learned this to be one of various forgeries.)

The 1601 version informs us, among other wonders of the elephant world, that 'this is known for certain, that upon a time there was an elephant among the rest, not so good of capacity, to take out his lessons, and learn that which was taught him: and being beaten and beaten again for that blockish and dull head of his, was found studying and conning those feats in the night, which he had been learning in the day time'. Another more educated specimen was known to the Roman consul Mutianus, who reported that this elephant 'had learned to make the Greek characters, and was wont to write in that language thus much: "Thus have I written, and made an offering of the Celtic spoils".'

As for their famed love and devotion... 'reported it is of one elephant, that he cast a fancy and was enamoured upon a wench in Egypt that sold nosegays and garlands of flowers ... Another there was, so kind and full of love, that he fancied a youth in the army ... that scarce had never an hair upon his face, and so entirely he loved him, that what day soever he saw him not, he would forbear his meat, and eat nothing. King Juba likewise reporteth also of an elephant that made court to another woman, who made and sold sweet ointments and perfumes. All these testified their love and kindness, by these tokens: joy they would at the sight of them, and look pleasantly upon them: make toward them they would (after their rude and homely manner) by all means of flattery: and especially in this, that they would save whatsoever people cast to them for to eat, and lay the same full kindly in their laps and bosoms. But no marvel it is that they should love who are so good of memory.'

Mark Rowlands (author of *The Philosopher and the Wolf*) gives memorable examples of how devoted elephants are to each other, including the way that they will care for elderly or disabled members of their herd, and an instance when an elephant named Eleanor seemed to die of grief, following the death of her mother. Masson and McCarthy explore the possibility that elephants have a concept of death – indicated partly by their very definite interest in elephant bones, and in one case by their casting vegetation and branches over a dead herd member, before surrounding the corpse in a curious outward-facing circle.

Their interest in human activities, meanwhile, is memorably captured by the example of Norma, a young elephant whose travelling circus was once pitched near a children's playground. 'When Norma saw children swinging she was greatly intrigued. Before long she went over, waved the children away with her trunk, backed up to a swing and attempted to sit on it … Despite trying periodically for an hour, she was never able to swing' (*When Elephants Weep*, 123-4, 149). Some consolation, perhaps, to anyone who's ever been forced off the swings by the bigger kids…

We have already heard about their musical abilities and tastes, and I hope to say more in my second volume about the various elephant orchestras of the late Victorian period. Londoners in particular had had some chance to see elephants in the flesh since the medieval period, when one was housed in the Tower, c.1255, by Henry III. In 1622 another was brought over from Spain for James I, along with two Spanish keepers, who insisted that the beast be given a gallon of wine to drink each day. Grigson adds that 'at least eleven live Indian elephants were brought to Britain during the reigns of Queen Anne, and Georges I and II' (1707-1760), and in 1706 one of these luckless animals perished in bad weather whilst being marched north from Edinburgh up the Scottish coast (*Menagerie*, 2, 22-3, 58). What would it have been like for some local crofter to chance on this extraordinary sight, after a life spent with sheep, horses and cattle? We will get some idea in a few moments, when we peer in at a more southerly encounter. We begin, however, with someone who seemed less than terrified by this spectacle, and who paid dearly for his insouciance.

191. Pulling an Elephant's Tail.

'A little fat journeyman plumber, whose name did not appear, was brought up to Bow Street, charged ... with having committed an assault upon Mr Cross, the proprietor of the Menagerie, at Exeter Exchange. Mr Cross did not appear himself, but it was stated by one of his keepers that, having let one of the elephants ... out on hire to a showman, and the time having expired, Mr Cross and several of his assistants went on Thursday night to fetch the animal home to his regular quarters. The elephant was making his way very peaceably along the Strand, under the guidance of his keepers, when the defendant came behind him, seized hold of his tail, and began twisting it about, laughing heartily, at the same time, at his own exploit. Mr Cross remonstrated with him upon his folly, and told him he was not, perhaps, aware of the mischief which he might occasion by enraging the animal. He, however, continued his "lark" as he called it, and Mr Cross attempted to remove him, upon which, being pot-valiant, the little melter of lead put his fist in the face of the elephant's master, and taking another twist at the animal's tail, he ran away laughing.

The elephant took umbrage at this last attack, and turning round, he pursued the fugitive plumber with all his speed, in spite of the efforts of his keepers to restrain him. Away ran the plumber, as fast as his short legs and his fat would permit, and close behind him strode the huge native of the East, roaring and throwing about his trunk in a manner than was quite terrible. The race, or rather the chase, lasted from near

Newcastle Street to St Clement's church, where the plumber's legs or his wind failed him so much, that the elephant got him within the reach of his trunk, and gave him a "wipe" (to use the phrase of his keeper) across the back, which assisted him to an elevation of several feet above his mother earth, and dispatched him in an horizontal direction a distance of some yards, [until] he came in contact with the railings of the churchyard, and found his natural level.

"I expected", said the keeper, "to find half the bones in his skin broken, but fortunately I was disappointed. I think it must be his fat that saved him." When they found that he was not materially hurt, they gave him in charge to the watch, as a punishment for his folly. They had considerable difficulty in appeasing the wrath of the elephant, and conducting him safely home. The keeper added, that Mr Cross had no wish to press the case, as he thought that the defendant's fright and imprisonment would perhaps deter him from meddling with an animal so much above his own calibre in future.

The defendant looked very silly, and said nothing. Sir Richard Bernie said that [the defendant's] … folly might have occasioned the death of half a dozen people. He should discharge him, with a caution never again to catch hold of an elephant's tail.
Defendant: That you may depend upon it, Sir Richard. I never shall, said the defendant, bowing very low. He was then discharged on paying the fee.'
Devizes and Wiltshire Gazette, 20 September 1827.

In this case, the problem seemed to be over-familarity breeding contempt… London elephants must have a been a reasonably common sight by this time. There had been menageries at Exeter Exchange since 1778, with Edward Cross taking charge in 1814. The Exchange building remained a key animal site until 1829, when it was demolished and the animals moved to Regent's Park Zoo and the Surrey Zoological Gardens.

192. A Flying White Elephant.
'One of the most remarkable phenomena ever seen in the metropolis was witnessed yesterday evening by the passengers on the George Peabody river steamer, just as Big Ben of Westminster was on the point of striking seven. This was the appearance of a huge white elephant in the sky, making straight, as it seemed, for the Houses of Parliament. There was some little doubt at first as to the precise character of the beast, as it charged through the air head first in a direct line for the centre of Westminster Palace, as though its purpose was to sweep away the halls and passages which connect the Commons house with the House of Lords. The apparition rapidly descended through the air, and speculations were hazarded as to what it was. Men looked up and trembled, while timid women screamed "The end of the world is come, and we are all lost!" The captain of the George Peabody kindly moored his boat to the pier to give those who desired it the chance of escaping by way of Lambeth Palace. In an instant the monster was close upon the boat and a chorus of startled voices shouted, "A white elephant!" There was no longer any doubt about the fact. It was an elephant whose trunk was rapidly moving from side to side. With

furious speed it passed over the stern of the George Peabody, and dashed into the Thames. The spectators breathed more freely. As soon as the elephant touched the water half a dozen boats dashed from the pier to investigate the phenomenon. One oarsman was far in advance of the others. He was seen to thrust a hand towards the struggling monster – and instantly it collapsed. It was a gigantic elephant made of laths and paper.'
Portsmouth Evening News, 24 July 1880.

Although I have not managed to find out who pulled off this prodigious stunt, we can assume they must have been skilled, wealthy and determined. We might imagine the incident to have been some kind of advertising ploy – but the first visit of a white elephant to London seems to have occurred in early 1884. In that notorious episode, the supposedly rare creature, Toung Taloung, turned out to be a standard grey elephant which had in fact been whitewashed.

193. An Elephant Meets His Fans.

'On Monday night, Mr Cross's elephant made his first appearance at Astley's Ampitheatre, in the melodrama of *Blue Beard*, to a very crowded audience. The piece was most splendidly got up, and went off with great *éclat*. After the performance it was announced in the bills that the elephant would go through a variety of tricks in the circle, but he no sooner entered than he became quite unmanageable, and appeared terrified from the number of persons around him, and the keepers who attended lost all control over him. The affrighted animal made a plunge toward the back part of the pit, and got his forelegs and trunk over the panels which surround the circle. The screams of the females were terrific, and a general rush took place towards the doors, and the confusion that took place it is almost impossible to describe.

Several ladies were slightly injured by the elephant's trunk, and one lady was so much hurt that she was taken to a surgeon's and bled immediately. With some difficulty the elephant was secured and taken out of the circle, when it was announced that he would again be brought in to proceed with his performance; upon which a general cry of "No, no" resounded through the house, and he was at last brought out upon the stage, when he went through his tricks with the greatest docility imaginable. The house was numerously and brilliantly attended.'
Bell's Life in London, 7 September 1828.

194. The Adelphi's Biggest Star.
'The great elephant of Siam made her appearance on Thursday night at the Adelphi. Of the splendour of the spectacle in which she takes so prominent a part, too much cannot be said. The great interest of the piece turns upon the many perils to which a young Prince and his intended bride are placed by machinations and sorceries, from all of which they are successfully delivered by the extraordinary sagacity and presence of mind of the elephant. On her first entrance, she presents bouquets of flowers to the Princess and her attendants. She afterwards apprises the Prince of the conspiracy against him, by conveying to him the Princess's tablets, in which she warns him of his

danger; she subsequently decides the contest for the crown, by taking it from the head of the usurper and placing it on that of the rightful Prince. She next releases the Prince from a chest, in which he was enclosed by the usurper, in order to be cast into a torrent; and seeing him exhausted, plucks some fruit from neighbouring trees, which she gives him to eat, and finally releases him (and this was one of the most clever performances) and his attendants, by tearing down the grating of their prison, and seating herself on her hind quarters, under the window of the prison in such a position, with her head raised to it, that her back forms an inclined plain, down which the attendants slide and escape.

There were many other clever parts of the performance, which we have not room to notice; but we cannot omit the gravity with which she sat down to supper, and the ingenuity with which she helped herself to two bottles of wine, from which she regularly drew the corks and *handed* them to the attendants … On the whole, this ingenious animal is entitled to great praise for her skill as a "dramatic artist" (as she is called in the bills). The punctuality with which she seemed to attend to her cue, in coming on and going off, would well deserve imitation of some of the human performers.

The piece was announced for repetition amidst thunders of applause. At its conclusion, there was a general call for the elephant. This was kept up for some time, and at length she made her appearance, walked from the back of the stage to the footlights without any attendant, and seemed by the extraordinary movements of her trunk and tail, to enjoy the roars of laughter and

applause which she excited. At the conclusion she gave a loud breathing, a sort of grunt of satisfaction through her trunk, and retired.'
The Sheffield Independent, 19 December 1829.

If you were a Londoner born around 1800 you would have had the chance to see a fair number of elephants gracing the stages of the capital – albeit with varying degrees of success. An early example was Chunee, who briefly featured in a pantomime, *Harlequin and Padmanaba*, just after Christmas 1811 – briefly, because the cries and plaudits of the audience unnerved him on two successive nights, causing him to hurtle off-stage in fright (*Menagerie*, 191).

The elephant of the King of Siam had (*The Times* remarked) arrived at Calais on Monday 23 November, after taking farewell of the Parisians, and reached London on Wednesday evening. Perhaps emboldened by the news that she had been insured for £4000 with Lloyds of London, the animal was 'very playful with her keepers, the hat of one of whom she threw into the sea for some slight affront passed on her' (*Bell's Life in London*, 29 November 1829). Come February 1846, the revived drama, *The Rajah of Nagpore*, was delighting audiences at Astley's Theatre, and now featured two Indian elephants, as well as camels (*The Morning Post*, 11 February 1846).

We can now only guess just what that final 'loud breathing' of our weighty diva really meant. But it has been observed many times that when pleased or relieved elephants do more or less purr.

195. Mademoiselle d'Jeck.

'On the night of Wednesday last, Mademoiselle d'Jeck, the celebrated elephant, arrived at Ashburn, on her way to Birmingham. This celebrated actress performed the journey on foot, accompanied only by an attendant on a

pony, which she followed like a spaniel dog. When the toll-gate keeper near the town gave his attendance at the gate, he was saluted by a friendly bow from the stupendous quadruped. On her going down the town, several individuals were a good deal astonished; and one in particular was so terrified as to be unable to stir from his position, exclaiming, "Will nobody tell me what it is? Will nobody stop it?" The sagacious animal was accomodated at The Green Man Inn, and exhibited to the public on Thursday; and early on Friday morning left for its destination, accompanied some distance on the road by several of the curious. The animal is seven and a half tons in weight, and is the same which killed a man at Newcastle a short time ago.'
The Times, 6 October 1830.

As promised, here we have a man who had not only never seen an elephant before, but seemed to have no idea what it was. To put it another way: he was terrified not by what it might do, but that it could even *be*... by the sheer impossible fact of its existence. The story also reminds us that, in the days before extensive rail networks, walking your elephant from one place to another was one of only two options available. Gilbert Pidcock was the owner of Britain's first commercial menagerie, based at that long-running site of animal exotica, London's Exeter Exchange. When transporting various creatures to Scotland in autumn 1797 Pidcock had an elephant caravan drawn by eight horses – obviously a more expensive method than one man on a pony. Added to this was the occasional cost incurred if you met one of the more officious types of toll-keeper. Grigson notes that when Pidcock's menagerie had reached the Wragby toll bar earlier that same year, the turnpike man 'had insisted on weighing the elephants and charged Pidcock £1 19s 6d'

(*Menagerie*, 109). The death alluded to here resulted in Mademoiselle d'Jeck undergoing a trial of sorts, in September 1830. Read on…

'On Friday last, the following dreadful event took place at Newcastle upon Tyne. It is well known to the public that Mr Yates, one of the proprietors of the Adelphi Theatre, has been travelling in the north of England with the sagacious elephant that nightly attracted such crowded audiences last season at the above theatre. Two keepers travel with this stupendous animal, and it appears that one of them, M. Baptiste Bernard, a Frenchman, had given some offence to the elephant. It is well known that these animals will generally resent an injury be it of ever so long standing, and so it unfortunately happened for poor Bernard. On going into the place where the elephant was confined on Friday, she seized Bernard with her trunk, who called out murder with all his strength, when Tom, the Yorkshireman, the other keeper, ran to his assistance, but the elephant heeded him not, and dashed the unfortunate Bernard on the ground and killed him. The enraged animal then attacked Tom, who luckily escaped, but not before his leg was dreadfully lacerated.' *Jackson's Oxford Journal*, 4 September 1830.

The Elephant.
'The natural history of this sagacious animal shows that it has its affections and its antipathies, and many anecdotes have been recorded of both feelings which almost exceed credibility. It has, however, one peculiar feature that it never loses sight of, and that is revenge,

and this passion it has been known to harbour in its breast for years, till an opportunity offers for its effectual development. To this may be attributed the death of Baptiste Bernard, the Italian keeper of Miss Djeck, the celebrated female elephant which lately performed at the Adelphi Theatre. On an investigation by a coroner's jury at the Phoenix Inn, Morpeth, into the circumstances of his death, it appeared from the evidence that the man had stabbed the elephant in the trunk with a pitchfork, about two years ago, while in a state of intoxication, and that the animal never felt cordially towards him; that on Tuesday evening previous to the inquest, the *lady* caught hold of him with the trunk, and did him so much injury that he died on the succeeding day. Verdict: "Died from the wounds and bruises received from the trunk of an elephant. Deodand. 5s."
Berkshire Chronicle, 18 September 1830.

Elephants, as they say, never forget… which could of course be a very long time, given the possible 70 year lifespan of the African elephant. The first such beast which Pidcock acquired in the 1790s seemed to be a friendly and highly-skilled animal on the whole. But it also had its pride. Grigson tells of how 'every evening Pidcock would treat himself and the elephant to a glass of spirits, always serving the elephant first'. One day, however, he served himself first – upon which 'the elephant was so offended that he refused his glass with disdain and never drank with Pidcock again' (*Menagerie*, 108). Interestingly, this suggests that an elephant could have not only pride, but the intelligence to see when it was being slighted, as well as the memory to persist in a state of resentment. We might then suspect that Mademoiselle d'Jeck personally resented Bernard's assault, rather than merely viewing him as a dangerous physical threat.

'We can contradict, from the best authority, the report that the elephant was thrown overboard during a storm, in order to lighten the ship, which was conveying her elephantship to America, and also that the ship was lost. No news of the kind has reached Lloyd's, where she was insured, nor has Mr Yates heard any fact of this kind. We learn that the tale was trumped up at a well-known theatrical gossiping shop.'
Northampton Mercury, 18 December 1830.
Mademoiselle d'Jeck had embarked on the Ontario on Saturday 30 October.

196. 'Indian or African, Sir?

'The one idea of generalising trade, borrowed from the Americans, has taken deep root in London, and the struggle now amongst the shopkeepers is not to furnish any one "speciality" ... Whiteley ... has undertaken to enlarge upon [Stewart], the trading leviathan of New York, and claims that he is ready to furnish the human being ... with every article necessary to his or her condition in life ... A bet was laid between two sporting men that Whiteley should be asked for something he did not possess and could not procure. So the friends went together one morning and inquired of the "universal man" if he could sell them an elephant. Whiteley was by no means taken aback at the strange demand, although fain to confess that he had not "that description of article in stock", but could procure it for them in three hours' time. The friends, who thought that Whiteley had

treated the affair as a joke, were somewhat astonished by the receipt of a paper which stated that the elephant ordered in the morning had arrived at Whiteley's stables and was ready for delivery. With the intuition of genius he had sent to "Jamrach, purveyor of wild beasts to the Queen" and bought up the elephant on trial. Needless to say that the friends were all too glad to pay up all expenses and an indemnity to be rid of their onerous bargain.'
Freeman's Journal, 16 September 1875.

197. Elephant Power.
'A few days since an enormous waggon with ten horses on the road from Lyons to Marseilles, got into a hole, from which the waggoner found it impossible to extricate it, notwithstanding the employment of several hours' labour. The celebrated elephant Kiouny happened to pass at the moment on its way to Marseilles. Ropes and sacks were tied together to form traces, and the stupendous animal being attached to the imprisoned vehicle, drew it and its team on the high road with the greatest facility, and then continued its march.'
Bath Chronicle, 9 October 1834.

198. An Elephant Takes a Stroll.
'A bull elephant, named Jim, which for many years has been one of the features of Mr George Sanger's circus entertainments, was yesterday afternoon taken by Mr Turner, the manager, from the depot in Woodhill Park, with two Indian llamas, for a walk through the streets. Mr Turner led the elephant with a hooked stick,

attached to one of its ears. When outside the Manor House, the animal broke away and dashed into Finsbury Park, breaking through or tearing up all obstructions to its straight course over the ground. It charged the grandstand, to which it did considerable damage, and then ran into Blackstock Road, followed by policemen and a large crowd.

It looked into open gateways, and entered a fishmonger's stable, where it knocked down a man who ran to protect a horse. Clearing the crowd from its path, the elephant ran by way of Highbury Vale to the rear of some houses in Highbury Park, where it knocked down six stout walls and trampled the gardens. To regain the road, it walked through a wooden fence and a garden wall, after which it walked leisurely through different thoroughfares to the New River*, where it quenched its thirst. Passing through the fences of the Willows Building Estate, Park Lane, it reached Albion Road, where the police unsuccessfully endeavoured to secure it with ropes. It would allow none to approach it, but a man named Long, who took hold of it by the ear. It was coaxed into a carman's yard in the Boelyn Road, Kingsland, and the gates were closed. It walked through them on its way to Clapton and Dalston.

At Lea Bridge a young man sought to turn it, and received a blow from the tip of its trunk which tore his hand open, and another which caught him in the stomach, driving him eight yards along the road. It lifted the iron gate, and its supports, of the Clapton Cricket Club's ground from its position, and laid it aside. From Stamford Hill it took the main road to Tottenham, and devastated the gardens of the Drapers' Almshouses.

Eventually, near Brucegrove Station, where it had been encamped some years ago with other elephants, the keeper succeeded in quietly chaining the forelegs of the animal, which then walked quietly to the depot, after having committed a large amount of damage along the route it had taken.'

The Standard, 21 September 1893.

*The New River was an artificial waterway cut between 1604-1613, to supply London with spring water from Hertfordshire. It now flows only as far as Stoke Newington.

199. The Elephant's Late Supper.

'A correspondent living at Woolwich sends the following ... "Early this (Thursday) morning one of a herd of elephants belonging to a circus which has been exhibiting at Woolwich escaped unobserved from an enclosure at the back of Trinity Street, near Charlton Pier, by breaking down the barrier. Smashing the fence in rear of No.1 Trinity Street, a house which is in the occupation of an artisan named Adams, the huge animal attempted to break in at the back door. The door itself was easily crushed in, but the elephant could not so much as get his head inside the house, and thereupon had recourse to the window, where a breach was promptly effected of sufficient capacity to admit at least his trunk. The remains of the family supper was on the parlour table, together with the master's breakfast tied up in a cloth for him to take to his work when he arose. The elephant quickly cleared away the remnants of the feast, and then carefully untying the knots of the bundle shook out the food, and disposed of that also, after which, finding no more refreshment, he swept all the crockery off the table with a wave of his trunk, and proceeded to further mischief with the household furniture.

It was about four o'clock when Mr and Mrs Adams were awoken by the clatter, and the lady, armed with a poker, came down to the scene. She could just discern some dark object in the room, and, suspecting that it was a burglar, she shouted a summons to retreat or surrender, but the object approached her, and she smote it heavily with her poker, whereupon the trunk curled up, and the elephant emitted a roar which frightened the inmates more than ever. The man took to the street in search of a policeman, and a light revealed the state of the case. One of the keepers from the circus then came and took charge of the runaway.'
Daily Telegraph, 19 October 1886.

200. The Elephant and his Toys.
'At about two o'clock yesterday morning, an elephant, which belonged to a circus travelling the country, broke out of the stables at Rugby and burst open the door of a small cottage adjoining, squeezed in and unfastened the cupboard, and ate a dozen pots of jam, a gallon of pickled onions, a supply of damsons, a joint of meat, a loaf, a pound of butter, and a quantity of sweets. Having demolished everything in the provision line, he browsed on the window plants, and then examined some small ornaments on the chimney-piece, laid them carefully on the sofa, and enjoyed himself for nearly two hours before he was got out.'
Daily Telegraph, 27 September 1887.

Presumably this was a baby elephant – as we have just seen, an adult one was unlikely to get through a cottage doorway, even before it had eaten. If this guess is correct, we might also wonder: was this why, after its late night feast, this infant was so happy playing with his toys from the mantelpiece?

For reading, listening, answering queries and offering specialist knowledge, many thanks to Adriano, Ann, Ash, Chris, Dan, Eiffel, Ella, Gillian, Ian, Irene, Isabelle, Jessica Borge, Julie, Marek, Marina, Matina Kalcounis-Rueppell, Matt, Michael, Nina, Paul, Phil, Rupert, Sree, and Suzi.

The cover shows a detail from *The Orphans* by James Yates Carrington (1857-1892).

Further Reading and Listening

Jan Bondeson, *Amazing Dogs: A Cabinet of Canine Curiosities* (Amberley, 2013).

Caroline Grigson, *Menagerie: The History of Exotic Animals in England* (Oxford University Press, 2016).

N.N. Ladygina-Kohts, *Infant Chimpanzee and Human Child* (Oxford University Press, 2002).

Elizabeth Marshall Thomas, *The Hidden Lives of Dogs* (Gallery, 1996).

Jeffrey Masson and Susan McCarthy, *When Elephants Weep: The Emotional Lives of Animals* (Vintage, 1996).

Irene M. Pepperberg, *Alex and Me* (Scribe, 2013).

Mark Rowlands, *Can Animals be Moral?* (Oxford University Press, 2015).

Rupert Sheldrake, *Dogs That Know When Their Owners are Coming*

Home and Other Unexplained Powers of Animals (Arrow Books, 2000).

John Simons, *The Tiger That Swallowed the Boy: Exotic Animals in Victorian England* (Libri, 2012).

Dave Soldier, Richard Lair, and Assorted Elephants, *Thai Elephant Orchestra* (Mulatta, 2001).

---

[1] https://www.youtube.com/watch?v=-HJTG6RRN4E (cited by Rowlands, *Can Animals be Moral?*, 6).

[2] Sara C. Nelson, 'Stray Dogs Attend Funeral of Elderly Animal Lover Margarita Suarez, 30 March 2015.

[3] http://www.huffingtonpost.com/2013/01/20/ciccio-the-dog-attends-ma_n_2511351.html

[4] https://www.historicmysteries.com/lady-florence-dixie/

[5] http://www.bbc.co.uk/news/science-environment-38665057

[6] Willy Newlands, 'Can animals really find their own way home?', *Daily Mail*, 28 November 1980.

[7] *Land and Water*, repr. *Dundee Evening Telegraph*, 21 November 1877.

[8] *The Sheffield & Rotherham Independent*, 6 May 1876; *Lincoln Mercury*, 2 May 1879.